RANDOM SHOTS

SHOOTING TIMES.

SIXTH YEAR OF PUBLICATION
ILLUSTRATED

SHOOTING TIMES.

Shooting Times,

AND KENNEL NEWS.

Edited by LEWIS CLEMENT, ("WILDFOWLER,")

Ex-Contributor and Kennel Reporter-in-Chief to the London "Field."

Author of "Shooting & Fishing Trips," three series; "Tables of Loads;" "Public Shooting Quarters;" "Modern Wildfowling;" "Dog Breaking," etc., etc.

REGISTERED AS A NEWSPAPER AT THE GENERAL POST OFFICE]   [FOR TRANSMISSION ABROAD.

VOL. VI. No. 266.]   PUBLISHED EVERY FRIDAY.   LONDON: FRIDAY, OCTOBER 7, 1887.   EIGHT PAGES.   [PRICE TWOPENCE.
POST FREE, TWOPENCE HALF-PENNY.

AN INTERESTING BIT OF NATURE.
BY "WILDFOWLER."

Some years ago, whilst shooting over a friend's land along the North Sea, I happened to notice a rather interesting occurrence which is sure to entertain our readers, and for that reason I will detail what occurred.

The downs over which we were shooting, held a good many rabbits, but the great attraction to me was the sea shore itself, which was, at low tide, literally swarming with waders of all kinds, and not a few birds of the duck tribe either. Now, what I am going to relate took place towards, as far as I can recollect, July 15th. I was lying in the downs on a bright sunny morning, and with my "Dollond" glasses I was scanning the shore, spying the various birds' doings when, to my great surprise I saw, coming from sea towards the land a shelduck evidently in a great hurry, for, she flew straight and swiftly to a spot about 100 yards from where I was reclining, and there she suddenly disappeared. I knew she had not gone over the downs, because I stood up to watch her flight, and, therefore, she had stopped somewhere (and very abruptly too), near a certain sand hill which I carefully marked in my mind's eye.

Of course, I knew of old, that shelducks lay their eggs in rabbits' burrows, for choice, wherever they can get any handy; failing which they will, themselves, burrow a hole wherein to lay their eggs and as the downs were perfectly honeycombed with rabbit-holes, I came to the conclusion that dame shelduck had her nest in one of those holes.

"Now," I thought, "I will walk along the tide, so as not to disturb her, and find out her abode."

No sooner thought then carried out. I sallied forth, and stalked straight ahead over the sands for about 100 yards, than walking parallel to the shore, I scanned the burrows with my glass. I made pretty sure of the very spot, but could see no sign of the bird. She had gone in, evidently, and the place seeming to me to be a very handy one over which to keep observation, I gradually got into the downs again and edged towards it. I chose a nice clump of rank grass to lie by, and, putting my gun down, I intently watched the hole, and then happened the little scene which I want to narrate. Whether I can do so graphically enough remains to be seen. However, I will try. Well, I had not been 10 minutes waiting (and, to tell the candid and solemn truth, I was getting rather tired of it), when something seemed to move at the mouth of the burrow. I focussed it at once, but there was nothing to be seen. So I put the glass down again, but, presently, I observed another movement at the hole, and I then distinctly saw a bird's head. I kept still and "skinned" my eyes wide, and this is what took place :—

The odd bird waddled out a foot or two, followed by two tiny bundles of wool, which, of course, were her progeny. The poor little things appeared hardly able to stand, but the mother-duck kicked the soft and warm sand about, ensconsed herself into the hole thus made, and presently the two little ducklings half-rolled and half-clambered on to her back. Well, I had often seen chickens do that trick with their mothers, so I was not surprised at it, neither was I astonished when, upon the shelduck spreading her wings, both youngsters rolled off her back, head over heels, on to the sand. But, when she resumed her place in the hole she had scooped out, and when the two youngsters climbed once more on her back, *and got hold of the feathers near her wings with their beaks, and when she spread her pinions and started off, flying for the open sea, with her tiny beloved cargo on her back, you may believe me or not, but I stood open-mouthed at the strange and affecting sight.*

In the face of *that*, who can dare say that birds have no instinct, and that there is no Being above us all to instil such thoughts and instincts into created living nature! I never was so struck in all my life, and there I stood, hat in hand, a mere speck, so to speak, amidst that vast wilderness of sand and sea, and if I did not say much you may depend upon it that, like Pat's parrot, I thought "a lot."

Well, I went to look at the burrow, just for curiosity's sake, and you may not credit it, but it is a fact, that there were no duck's footmarks *leading* to the hole. So, evidently the old woman had actually sailed into the burrow for fear that by landing near it she might have betrayed its whereabouts! How is that again for artfulness !

BLAND'S PATENT DIAMOND SIGHTS.

In this patent, diamonds are utilised in sighting sporting arms and revolvers. For rifles, the new plan has been proved to be of the utmost importance, and of its utility in stalking several glowing reports are to hand, whilst one gentleman, shooting a rifle fitted with diamond sights, did not have a single miss, and killed during his "out" nine stags and two hinds. Diamonds, cut brilliant, are set thus :—

FIG. 1.

BLAND'S PATENT DIAMOND SIGHTS.

In the front sight one stone is set, forming, with its silver setting, the bead, as shown above. In the back sight a single stone is set

FIG. 2.

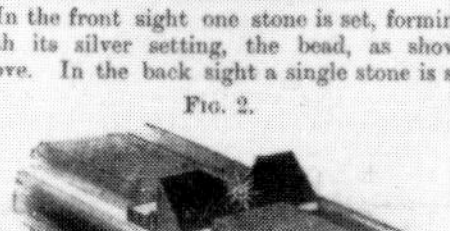

BLAND'S PATENT DIAMOND SIGHTS.

in the centre below and touching the apex of the V, as illustrated above. These small stones, of course, instantly become most conspicuous objects, as from their many facets they reflect light and catch the eye at once.

The nesting of the diamonds (Figs. 1 and 2) will convey to the reader important results as instantaneously perfect alignment is given. The weapon when brought to the shoulder gives this on to the quarry without that trouble attached to the platinum line and V so that it quickens the aim, and an effective shot is the result. Thus we have a naturally clearly defined sight, supplying a want felt by sportsmen which other expedients have failed to satisfy. These patent diamond sights can be seen under the most difficult circumstances such as bad light at dusk, and after a hard stalk, etc. The new invention will also prove to be beneficial to sportsmen whose eyesight is failing, their brilliancy being easily discerned.

FIG. 3.

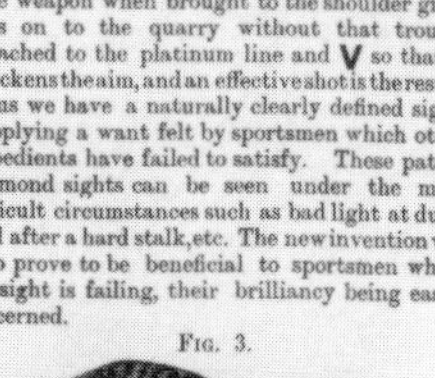

BLAND'S PATENT DIAMOND SIGHTS.

For night-shooting in India, over dead decoys (a sport common in that country when vermin-killing), they give important aid.

The sight can be used on wildfowling guns with advantage for flighting at night, and the diamond is a very useful adjunct to a revolver. For simplicity and strength this sight is unsurpassed by any other.

We may add, as our own opinion, that there is absolutely nothing to be compared for efficiency to these sights in the market. We intend shortly to try a rook rifle and a double Express, fitted with these "Diamonds," and will duly report thereon in the columns of the SHOOTING TIMES.

THE HON. WARNER MILLER has leased for 50 years a tract of 50,000 acres of forest in the Adirondacks, which he will protect as a game preserve.

THE EARL and COUNTESS of HOME are staying at their seat, Douglas Castle, Lanark, with a select party.

RANDOM SHOTS

An anthology from the first 50 years
of the *Shooting Times*

Selected and edited by
JAMES IRVINE ROBERTSON

PELHAM BOOKS
Stephen Greene Press

With thanks to:

Ned Goschen, Philip Caraman S.J.,
Norman di Giovanni, Lance Nicholson,
Pat Veale and Jonathan Young [Ed.]

PELHAM BOOKS/Stephen Greene Press
Published by the Penguin Group
27 Wrights Lane, London W8 5TZ, England
Viking Penguin, a division of Penguin Books USA Inc
375 Hudson Street, New York, NY 10014, USA
The Stephen Greene Press Inc., 15 Muzzey Street, Lexington, Massachusetts 02173, USA
Penguin Books Australia Ltd, Ringwood, Victoria, Australia
Penguin Books Canada Ltd, 2801 John Street, Markham, Ontario, Canada L3R 1B4
Penguin Books (NZ) Ltd, 182–190 Wairau Road, Auckland 10, New Zealand

Penguin Books Ltd, Registered Offices: Harmondsworth, Middlesex, England

First published 1990

Copyright © James Robertson and *Shooting Times*, 1990

Typeset in 11/12 pt Goudy Old Style by Goodfellow & Egan Ltd., Cambridge
Printed and bound in Great Britain by Butler & Tanner Ltd., Frome

A CIP catalogue record for this book is available from the British Library.

ISBN 0 7207 1945 3

FOREWORD

Whether delivered to a crumbling Irish mansion, bought from the news stand at Waterloo, or carried to the middle of the jungle by a sweat-soaked coolie, the Sportsman welcomed the weekly arrival of the *Shooting Times* like an old friend. A gentleman's club in print, willing to admit the like-minded amongst the lower orders to its readership, down the decades the magazine instructed, admonished and entertained its readers and provided a forum for their esoteric arguments, complaints, observations, boasting, and gossip.

How to shoot a lion, how to avoid being eaten if you miss and, if you are eaten, how much it will hurt. What size shot is best for birds-of-paradise? Can one shoot seagulls after sunset on summer Sundays in Sussex? Does a violin G-string round the waist cure arthritis? Have you heard the one about the bishop and the buffalo?

Sportsmen prowled obscure parts of the globe, shooting whatever they found, and then reported back to the *Shooting Times* on the quality of the sport provided. Sloths were not recommended, nor was the sperm whale, although 'with a razor-sharp lance' one could 'stir up his vitals in a highly artistic manner'. They shot okapi, peacocks, gorillas, flamingos, sparrows, turkeys, mullet, eagles, humming birds, porpoises,and even a great auk, although the latter, after the editor had inspected the remains – posted, like so much else, to him for examination – turned out to be an escaped penguin.

The denizens of the field seemed to be regarded as one more layer of the great social order of the days of the Empire. At the top was the Sportsman, an officer and gentleman, and those who aspired to be like him. Beneath him, the peasantry who, although occasionally truculent and consequently shot or imprisoned, furnished gamekeepers and beaters. Her Majesty's dusky subjects constituted the next layer, providing trackers and sources of dubious anecdotes, whilst way beyond the social pale were Huns, Frogs, and Dagoes, if not grand enough to be guests on Scottish grouse moors. A special opprobrium was reserved for Killjoys, those sufficiently deranged to be anti-Sport.

Last were the beasts, and since virtually nobody but the Sportsman took much interest in their welfare, they became his responsibility. The reader of the *Shooting Times* was as much a naturalist as a hunter, taking a keen interest in the environment and threats to the habitat of anything he might want to shoot. Then, as now, he raged against oil pollution on the seashore and the leechings from tarred roads into the rivers, bemoaned the decline of the corncrake, the decimation of elephant populations, and scarcity of the bittern in his game bag. He formed conservation societies, natural history societies, and reviled those who shot birds out of season and failed to give the quarry a good, sporting chance.

Readers died of fever in the outposts of the Empire, of Boer bullet, at the Front – wherever skills in shot and shell and sport and duty were most needed. As they met their country's demands, their hearts were back in the meadows, marshes, and moors with a 12-bore in the crook of the arm and faithful spaniel at heel. The *Shooting Times* took them there, seeing the world through the eyes of the Sportsman. The outbreak of the Great War was mentioned only in relation to its effect on partridge prospects for the approaching season in Europe.

An anthology of 50 years of the *Shooting Times* in 219 pages is the proportional equivalent of reducing *Hamlet* to 'To be or not to be, that is'. With such wealth of material, the only criterion for selection can be what catches the eye, imagination, or sense of humour of the reader. Such an anthology cannot hope to reflect or represent the totality. Apart from shooting and what struck the three editors of this period as interesting or bizarre, the other areas of interest to the *Shooting Times* were angling and dog shows and trials, which are scarcely touched on in this collection. Even then, the anthologist has to leave out much of what he would like to put in. There is no space for the safari through Africa, where the game was tame, nuzzling the porters as they marched, because no man – let alone a white man – had been there before. Or the Wild West lynching of Joe North, told by one of the participants (it had been a dull evening in the saloon until one of the cowboys remembered that Joe had murdered somebody the year before). Or the exploits of the battling poachers of Portree.

The herds of Victorian commas have been lightly culled; ghillie has been chosen rather than gillie, gilly, ghily or ghilly; some introductory headings have been added; a few cuts made, and, where meaning had to be worked out like a crossword clue, the text has been clarified. Otherwise nothing has been altered or added. These are the voices and the interests of the English – which, of course, included the Scots and the Irish – sporting gentlemen, the creators of the legend of stiff upper lips, understatement, eccentricity, and honour from which the British still benefit in the world today. Bulldog Drummond, Richard Hannay and Allan Quartermain stalk through every page.

J. I. R. January 1990

1884

A BIT OF A TIFF

I WAS ALLUDING to a stay of mine in Boulogne with my chum, Charlie, in one of the last numbers of the *Shooting Times*. There are as, doubtless, several of my readers are aware, several small but very good marshes in the neighbourhood of Boulogne, notably at Wimereux, at Slack, and at Tardighen. The one at Wimereux was not much to speak of; still, along the brooks, I have often killed my two or three couple of snipe on about 200 yards of brook – which was not bad, considering the deed only took me ten minutes each day to perform. The shore-shooting was fair there, as vast flocks of oxbirds, etc., used to fly past the mouth of the river. Of course this was then all free shooting. What it may be now I do not know. At Slack one side of the river marshes was preserved, but the other was open to all. And at Tardighen there were about 200 acres of very good marshy land, where good fun was to be had with snipe in the daytime and with ducks, etc., at night, there being several decoying-huts constantly occupied throughout the long winter nights. As regards the snipe, the sport would have been still better than it was, had there not been a son of the communal keeper setting snares all along the likely places, and consequently nailing a good many of the long-billed customers.

Some official complaints, I understand, had already been sent to the authorities, but they took not the slightest notice of them, and there the matter remained, so that whenever any sportsman tramped over the marsh, every now and again he came across a loop from which dangled a dead snipe – which was *not* a cure for *his* sore eyes!

Oh! how I did – inwardly – swear!

However, it could not be helped. We, strangers in the land, were there simply on sufferance and none of us even lived in that commune, and so we had to grin and bear it, but it was very, very hard to do that same.

'Why not have picked up the dead snipe from the snares?' some reader will suggest.

Well, to tell the candid truth, we tried it on once, hoping thereby to make the snarer tired of setting up his loops, but no sooner were we observed from the village – which stood on a small hill facing the marsh – than some dozen roughs rushed towards us, swearing and cursing, threatening to spoil all sport if we interfered with their chum's proceedings. And yet there are some people who have the incomparable cheek to say that 'they do these things better in France!'

Hum! Do they? Well, 'I leave it to you,' as London cabmens' catch-word now runs!

Well, to come back to our snipe, every shooter who does me the honour of reading these lines will, I am tolerably certain, agree with me when I say that, when a man is snipe shooting and sees dead birds caught thus every 100 yards or so and gets no sport himself, he is apt to get slightly riled. Now, I am myself a little bit quick-tempered at times and under such circumstances as those, I can't say that it improves the said temper. Therefore, one day when I was so situated, I was not at all pleased with things in general, and with that day's sport in particular. I had an excellent snipe pointer with me, but all he could find was dead or dying snipe caught in the infernal nooses. I was deliberating whether it would not be better to make tracks and go, when, on getting about half-way through the marshes, I saw Ponto once more as stiff as a poker, moving his stern slowly as he used to do on snipe.

'Now,' I thought, 'another dead 'un, I expect.'

And of course when the snipe arose, I missed it but, to my extreme gratification, my left fetched it such a thwack that down it came like a stone.

Ponto retrieved it and I was admiring it as usual, when I saw another fellow coming down the road as fast as his legs could carry him, evidently intending also to patronise the marsh. He, of course, had as much right to come there as I had, and likely more – but I did not like the idea, so I instantly set to work to try and do my best to make a bag before he had much time to interfere. But he was too near to be outdone, and by-and-bye we came to be very close together. He was a Boulogne shopkeeper – one of those fellows who sell lobster shells and things, you know as *ornaments*, ha! ha! Well, he was a man who made money in his business and, of course, he was full of his own importance. He was a dapper little man of some 45 summers, with a tremendous moustache and imperiale, and he had the loveliest and whitest teeth I had ever clapped eyes on. He had with him a beast of a dog who flushed every bird he came to, and at last put up a hare, chasing it across the marsh

and over the ploughed fields and finally disappearing in full cry over the brow of a hill.

And a good job too!

'Moly Hoses! may he never return! Amen!' said I, inwardly.

Naturally enough, the little man was grinding his lovely teeth and giving vent to his outraged feelings in choice language.

'When Medor comes back,' I thought, 'he will get a clipping good hiding – but if he has any respect for his hide and wishes to please me, he will keep away and hunt hares till Doomsday.'

Of course, I never took any outward notice of Medor's misbehaviour, or of his master's rage, but went on as if I had been alone, quite alone; but presently, when I knocked over a snipe, a gun goes off behind me and this fellow rushed up breathlessly and claimed the bird!

I looked at him from head to foot with unutterable scorn and, without saying a word, turned my back to him and put the bird in my bag.

At this, he flew in another tremendous rage and told me a lot of things which, being more likely than not slang, I did not quite twig, but I could see by the light in his eye and his gesticulations that he was not exactly well pleased at having made my acquaintance there. Howbeit, as he was getting a bit noisy: 'If you give me any more of this,' I said to him with my best manners, 'there will be a row directly.'

And I left him. But he stuck to me and whenever I fired, he fired! This went on three times. At the third I put down my gun, went right up to the beggar, who looked at me with puzzled astonishment depicted on his countenance, and I said: 'Why don't you let me go my way and you go yours?'

'Shan't!' he exclaimed.

The birds rose.

'Je suis tres sorry que je spoke,' I remarked and, straightaway acting on the never-to-be-departed-from rule, and the-never-to-be-forgotten principle, that if you ever get into a shindy, always place in your fist first if you can, I landed what the 'fancy' would call a 'cracker on the 'tater trap.' Over he went, gun and all. But my horror was simply indescribable when I saw the poor devil getting up with his hands to his mouth and, into the said hands, he was dropping his teeth, one after the other, to the tune of 32, neither one more nor less! Then he pulled out the plates and the mechanism! Heaven be praised! His teeth were but a false set! When I left him he was trying to say 'Sacre' this, that, or the other, to me, but he couldn't having no teeth left in his mouth to pronounce the 'r' with.

Vat a larks!!!! – WILDFOWLER.

THE VERY EARLY CUCKOO

SIR, I HAVE just heard the cuckoo. Is not that early?

Yrs., READER, London,
Mar 8th.

[What time was it when you heard this cuckoo? And are you quite sure it was not a cuckoo clock? What were you up for so early in the morning? – Ed.]

Sir, it was at 3 a.m. that I heard it, and the place was St John's Wood. I was waiting for the sunrise. And to make sure, I have just gone back to the spot, and you are quite right, it was a cuckoo clock.

Yrs., READER, London,
Mar 11th.

[We thought so. We always like to ascertain true facts in such cases. Now, those readers of *The Field* who are anxious to hear a cuckoo clock early in March will know where to go to hear it, and the best time for hearing it. – Ed.]

WILD TURKEYS

LORD LORNE'S attempt to acclimatise moose-deer at Inverary has failed, but the musk-rats and other animals and birds are doing well and the wild turkeys appear to be flourishing. There seems no reason why wild turkeys should not be bred throughout the country. Not so long ago there was a breed at Holkham which used to afford good sport; and 100 years ago there were several flocks at Windsor Forest, which had been introduced by the Duke of Cumberland. During the reign of George II, Richmond Park contained over 2,000 wild turkeys.

PRICE OF GUNS

SIR, PRAY WHO is Mr. Charles Boswell? He, in the paper of the 28th March, writes as follows:– 'As far as price goes with guns, if the public will have great names, they must pay great prices, etc. . . . Nearly all the gun-trade in London is put out to workmen in its different branches, as very few make their guns on their own premises; there may be one or two exceptions, and no gun should cost more than £40 complete. The finest gun can be turned out at that price, and the best skill that money can find should be employed to make it. *This I can satisfy any gentleman upon.*' Indeed! According to Mr. Charles Boswell then, Dougall and Grant are not far removed from robbers and Purdey little short of a swindler – the prices asked and paid for their guns running from £50 to £70. What right has Mr. Boswell to assert that he is more honest than the above celebrated makers? What would you rather do sir, give Dougall or Grant £50 for one of their guns, or pay Mr. Charles Boswell £40 for one of his manufacture? I should not take long to decide. And in the same paper, in which

Mr. Boswell thus casts a slur upon our leading gun-makers, appears the following advertisement: – 'Charles Boswell, established 1869(!) has about 100 second-hand guns and express rifles, by all leading makers, Purdey, Boss, Grant, Rigby and Co. . . . These guns would wear out a dozen common Birmingham guns . . . Why buy common new ones!' Then follows: 'Gentlemen favouring me with their orders for new guns can rely upon having a first-class gun in every sense of the word, as not only being a practical man, I have proved myself one of the best pigeon shots in England.'

I wonder what our tip-top men have to say in an answer to the above. It certainly needs a refutation. If Mr. Charles Boswell is the dealer (of Edmonton) in second-hand guns, he is a very ungrateful man, as he has, to a considerable extent, prospered by means of the inventions and brains of our foremost West-end gun-makers.

Yrs., 'GENUINE ARTICLE',
St. Leonards.

MEMORABLE BAT SHOOT

THE ANNOUNCEMENT that Dr. Carver would attempt to shoot 1,000 bats in 80 minutes, after his regular Wild West performance, attracted an audience of nearly 3,000 to the enclosed grounds on Canal and Olympia Sts. Not a man who knew anything of bat shooting would believe that Carver would accomplish his task, in fact the doctor himself did not express any very

decided belief in his ability to win; hence bets were freely made that he would not succeed. After the performance, preparations were made for the event of the day. A large table was placed in front of the grand stand, on which were placed the shells, guns, a bucket of iced water and other necessary articles. Nearby were several large barrels of iced water which were used

to cool the guns after rapid firing. Eighteen yards from the table were two cages filled with bats, in the charge of four attendants, two of whom were selected to furnish the bats and the other to throw them in the air. Mr. Edgar Leche was selected as the referee, Mr. G.C. Dawkins, the timer and Messrs. William Dupré and Edward Dronet, the scorers. Dr. Carver wore dark pants, high boots and a dark-blue shirt. He wore on his left hand a heavy buckskin glove in which the barrel of his gun rested. He used his celebrated old widow, a Greener double-barrel, choke-bore gun which he had used in all of his famous matches; he also used another choke-bore gun of a different pattern; he had two other guns ready in case of necessity, but did not use them.

At 16 minutes to five o'clock, the attendants began throwing the bats in the air, one at a time. With his old reliable shotgun, Carver began finely and before the bats could begin their pirouettes in the air he brought numbers of them to the ground. When the doctor got hold of the other gun, however, he experienced some difficulty, and scored a number of misses, being unaccustomed to it because of the difference in the sight, and the fact that the guns snapped several times; many of the cartridges did not explode well either and one of the attendants failed to throw the bats properly, so that for a few minutes the shoot did not progress brilliantly. However, an old time bat thrower, a coloured man, was directed to do all the throwing, and the doctor becoming more accustomed to his guns, execution soon became rapid and brilliant. The large number of spectators crowded on either side of him and caused many shots to be missed by the doctor, which he could have made had the people not been in the way.

His shooting was watched with rapt attention, and several times the spectators broke forth in wild applause over the magnificent work done. The referee and scorers performed their duty well, and rapid firing kept them busy attending to their duties so that Dr. Carver had very little idea of how he stood at any time of the match. The quick firing kept the guns exceedingly hot all the time, causing Dr. Carver to have constant recourse to the pail of iced water to relieve his hand from the heat of the gun. Several times he brought down two bats at the same fire, and again he would kill the bats while they were pursuing the most difficult flight in the air.

After the first 20 minutes, Dr. Carver kept the coloured man busy throwing the bats, his shooting from this time on being of the finest character, with very few misses. Finally at 5.55 o'clock, just as the scorers arose to announce that the thousand bats were killed, the coloured man threw into the air three bats at the same time and Dr. Carver, with one beautiful shot, brought all three down together. It was then announced to him, amid the wildest enthusiasm of the spectators, that he had killed 1,003 bats in 71 minutes, thus having nine minutes to spare and three bats more than necessary. The crowd surrounded the renowned marksman and showered their congratulations upon him, which he accepted in his usual pleasant and dignified manner.

This feat of Dr. Carver's was undoubtedly a magnificent piece of endurance, as can be readily understood when the immense amount of work required in the loading and firing is considered; the recoil of the gun after each shot, the pulling of the trigger, the loading and the raising and the lowering of the gun, required an extraordinary amount of endurance. After the match, the doctor's left hand was fearfully blistered, bearing evidence of the hot work and suffering he experienced. Of course, a more difficult test of bat shooting would have been in the open fields, where a bat would have had more opportunities for flying, but, seeing how easily the doctor did shoot these bats that did do very much flying and were out of range of the crowd, there can be no doubt of his ability to repeat his performance.

Dr. Carver had never engaged in this style of shooting until this week, yet he has done the best bat shooting on record.

PIGEON SHOOTING MATCH

16 May

SIR, MR. CHURCHILL, Mr. Baker's assistant of Cockspur-street, has challenged Mr. Charles Boswell to shoot a match at pigeons at the trap. If rumours be true, Mr. Charles Boswell does not seem disposed to take up the challenge. I trust, however, that the friends of Mr. Charles Boswell will dissuade him from crying off this, which would be to many a most exciting contest.

Yrs., 'PIGEON TRAP'.

23 May

SIR, I HAVE offered to shoot Mr. Churchill for from £10 to £50 a side at 25 to 50 pigeons each in any open grounds in England, and he will only shoot in one ground, namely the Junior Gun Club Grounds where he is in attendance on gentlemen three or four days a week, so he sees 'exactly' where the pigeons make for. All I want is a fair contest, which he does not seem to care for or he would not limit me to one ground. A match well made is half won, perhaps this is Mr. Churchill's idea. Loser to pay for all the birds or pay for our own, whichever Mr. Churchill likes – both to shoot at 30 yards from five traps.

Yrs., CHARLES BOSWELL,
Gun Maker, 126 Strand,
LONDON, W.C.

30 May

SIR, MR. CHURCHILL did not seem to care to shoot in any other field than the International Gun and Polo Club Grounds, Hendon. I thought it best to let him have his choice of ground, so that if he cannot win there, he cannot win anywhere, but it seems rather hard, as I have never been in the grounds. But I was afraid the match would fall through if I did not agree to this. I hope, Mr. Editor, I shall have the pleasure of seeing you and many of your readers. I will endeavour to give my opponent a lot of trouble to win. Let us hope it will not be like the Derby of this year!

Yrs. CHARLES BOSWELL.
[We will try to be there. – Ed.]

6 June

SIR, I SEE that Mr. Charles Boswell has offered to shoot Mr. Churchill on his own

[14]

grounds, so that reads very much as if he were afraid Mr. Churchill was likely to cry off which meant striking while the iron was hot. I am glad to see that the match is made. It does not look as if Mr. Boswell were afraid of his opponent or he would not offer to shoot him on his own grounds.

Yrs., 'BLUE ROCK'.

6 June

SIR, LIKE MANY of your readers I shall have great pleasure in witnessing the match between Messrs. Boswell and Churchill, which must be a treat worth seeing to lovers of the trigger. I have not had the pleasure of knowing Mr. Churchill, but if he is as good a shot as Mr. Boswell it will be worth going a few miles to see. The latter shot at our club meeting on Tuesday and killed 37 out of 40. He won the silver cup on this occasion, also at our last meeting. Hoping you will give a full account of the match.

Yrs., T.D.
[We will. – Ed.]

13 June

The match between Mr. Boswell and Mr. Churchill for £100 a-side took place on Monday last. The total of the individual scores were: Mr. Churchill, 42 birds, 35 kills; Mr. Boswell, 41 birds, 26 kills. The result was rather startling to the cognoscenti, as two and three to one had been laid on Mr. Boswell. At the conclusion of the match Mr. Boswell offered to shoot Mr Churchill again for a match of £50 a-side, and, although it was declined on the ground, it is more than probable that it will eventually take place.
[Considering the form shown lately by Mr. Boswell, we think that something must have occurred which upset him. One of our friends also tells us that Mr. Churchill had a rare run of luck with the centre traps, getting no less than seven or eight in succession. – Ed.]

20 June

SIR, I WAS PRESENT to witness the match and I must agree with you, the result was extraordinary. For Mr. Boswell to go off his form like this cannot be accounted for, unless it was because he saw his opponent was having nearly all centre traps which might have upset him. So I think as you do, that Mr. Churchill had a rare run of luck. The birds out of the corner traps were a very different class of birds to those that came out of the centre traps.

Yrs., W.H.G.

SIR, YOUR REPORTER is incorrect when he states at the conclusion Mr. Boswell offered to shoot Mr. Churchill again. I was there when Mr. Churchill left, and neither myself nor Mr. Churchill heard anything of such a challenge. The form shown by Mr. Boswell prior to the match was good, killing some 16 or 17 birds without a miss, but as you seem doubtful as to the cause of him falling off in the match, I venture to suggest that the birds provided for the sweepstakes were inferior to those furnished for the match. The latter, being supplied by Hammond, were all that could be desired, which, with the good shooting of his opponent, beat Mr. Boswell.

Your reporter is also in error when he states Mr. Churchill had more birds from the middle trap than his opponent. Of the first 10 birds Mr. Boswell had two from the middle trap, Mr. Churchill none. The birds afterwards were evenly divided. Mr. Boswell's style of shooting is strictly 'snap' whereas Mr. Churchill carefully timed each bird, showing marvellous accuracy, as the issue proved.

Yrs., CHARLES MASON,
Brixton, S.W.

27 June

SIR, MR. MASON says he was at the match and never heard me offer to shoot Mr. Churchill again. Perhaps not. Allow me to tell him that nothing would give me greater pleasure, as I was anything but satisfied with the last match. Mr. Mason goes on to say that the birds in the match were supplied by Hammond, insinuating that the birds in the sweepstakes were not. 24s. per dozen were charged for the sweepstake birds. How was it I killed the first five birds in the match without a miss, Mr. Churchill missing two out of the first five? He also missed the 'sweepstake' bird he had before the match. Perhaps it did not fly fast enough. I thought the reverse. Mr. C. has the 'credit' of winning which ought to be satisfactory to him.

Now, I will shoot Mr. Churchill a match for £25 a-side, 25 birds each to find trap and pull against each other, and, to show Mr. C. what I think of his shooting, I will wager him another £25 that he cannot kill 35 out of 50 at 30 yards. Two things I will promise Mr. Churchill, namely, that he won't know where the birds are coming from, and that he won't have many centre traps; I shall pull which I like, he of course to do the same.

Yrs., CHARLES BOSWELL,
Gun Maker.

SIR, AS REGARDS Mr. Churchill's shooting, I am not in the least surprised at it. His quiet behaviour over this match deserves commendation, as anything like modesty in a pigeon match requires encouragement just now.

No doubt Mr. Boswell would like a fresh match, perhaps another after that, but he must remember that not everyone has sufficient spare time to avail themselves of his kind offers, and we should also think as to whether it would be desirable to start a match in which the loser is pretty sure to intimate he has not been fairly dealt with, and so end in anything but a satisfactory manner.

Yrs., A.B. BARNSBURY.

BEATERS ETC.

THERE IS nothing the agricultural labourer enjoys so much as employment as a beater on a grand day in the preserves. He is the severest of critics and woe to the duffer who figures before him. He is apt to get it very hot. Beaters are very keen, and the cheerful confidence with which they ask you to shoot a rabbit between their legs is quite touching. We were once told by a keeper that one of his beaters had lost an eye in a bramble bush. I pitied the man and the answer was, 'Oh, he's a hard man. He doesn't care about his eye.' The Duke of Gloucester, a very wild shot, deprived his equerry of half his sight, and then complained that the wretched unfortunate made 'such a fuss about his eye'. An old gentleman in the eastern counties once shot and killed a boy and an under keeper in the same year. On asking one of his beaters whether his master felt the matter very much, 'Well, sir,' he answered, 'he didn't care very much about the boy – he gave his mother £5 – but he were very much vexed about the man. He did not go out shooting for a whole week.'

GUN HANDLING FOR BOYS

THE FIRST thing you do when you go shooting with another boy, is to guard yourself against accident. The best way to do this is to shoot the other boy before he has time to load his gun. Then take both guns to the nearest stream and throw them in. Throw in the shot and powder after them. If you have any matches about your person, throw them in also. Then start at once and go home as fast as your legs can carry you. And if you are under 18, the chances are, even with these precautions, that you will get both legs and a section of your back filled to the brim with birdshot.

– ROBERT BURDETTE

ZINGARI

WE HAVE received a small tube of this new shaving extract for review, and can only say it is the best preparation we have ever met with. It leaves no soreness, leaves a lovely creamy lather, is fragrant, and undoubtedly allows you to shave closer. Having some left over, and it being our French poodle's shaving day, we tried it on him, and now the intelligent dog refuses to be shaved with any other. It is in tubes, price ls. 3d. each, post free, and is made by Mr. L.B. Bigglestone, chemist, Canterbury.

[This puff has been written by a Sub. who shaves – we don't – and we expect the inventor will have to pay dearly for it, for both Adelina Patti and the Jersey Lily's testimonials pale before it. – Ed.]

1887

MR. GILBERT'S ADDRESS

SIR, CAN YOU tell me the address of Mr.
Gilbert, of 'shooting corrector' fame?
        Yrs., W.H.B.,
        Market Harborough.
[We have not the slightest idea. – Ed.]

SPORT IN INDIA

THERE IS most delectable sport in the catching, snaring, shooting, and hooking of creatures. But to the sober-minded, practical, bearded man I appeal, whether much of the attendant satisfaction is not wanting in the absence of a comfortable assurance that these good gifts will not be marred in the cooking. And so, to my mind, there is no more fitting close to a good day's sport than a good dinner. Young fellows fancy that they like roughing it – that's because they have not tried it.

And herein consists one amongst other advantageous features that India, above all other game-abounding countries, offers to the sportsman. He has not to rough it. On the contrary, he carries with him into the wilderness all the comforts and luxuries of civilised life. After a hard day's shooting he returns to a lively and busy camp, where fires are blazing all round and the wives of his tired followers are cooking savoury curries; whilst from his own snug canvas kitchen there issues a stream of mingled odours suggesting the coming feast. There in the rear, is his little bathing tent which, entering, he finds furnished with a capacious tub flanked by half a dozen water pots, filled to the brim with purifying water after the manner universally practised in the East, and holding two to three firkins apiece. Hence refreshed, one step carries him to his sleeping and dressing tent where a comfortable cot with snowy mosquito curtains seems by turns to invite and to promise repose. His dinner toilet soon completed, he seeks the familiar mess tent where he knows from past experience that there awaits him the reward of a good day's work.

A handsome, spacious and well-lighted tent, double-roofed and double-walled. On the ground rich Jubbaulpore carpets, surpassing in softness and richness of colour the famous looms of Turkey. About a round table, covered with glossy damask and glittering with glass and plate, are set four chairs, though in truth the shooting

SHOOTING TIMES.

FIFTH YEAR OF PUBLICATION.
ILLUSTRATED

Shooting Times,

AND KENNEL NEWS.

Edited by LEWIS CLEMENT, ("WILDFOWLER,")

Ex-Contributor and Kennel Reporter-in-Chief to the London "Field."

Author of "Shooting & Fishing Trips," three series; "Tables of Loads;" "Public Shooting Quarters;" "Modern Wildfowling;" "Dog Breaking," etc., etc.

REGISTERED AS A NEWSPAPER AT THE GENERAL POST OFFICE. [FOR TRANSMISSION ABROAD.

VOL. V. No. 248.]   PUBLISHED EVERY FRIDAY.   LONDON : FRIDAY, JUNE 3, 1887.   EIGHT PAGES.   [PRICE TWOPENCE.
POST FREE, TWOPENCE HALF-PENNY.

SOME SENSATIONAL FERRETING.
BY "WILDFOWLER."

It was in the days when *Drink* had such a long run at the Princess's, I had gone to see that famous play, and, to my surprise, on coming out I fell in with Johnny, an old chum, who, on the strength of the play having been translated from *l'assommoir*, had evidently gone between each and all the acts to *entr'acte-come-more*. (N.B.—This joke has been registered, on account of its antiquity.)

Well, Johnny, I am sorry to say, clearly had, as usual, taken a little more than was good for him, and when I saw him home, he first told me (after more drinks) that (1) I was his only friend, then (2) he wept, and (3) finally he wanted to fight. I didn't. So I saw that he was duly put to bed, and at parting reminded him that he had promised to come ferreting with me on the next day.

To my great surprise he actually turned up at the station at the appointed time, and all the way down he was truly repentant.

by the way a few brace of birds and a hare or two. Then we had lunch at his cottage; after which he put two ferrets in a sack, and we made a start for the new wood. Johnny was much brighter then, and was getting quite jolly; in fact, he was in as bright a frame of mind as need be when he was posted in front of a big burry and one of the ferrets was put in.

I went about 30 yards further down to another burry, and slipped the other ferret in. Johnny was standing as still as a mouse, and I was going to devote all my attention to the job on my own hands when suddenly I heard my worthy friend utter an unearthly yell, which would have done infinite credit to one of Buffalo Bill's wild Injuns. And there he was, with his hair standing on end, and glaring at a rabbit hole.

"Great Scott!" he shouted.

"What's the matter? What's up?" And I ran up to him.

"Oh! oh! oh!" he moaned, "I've got 'em on!"

"What!"

THOSE NEW SPRING HATS!

WOULD-BE SHOOTIST.—"Will you do me the favour to stop your pony for a moment, madam? I've been following that woodcock (!) for two hours."

"Silly thing—to get tight, don't cher know, dear boy!"

"Quite right," I said. "It is a silly thing."

"It makes one feel so queer-like the next day," he went on, "and, do you know,that play *Drink* is fearful enough to give a fellow the horrors. Fancy Coupeau seeing monkeys and rats and snakes, and so on! B-r-r-r! It makes me shiver. You don't think last night's dissipation would have such effects upon me, do you?"

"Of course not," I replied. "Such hallucinations are the result of long-continued,steady, persistent drinking.

At this he appeared but slightly relieved. I expect his head was aching and he was not yet quite himself. Howbeit, as we winged our way (winged is, I think, the proper term to express speed when railway travelling), we discussed the prospects of sport, and I explained to him that part of the place we were going to was a bit of land belonging to an old lady who hitherto had never allowed anyone to sport there.

"The small wood particularly, has been sadly neglected, and I believe it to be full of vermin, as nokeeper has looked after it for years, but I know there are *some* rabbits, nevertheless, for I have seen a few cut when passing by. However, we will chance it, and do our best. The old lady at last has consented to let me have it, together with two or three large fields for £5 a year, and as the lot is just in the midst of my shooting, it will come handy."

Well, my old keeper met us at the station with a brace of setters and a retriever, and we worked our way up across the fields, shooting

"You know," in a plaintive tone of voice. I looked at him and thought he had gone cracked.

"Yes," he said, sitting down on the bank and burying his head in his hands, "a rabbit with great fiery eyes as large as saucers just looked at me out of that hole opposite!" and he shivered.

I looked at the hole, and, sure enough, two large round eyes were glaring at us!

And out flew an owl!

I floored it, like a man, in order to prove to Johnny that his fancy had not been playing him tricks.

And then he began to laugh.

"That infernal play last night *did* upset my nerves," he said. "But I am glad this is over, anyhow, for who the dickens would expect an owl out of a rabbit burrow!"

"Oh!" I said, "I had a similar case not very long ago."

"Oh, you," he rejoined, "what is it you have not seen, I should like to know!"

And we laughed, and then a rabbit bolting at my end, I went to watch after my ferret, but poor Johnny was bound to have another turn, for, presently, out of the same hole bounded a great white cat!

(Continued on page 314.)

(Continued on page 314.)

party consists of three only. A number of servants stand around, each arrayed in spotless muslin, but with a variety of gaudy turbans that would fill the heart of a British dowager with envy and despair. Every *met* is suggestive of sport and furnishes some undying memory. That mulligatawny soup is flavoured with the delicate juices of a pea-chick. The murrell, best of Indian fresh-water fish, was caught with a spinning-tackle by Jones and finds itself in strange company with oyster sauce. That splendid steak is a tender reminiscence of the grand old tusker who made such a gallant stand on Wednesday and died with two inches of fat upon his ribs. Could the designer of the New Law Courts have partaken of that raised *vol-au-vent* with its confused flavour of snipe, quail and mushrooms, what brilliant architectural conception might not have presented itself as he demolished its mimic walls and battlements!

But the curry – oh, that curry! you would never guess what it commemorates. I suppose woodcock toast is about the best thing to be found within these four seas. But snipe-toast, if the snipe be fat and well conditioned, is every whit as good. Fancy, then, a curry entirely composed of the 'trails of snipe. Of course this is not a common dish. How can it be, when it takes at least 50 snipe for a small curry? Many a gallant Indian sportsman has gone down to his grave without having ever tasted a 'trail curry. As for the ὁι πολλοι – by which I would be understood to mean all those poor creatures that are not sportsmen, such a dish, even if they could get it, would be much too good for them. – 'LONG-SPEAR'

THE GUNS OF A LIFETIME

SIR, AMONG my oldest and most valued friends are men who shoot with the following:- a pair of Purdeys, at 80 guineas; a Westley Richards, at 40 guineas; and a Powell, at 35 guineas – all good guns. I undertake to say that Cashmore would supply guns as valuable, except that his guns would not have the advantage of the eminent names I have mentioned. But, then, names don't shoot. My experience has been varied and extensive. I began (as a lad of 10) with *flint and steel*(!); that was on board the *Bellerophon* at

Colonel Hawker's famous gun.

the Battle of Trafalgar, the then owner being First Lieutenant of the ship and 'mine uncle'. Soon that gun was converted to percussion, but we did not keep company long. My next flame was a Joe Manton (a 16-bore), and about that time large bores came to the fore. Soon after that pinfires came in, and I had one of them – a double grip. Then the snap actions started – so did I. Presently central fires were brought out – I was let in. Then the guns were made to look like the old percussion gun. Immediately after I had bought this, rebounding locks came up. I came up too and have been coming up ever since, for hardly a year goes by without something fresh being started.

I was a member for some years of the Civil Service Stores, in Victoria-street, and of the Junior Army and Navy Stores, but I thought their guns very dear.

Yrs., J. THOMAS.

THE SPORTSMAN'S WIFE

SIR, MY HUSBAND is a shooting man, and I wish to know if any of the other ladies who see the *Shooting Times* experience anything of this kind. After a week's shooting he returns as jolly as a sand boy, full of fun and pride at the sport they have had. Well and good; that I can enter into and enjoy – to hear all the news. But now, sir, at night he lies on his back and takes up all the bed with his great long legs, and if I mildly suggest that he must move over a little, out he swings his huge arm, shouting out in a voice loud enough to raise the neighbourhood, 'Mark over!' 'Leg down bird!' and, on crying out 'Oh, George, you have hurt my nose!', he adds insult to injury by shouting out, 'Down, you cur!' At last I manage to awake him and his answer is 'Dear me, I'm awfully sorry, I must have been dreaming.'

Is there any cure for this?

Yrs., SUFFERER.
[Not that we know of. – Ed.]

LORD ASHBURTON'S PARTY

LORD ASHBURTON entertained the following distinguished company at The Grange, Alresford, and had some good sport in partridge shooting, the weather being favourable and the birds plentiful. The party of seven guns comprised H.R.H. the Duke of Cambridge, his Grace the Duke of Roxburghe, the Earl Ilchester, Lord Walsingham, Colonel the Hon. E.H.T. Digby, the Hon. Francis D. Baring, and Captain

St. John Mildmay (in attendance on H.R.H. the Duke of Cambridge). The bag totalled 4,076 partridges, six pheasants, 31 hares and one rabbit. This bag of partridges has not been beaten yet.

SHOOTING A FROG

SIR, LAST SUMMER I was out on a marsh with a friend when we met a fellow who had been shooting in an adjoining marsh. He picked up a frog and said he would blow it to atoms. So he put it on the muzzle of his gun – which, of course, he held pointing upwards – and pulled the trigger.

What was the result?

Why, the gun burst!

Yrs., R.J.M.

[Served the fellow right! – Ed.]

MISS ANNIE OAKLEY

SIR, JUST GOT back from game shooting in Shrewsbury. Rainy weather all the time, but killed plenty of game. Miss Oakley has done fine work. We leave in a few hours for the Continent. The 'E.C.' Powder Co. presented Miss Oakley with a large silver tea-pot – Hoping to see you in a few months.

Yrs., FRANK C. BUTLER.

SIR, I NOTICED a few weeks ago in some of the sporting papers that a question had arisen as to whether the above lady could perform on English game as she does on pigeons, glass balls etc., in her exhibition shooting.

Miss Oakley was shooting with me on Wednesday, Thursday, and Friday last, and during those days she killed pheasants, partridges, hares and snipe, her shooting being wonderfully clean; the wretched state of the weather prevented her getting a shot at grouse, but, judging from her shooting at other game, there is little doubt they would have stood a poor chance before her.

Not only did Miss Oakley prove herself an exceptionally good shot, but also a plucky walker over very heavy ground.

She carried one of the splendid pairs of 20-bores, built for her by Mr. Charles Lancaster, the killing powers of which in her hands seemed quite equal to any 12-bore.

Yrs., W.R.C. CLARKE,
Shrewsbury.

A WORD FOR STARLINGS

SIR, WHEN I was a boy I once stole my father's gun, and went off to have a day among the wild pigeons. It was bilberry time, and the birds were in flocks, but I didn't get near them. I could always get alongside rooks when I hadn't got a gun, but on that day I found even them shy, and the yellow hammers quite out of reach. I felt mad, but I wasn't to be done quite, so I started on the bumble bees. I got no end of sport, and blew the bees to bits too small to bag. It was fine fun, but just as it was getting fast and furious, my father bagged me, and I thought all the bees had got into my bonnet after that. Now why don't starling 'sportsmen' begin upon bumble bees? They would be doing far less harm. Starlings are not too numerous. True, they like a cherry, but they are among the best friends a sheep farmer has.

I do like a true sportsman, but I don't like to hear of anyone who kills 25 starlings at a shot, skins them and takes their back bones out and stews them. Why, sir, the man who does that must be uncle or cousin german to the little boys who, now the nights are long, go round with clip-nets and lights to catch birds in the ivy. They came round my way last week, but sud-denly discovered the weakness my Newfoundland bitch has for seats of trousers. Fifteen starlings at a shot! A yokel here beats him though. Eight and 20 sparrows and a blackbird at one discharge. I remonstrated with Garge for his cruelty and Garge replied:-

'Sparrers, sir? Whoy, dang 'em, doctor, I cawn't abear 'em.'

How's that for bitter, starling fanciers?

Yrs., GORDON STABLES,
M.D.R.N.

[What a whack you are having all round, doctor! You will catch it directly no doubt. By-the-bye, are you aware that Colonel Hawker (of wildfowl reknown) once fired his double-barrel punt gun, carrying *two pounds* of shot, into a large flock of starlings which were roosting on the reeds on Southampton Water, and he picked up hundreds of them! Moreover he wrote: 'The time to shoot starlings by wholesale is just before the dusk of the evening, when they come to roost among the reeds. Having swept down some dozens with your duck gun, let their heads be immediately pulled off, as this will in a great degree prevent them having a bitter taste.'

How is that, doctor? – Ed.]

THE DELIGHTS OF A DEER FOREST

SIR, I AM thankful to say that my lease on _ _ _ _ _ Forest has at length expired. I have had the confounded place for three years, and it has cost me not less than £3,000 per annum, all told, in addition to no end of clothes of all kinds. I have never worked so hard at any time of my life as I have done at the business of deer-stalking; I have walked for an hour at a time well over my boots in a running stream, twice I have been up to the chest in a stretch of moss, once I have fallen over a precipice,

---

and three times I have had an unsought for bath in the loch. On another occasion when I was creeping about in a plantation of young larches, I was fired at by one of my own ghillies, and narrowly escaped being killed. *Per contra*, I have on five occasions brought down my stag. I was, of course, sprinkled with blood on the first occasion of showing my prowess, at a cost of half-a-sovereign to each of the seven fellows who were in attendance, and two sovereigns to 'The McAllister', as I call my head-forester, who seems to be thought a much greater man than his master.

Yrs., 'HIGHLAND SPORTSMAN'.

[24]

MISS ANNIE OAKLEY

Sir, As I leave for America shortly, my departure being hastened by my health which is not of the best at present, I write to ask if you will kindly allow me space in the *Shooting Times* to thank the English Press and the Public for the many favours shown me during my stay in England. To the members of the Gun Glub, Hurlingham, and the Sporting and Dramatic Clubs, I am indebted for the many pleasant hours spent in their company. I am leaving England with regret, but I hope to return at some future time, and see my many English friends. Until then I will say good-bye, wishing all a Merry Christmas.

Yrs., ANNIE OAKLEY,
'LITTLE SURE SHOT',
151 New Bond St.

P.S. To your correspondents who complain of the English powders, I can suggest a permanent cure, viz. try the Foreign powders. I HAVE BEEN THERE!

ROUGH JUSTICE

A telegram from Bechuanaland says that Mr. Fred Seton, the celebrated hunter, with some English friends, Mr. Jamieson, of Dublin, Captain Fountain and another, who were on a hunting expedition to Le Benqulo's territory, were away in Mashonaland after big game, accompanied by a bodyguard of 150 Matabele warriors under an Induna. Their duty, while ostensibly acting as guides, was to watch the white hunters and thwart any attempted gold prospecting. The latter attraction, nevertheless, induced the whole party to deviate from the hunting grounds towards the northern goldfields, prospecting by the way. The Induna neglecting to prevent this, one of his followers, fearing the consequences, returned and informed Le Benqulo, the king, who dispatched a regiment to administer the inevitable punishment. The king's messenger overtook the party, and communicated the death sentence, which was immediately carried out. All the 150 natives died without a murmur, the mode of execution being two spear thrusts and a blow from a knobkerrie. The English hunters were simply cautioned, and conducted back. All this does not read pleasant for the natives – but then let us not forget that *they are only niggers*.

1894

DISAGREEABLE EXPERIENCE

MISS MARTEN, the professional English shot, had a very disagreeable experience the other evening during an exhibition of her skill at the Zoological Gardens in St. Petersburg. Whilst shooting an apple off the head of an assistant named Morris, the markswoman missed her aim and wounded her human target in the forehead. The bullet, luckily, did not pierce Morris's brain, otherwise Miss Marten would have been tried for manslaughter.

FRIGHTFUL DEATH

M. LEON SAVOURÉ, a country gentleman, aged 68, who was living at Morigny, in Seine-et-Oise, France, met with a frightful death on Saturday, while out rabbit-hunting. He had sent his ferret into a rabbit-hole, and getting impatient set about getting into the rabbit burrow himself. He managed to get in up to the waist, but there stuck until extricated some hours later by some neighbours. He had been suffocated, and his contorted features showed that he must have endured great suffering.

Ferreting in Belgium.

ROYAL PHEASANTS

Queen Isabella's shooting parties.

THE QUEEN, of course, is privileged to break the Game Law – or any other laws for that matter – so today (Saturday) the royal gamekeepers at Windsor will shoot a few brace of the best young pheasants, and despatch them to Balmoral so that they may grace the Queen's dinner table on Monday October 1st. There are plenty of birds this season. By-the-bye, it is estimated that every pheasant which is killed in the Queen's preserves costs 11s. 6d.

Her Majesty's first pheasants, which are prepared for the table in the early days of October, are cooked *à la chipolata*. They are trussed and nicely roasted, and when taken from the spit they are dished up and neatly garnished with a *chipolata ragoût* which is made as follows. Twist one pound of pork sausages into small round balls, separate these, fry them, and when they are cold, trim and put them into a *bain marie* containing a proportionate quantity of cocks' combs and kernels, button mushrooms, truffles, *quenelles*, carrots, and turnips turned into the shape of olives, and boil them down in their own glaze; also some round balls of braized streaky bacon, and an equal proportion of chestnuts peeled and boiled in the *consommé*; add a little essence of truffles and mushrooms, then set the *ragoût* on the fire to boil for two minutes, and serve with the pheasant.

LORD CARDIGAN

SOME GOOD stories are told of the late Lord Cardigan, who led the Light Brigade at Balaclava, and his shooting exploits. On one occasion, it is said, he was annoyed with his keeper about the scarcity of game, and ordered him to beat through another wood which he pointed out, promising instant dismissal if satisfactory results were not obtained. 'But, my lord,' urged the keeper. But he was interrupted by Lord Cardigan. 'Not a word, sir; obey my order at once!' Terrified, the wretched man slunk off, and the wood was duly beat up to the guns. There was scarcely a head of game in it. Limp and dejected, the unfortunate keeper now came up, and when his lordship had said all he had to say, and was compelled to stop for want of breath, the poor man meekly pleaded. 'But, my lord, it's not your wood at all – only you told me to beat it.'

DAD'S OLD MUZZLE LOADER

AH! THOSE happy times when we were lads. Some of us are turning grey now, and the hair is 'getting a bit thin on the top, sir', of others; but, thank goodness, the true sportsman always retains a certain amount of boyishness. And it is well that it is so. We are so rushed and knocked about in this busy, tearing world of ours that it is a relief, after the worry of business, to turn once more to the gun case; to lift out our favourite weapon and, gently caressing it with an almost boyish glee, to murmur,

'We'll be off again in a few days, old fellow.'

Hurrah for the stubble and the copse, hurrah for the bonny brown hare and the welcome whirr of the partridge. Let old 'Time' grizzle our locks as he may; let him stiffen our limbs with rheumatism and throw his misty vapours before the lynx eye of our youth. But, hark! we hear the merry laugh of assembled shooters; once again the sound of the rustling stubble falls on our ears, and we are young again, my boys; thank God, we feel young again.

An old friend called upon me the other day bringing with him a new gun which he had just bought. It was a 12 hammerless ejector, with all the latest improvements, as the advertisements say, and as my friend was extolling its beauty he suddenly burst into a laugh. 'I say, Tom, old chap, do you remember your dad's muzzle loader? It would look funny alongside my new gun, wouldn't it?'

Did I remember it indeed! Could I ever forget it? Handed down from goodness knows how many generations, it had hung over the mantle for years without being used or cleaned. But as I grew older and the shooting fever increased with my stature, its days of quiet were numbered.

I reached it down one fine afternoon to have a bang at a large hawk which was bothering the fowls in the farmyard a good deal. Shoot the hawk, forsooth, it is a wonder I did not shoot myself or one of my boon companions, who, lad-like, delighted in anything which showed the spice of danger.

We poured down about three times the proper charge of powder, followed by half an old newspaper for wadding and a quarter of a pound of chipped lead. And I was to have the first shot. Great Scott! it gives me a cold shudder to think of it, even after the lapse of so many years. Surely a special providence looks after boyish pranks.

The first shot! The first earthquake I thought afterwards. I could remember pulling the trigger and then, as the novels say, all was a dreary blank. A black eye and a contused shoulder were the result of this, my first essay with the old gun, besides a general sense of soreness as though I had been soundly thrashed, which pervaded my system for the next few days. But as I got better I longed for another try.

On examining the gun I found the stock was so much shattered that it was necessary to fasten it together, and to the breech, with a piece of rope. The spring of the lock was broken also, and the trigger useless. The latter difficulty did not appear insurmountable, we were youths of resource I can assure you. We got an old hammer from the tool house and we thought that by dropping the cock on the nipple, and giving it a smart tap we should do nicely. But how about aiming; was one to hold the gun and another to do the tapping? No, this division of labour did not commend itself to our eyes, so we rigged up a sort of tripod affair to carry the gun and thus leave both hands of the gunner at liberty.

Did we ever shoot anything? Oh, yes; my first kill was an old ram, of famous pedigree, which my father prized highly, and after this exploit I am afraid that my efforts to become a sportsman were to be rudely checked.

You see it was this way. On the farm there was a small plantation of about an acre in extent, and this having a dry, sandy soil, and being rough and hilly, someone in years gone by had turned it into a rabbit warren.

The rabbits would come out by the score at dusk and in the early mornings, and as they generally used the same old 'runs' we thought that by fixing the gun in a hedge about 20 yards away, and laying upon one of these 'runs', we might, if fortune favoured us, bag at least one rabbit.

Our ordnance being fixed in readiness, we went down one fine night at dusk and, after waiting a short time, a big bunny popped his head out on the very 'run' we fondly imagined we had aimed for. A smart tap with the hammer, a loud report, and a cry of pain following, told us we had hit *something*. But, horrors! On rushing out to bag the game, we found the poor old ram kicking in his death agony.

The gun must have got a twist, or we had mistaken the 'run', I never knew which; but there was our victim as dead as a doornail in five minutes.

The dad refused to be comforted, although I imagine he derived a grim sort of satisfaction from the tremendous hiding he gave to yours truly as soon as he heard of our mishap.

The old gun was locked up, and I had to be content with a catapult for a few weeks. Still yearning after a firearm of some sort, I got an old flute and by carefully blocking up all the holes but one (which I had left for a touch hole), and carving a rough stock, I made such a weapon as surely never existed before or since. This 'gun' had certain disadvantages, not the least being the way the charge had of finding its way through the touch hole as often as through the muzzle. After setting fire to my clothes twice,

and burning off my hair and my eyebrows as fast as they could grow, my father thought it best to get me a proper gun and allow me to use it in a legitimate way.

Perhaps this pleasure would not have been granted me so soon but for the following incident. My powder had to be hid from prying eyes, and I had put it in an old mustard tin and buried it in the garden. Naturally enough it became damp and would not ignite, so I took it into the kitchen and put it into the oven when the servant's back was turned. My ill luck followed me as usual and I forgot to take it from the oven before going to school. Of course it was baking day, and equally of course the oven plate got red hot, and a mighty explosion ensued. Fortunately no one was hurt, but the incident helped my father to make up his mind, and after this I had my own little ammunition chest, and

For your neighbour's peace of mind
— don't swing across the line

kept all my shooting requisites in good order. Father used to say he never regretted the day he bought me a gun and gave me permission to use it without restraint, and personally I feel it was a red-letter day in a most uneventful life.

It is singular how boyish pranks cling to our recollection in after life. To this day my sporting friends twit me good humouredly about my exploits with dad's 'old muzzle loader'. – 'WHIMBREL'.

EXTRAORDINARY HUNTING INCIDENT

BARON VEITINGHOFF and Prince Hohenlohe went together to shoot stags, and agreed to decoy the animals by imitating their call on a special kind of horn. When they reached the hunting ground, therefore, the two hunters separated and, each accompanied by a gamekeeper, went off in different directions. During the course of the day they unknowingly approached each other, and each heard the other's decoy call, and believed that a stately stag was before him. They, imitating as usual the heavy steps of the animal, noisily drew still nearer, and the imitation of steps and call was so well done that they finally arrived within ten paces of each other without perceiving their mistake. The thicket was so dense that they could not see each other. They both stood still, repeating the challenge from time to time; neither perceived any difference to the natural challenge, and each firmly believed he was within a few

paces of a real stag.

At last Prince Hohenlohe got tired of waiting, and fired thrice rapidly in the direction where he believed his game to stand. The first bullet glanced off the cartridge belt of Baron Veitinghoff the supposed stag; the second struck his watch; the third fell dead from a pocket-book well filled with papers, and the young Baron though hit three times, was unwounded. He was so convinced that, not his fellow hunter, but a stag was before him, that he attributed the three shots to explosions in his cartridge belt and was busy in unfastening the belt and throwing it away. The astonishment of both comrades when at last they found out what had happened must have been very great, and their joy at the happy ending of what might have turned out a tragedy equally so. The Prince Hohenlohe of this curious adventure is the son of the new Imperial Chancellor.

GALLIC GULLIBILITY

AN ABSURD story has been published in the columns of a Parisian contemporary, which

further stated it could absolutely vouch for its truth. It was to the effect that the

French government had received information that several well-known English sportsmen had started for Madagascar for the express purpose of seeing how many Frenchmen they could bag. It was a match got up by a party of 'honourable gentlemen' belonging to an association, who, being tired of tiger shooting, had decided on organising 'La Chasse à L'homme,' but preferably of the Frenchman because he was the most redoubtable and the most noble type of manhood. The journal also asserts that this was not the first occasion on which this sport had been indulged by France's 'amiable neighbours on the other side of the Channel', as they had already tried it in Tonkin and Dahomey. The hope was expressed that the French generals, being duly warned, would see that their soldiers would treat these *fous furieux* like the wild beasts that they were, and gave themselves 'the great attraction of a very select shot'. Our Gallic friends are wonderfully gullible if they can swallow such trash as this.

BETTER THAN SANDRINGHAM

Mr. Clarke-Thornhill has had a most successful shooting party at Rushton Hall, Northamptonshire, where nearly 1,400 pheasants and a heavy bag of other game were killed by seven guns in three days. Rushton is a very pretty old place, near Kettering, with a well-wooded park. In 1862 the estate was nearly being purchased for the Prince of Wales, and it would have been a much better bargain than Sandringham has proved.

DOG SPEARS

Sir, I shall be glad if you can inform me if it is legal to set dog spears in plantations without giving notice on boards that such instruments are set.

Yrs., JUSTICE.

[Dog spears can be set in woods, and the owner of a dog injured by them has no redress against the person who set them. No notice is required. – Ed.]

1895

VANISHING FRUIT

IT IS NOT generally known that an orange hit in the exact centre by a rifle ball will vanish at once from sight. Such, however, is the fact. Shooting it through the centre scatters it in such infinitesimal pieces that it is at once lost to sight.

ELEPHANT COURT MARTIAL

ELEPHANTS EMPLOYED in the military service are not only drilled in the ranks, but are also tried by court-martial, like soldiers, for insubordination or breaches of discipline. A case of this denomination occurred in the ranks of a garrison battery or artillery station near Rawal Pindi, Bengal, for the purposes of trying Elephant Abdul for causing the death of Syce (grass cutter) Ramboucles. The court-martial was most impressive. The prisoner marched between two comrades, all the witnesses bringing up the rear, till the place of trial was reached. The president of the court-martial – a major of native infantry – then read out the charge: 'Elephant Abdul is charged with causing the death of Syce Ramboucles by catching him by the legs with his trunk, and beating his brains out against the wall of the grain hut.' The first witness called was a bombadier who stated he was at the lines at noon watching the elephants being fed. When the trumpet sounded 'feed', he saw Syce Ramboucles run with a bag of grain to elephant Abdul. By this time all the other elephants were fed, and consequently the Syce was late in feeding his animal. Abdul, greatly angered at the groom's neglect, on his approach to the lines seized his legs and killed him. Eight other syces gave similar evidence, and the charge being fully proved, the court found Abdul guilty, and sentenced him to 50 lashes and two years imprisonment. Right well the prisoner knew he was in for punishment, for, on being taken to the prison shed, the inside of which he had seen before, he, quickly remembering previous chastisements, roared piteously.

Three days later the sentence of the court was carried out. At morning parade the whole battery was drawn up in square, 14 elephants forming one side, the non-commissioned officers and men on the other three. In the centre were the prisoner, two huge elephants as escort, and the flogger elephant, Lalla. The officers of the battery, the brigade-Major and the doctor were also within the square. Four great iron pegs were driven into the ground, to each one of which the prisoner's legs were chained. Lalla stood by with a huge chain fastened round her trunk, waiting for orders. Everything being ready, the doctor, who stood with a watch in his hand, gave the signal to begin. Lalla raised her trunk, then gave it a couple of turns, and down came the iron 'cat' with terrific force on Abdul's back. A loud thud was heard, followed by an unearthly roar from the prisoner. Again the doctor gave the signal, and down came the chain, causing more roaring. And so lash after lash were administered until the 50 were completed, after which the prisoner was marched back to prison trembling in every limb, a few lumps on his back being the only sign of the severe punishment.

FIVE BIRDS A MINUTE

SOME REMARKABLE shooting took place on the Highclere estate of the Earl of Carnarvon last week, notwithstanding the extremely wet weather. The party, including Earl Carnarvon, Earl De Grey, Prince Victor Dhuleep Singh, Prince Frederick Dhuleep Singh, Lord Ashburton and one other – six guns in all – shot near the lake and killed no less than 1,300 pheasants in three-quarters of an hour. On two previous days this week the same party shooting over Lord Carnarvon's preserves had killed some 6,000 head of game. To kill 1,300 pheasants in three-quarters of an hour, means 216 birds per man, or five birds a minute for each gun.

Bag of nine guns – 150 ducks and nine swans.

1896

FAITHFUL SERVANT

UPON A GENTLEMAN'S tomb, in Warwickshire, we read that he was 'accidentally shot by his gamekeeper'. Under this piece of information is the text, 'Well done, thou good and faithful servant.'

SEAL HUNT

ON THURSDAY last a remarkable capture was made at Brown Hill Staunch, about six miles from St. Ives. A party of anglers from St. Ives discovered a seal in the river and immediately gave chase. After some time, one of the party succeeded in shooting it in the head, when it sank to the bed of the river. A reverend gentleman, who was in the vicinity and joined in the chase, dived and fetched it up, and was rewarded for his trouble by having it presented to him. It turned the scale at 24lb.

FIRST BREECHLOADER

IN MY YOUNG days it was just beginning to be talked about in the field at lunch times, of a certain Frenchman who had invented a gun which loaded at the breech. It was treated with roars of laughter and the smile of contempt. I have since seen much the same thing applied to hammerless and one-trigger guns. I remember an uncle of mine coming to our place to shoot and he had a breechloader, the first we had seen; it was shown round overnight and handled and looked at and scanned and quizzed and put up and pulled off, and at the finish declared by all the old hands to be a dam'd dangerous thing and worthy of a Frenchman, for at that period the French were looked upon with very different feelings to what happily they are now. The sting of victory is sometimes in the tail, and our country village has now recovered from the awful strain upon the young men who had gone to the wars and never returned. Our old nurse used often to tell me, if I did not go to sleep she would send up 'Old Boney Party'.

The next day the breechloader was to be in the field, and my father, who was a true sportsman, advised Uncle George to work on the left in case of accidents. I was warned on no account to try the weapon, which, of course, being a radical turn of mind, I did on the first opportunity, and liked it much.

Five or six years ago I took a hammerless partridge shooting with some old friends I had shot with for years. The same thing over again, no one liked the look of the thing, 'Like a dog with no ears,' says one. 'Not safe,' says another and so on. Yet, in years to come I fully believe, that is if we have anything left in dear old England to shoot, bar claybirds, that the gun of the day will be a straight bar of iron, loaded with greased lightning, and you simply press a button, and there you are, don't you know. – 'JUPITER'.

DUKE OF MALAKHOFF

A CURIOUS STORY is related by Lord Blackford of the Duke of Malakhoff. He (Malakhoff) was at a battue at Stratfieldsaye and shot nothing, much to his disgust, and when the day was over it appeared that he would be extremely put out unless he was allowed or enabled to kill something; so, in spite of all the gamekeepers could think, feel, or say, a pheasant was procured, tied by its legs to the top of a post, and Malakhoff was put some 30 yards off with a double-barrelled gun. It was supposed that he would thereupon and from thence take two shots at the bird. Not a bit of it; he loaded his two barrels, walked close up to the pheasant, put the muzzle close to him and discharged both barrels into him with *'He! coquin!'* The next day the Duke of Wellington told the keeper that Malakhoff was a great man who had smoked to death 500 Arab men, women and children in a cave, to which the gamekeeper replied, 'Like enough, your Grace, he'd be capable of anything.'

AN UNFORTUNATE ACCIDENT

COUNT MEDRANO, owner of large game preserves at Tirault, near Mons, in Belgium, was so annoyed at the constant poaching that took place that he ordered a loaded gun to be placed in the gateway leading to his land in such a manner that it should be discharged by the opening of the gate. A few days later he fell victim to his own device, for on opening the gate for some friends, the gun went off, and he received the charge in the breast.

1897

HACKNEY MARSHES

THERE IS IN THE East of London a rendez-vous for the poorer sporting world of the metropolis known as Hackney marshes. A strange crowd gathers on the marsh on Saturday afternoons and Sunday mornings – labourers, publicans and sportsmen who 'have seen better times', all intent on inexpensive amusements, few of which, however, can be called 'sport'. The favourite pastime is sparrow shooting. Matches are arranged between rival shooters, and a dozen or two of sparrows are bought from a dealer on the ground at about sixpence a dozen. A sparrow is placed in a collapsible box, the shooter takes up a position about 20 yards away, and a string is pulled from behind. The box collapses and, as the sparrow flies, the shooter fires. He generally brings it down. A number of scouts post themselves at a certain distance from the shooter and, if he misses, the sparrow has to run the gauntlet of the scouts. It is seldom that a sparrow gets clean away. Even crack pigeon-shooters might envy the skill of some of these men. The writer has seen a labourer in his shirt sleeves kill 25 sparrows in rapid succession, a more difficult feat than the shooting of 30 pigeons. The small size of the mark and its uncertain flight make it really difficult to hit. Many hundred sparrows are often killed in a day.

HOSING RABBITS

MR. OSWALD VON LENGERKE of the firm Von Lengerke and Antoine, Chicago, recently, when out shooting with a friend from New York, learned something about catching rabbits which beats half a dozen ferrets. While hunting they came alongside an express wagon standing on the roadside, and in the bottom of the wagon were a number of dead rabbits. The driver of the wagon had no gun and Oswald was about to enquire how he got the rabbits when, on looking round, he saw a couple of men coming towards the wagon, each carrying a number of rabbits, and neither of them had a gun. Mr. Lengerke was dumbfounded for a moment, but he finally ventured to ask them how they caught the rabbits. 'With this rubber hose,' replied one. 'How do you catch rabbits with it?' queried Mr. Lengerke, still unable to see how it could be done. 'Come along,' said the man with the hose, 'and I'll show you.'

Mr. Von Lengerke and his friend followed a short distance, when a little cur

BILL COX, 36, Manchester St., LIVERPOOL.
High Class Taxidermist and Furrier
Workmanship and Satisfaction Unconditionally Guaranteed.

and, stationing himself near it, he spread a small net supported by two short stakes in front of it. Meantime rabbit hunter no. 1 wormed the hose down into the first hole as far as he could and, placing his mouth over the end of the hose which he held in his hand, shouted through the hose at the top of his voice. In a second from the hole being watched by his comrade came the rabbit, landing squarely into the net and rabbit hunter no. 2 pounced upon bunny and dispatched him. This was quite pleasing to Mr. Von Lengerke and his New York friend, and they laughed heartily. Finally the man from the East said he did not believe the net was a necessity, and that he could catch a rabbit without it.

Another rabbit den was soon found, and the New Yorker fixed himself in front of the exit close down near the opening and told rabbit hunter no. 1 to 'let 'er come'. The hose was inserted into the hole as before and the alarm was given, when out came the rabbit with great force, striking the New Yorker square between the eyes, and knocking him end over end. The rabbit broke its neck and was added to the pile on the wagon. The New Yorker is quite satisfied that a net is indispensable to a man who has any regard to his personal appearance and Mr. Von Lengerke says the hose and the net is the slickest rabbit catching device he ever saw.

that accompanied the rabbit hunters sniffed at a hole in the ground, indicating that it contained game. 'Now,' said the man with the hose, 'come up close and I'll teach you the trick.' In the meantime, rabbit hunter no. 2 had found another hole out of which he supposed the rabbit would come

BOAR HUNT

AN INCIDENT, unique of its kind, has recently occurred at Rodez. A herd of wild boar, 17 in number, driven by a hurricane, took refuge in a stable above the wood at

Palanges, a few miles from Rodez. A shepherd who wanted to shelter his flock there heard, as he was nearing the spot, an unusual noise, and thought that the stable

Poachers caught in the act!

must be full of wolves. In his fright he ran off to the nearest village, Trehosf, to give the alarm. The inhabitants quickly armed themselves and made in the direction of the stable. When they arrived, they ascertained they had wild boar instead of wolves to deal with, six of them full grown, the rest suckers. Closing the door with care they made a hole in the roof, and through the aperture directed their fire until they had shot them all down.

POACHERS' MORALS

NOTHING SHOWS more completely the decadence of poachers' morals than the fact that a man who admits he is an old hand at the game has fallen so low as to steal dead pheasants. An old-fashioned poacher with a pride in his profession would have scorned such an undignified method of acquiring spoil. Thomas Jackson was caught in the act of stealing two dead pheasants from the shop of Mr. Webb, Streatham, and when brought before the South-Western magistrate said, 'I am an old poacher and have more at home.'

There is, however, a great difference between stealing 'still' game and capturing the flying birds on their native heath. The latter may be wrong, but it has in it an element of sport as well as of danger: but the former, as the magistrate remarked, is simply larcenous impudence. For this offence Jackson was relegated to the tread-mill for 14 days.

UNSINKABLE BATTLESHIP

So DENSE is the water in the deepest parts of the ocean that an ironclad, if it were to sink, would never reach the bottom.

IRISH WITNESS

AN IRISH witness was being examined in his knowledge of a shooting affair. 'Did you see the shot fired?' the magistrate asked. 'No, sorr. I only heard it,' was the evasive reply. 'That evidence is not satisfactory,' replied the magistrate sternly, 'stand down.' The witness proceeded to leave the box, and directly his back was turned he laughed derisively. The magistrate, indignant at this contempt of court, called him back and asked him how he dared to laugh in court. 'Did you see me laugh, your honour?' queried the offender. 'No, sir, but I heard you,' was the irate reply. 'That evidence is not satisfactory,' said Pat quietly, but with a merry twinkle in his eye, 'so stand down.' At this everybody laughed – except the magistrate.

TSAR'S HEALTH

THERE IS NO foundation for the alarming rumours regarding the health of the Emperor of Russia which have been industriously circulating during the last few months. His Majesty does not suffer from any cerebral symptoms, as has been alleged; he is out every morning as soon as it is light, and keeps himself in condition by running a verst (1,160 yards, or about five furlongs), watch in hand, to see that he can do it in his average time. One of his amusements is said to be shooting from a bicycle, and he can bring down a crow even when he is going at a good speed.

A LADY'S FIRST SNIPE

ALTHOUGH THE snipe is the smallest bird that attracts the lover of sport, it affords more discussion than any other. Woman as I am, the prospect of getting one of the swiftly flying fowl, here in beech-tree country, allured me, and attired in rational costume, with a light fowling piece under my arm, I braved marsh and heavily-ploughed fields. It was a speculative quest, for in this part of Buckinghamshire would-be snipe shooters are likely to meet with about as much sport as did the visitors to that French land-owner who kept a hare on his preserves for the accommodation of his friends.

We considered ourselves fortunate when a farmer with whom we had scraped a speaking acquaintance informed us that he had seen a snipe, only one, down in the bottom; and we were welcome to bag it, if we could. There was no time to be lost if we, my brother Alick and I, intended to avail ourselves of the opportunity; for the speedy long-bill, who can scarcely be made sure of until he figures on toast, is proverbially uncertain in his movements. There was a snaw, and a blaw, with a suspicion of thaw; and when the weather is variable, Jack Snipe is seldom found in the same locality for two days together.

Our route took us past Waller's Oak, and early though it was, and with a few scattered snowflakes falling, a Corydon and Phyllis were love-making beneath the venerable tree. The man was as clownish as any old-time Puritan, while the 'damsel' appeared of the type of modern servant-girlism, in her tawdry jacket and imitation fur boa. As we walked briskly past, the man stooped to whisper something in the maiden's ear; at which she laughed out loud immoderately. He may have called attention to my dress, as my feminine instinct suggested he did; or perhaps, the spirit of Waller prompted him to repeat the poet's high-flown lines to Sacharissa:

'In heaven itself thou sure wert drest
With that angelic-like disguise.'

The farmer considerately provided us with a boy and a dog, one of which proved as useless as the other. The urchin did not know a snipe from a thrush; while the cur evidently imagined that the object of our excursion was rats. Before the end of half an hour we wished them both back at the farmstead. The boy conducted us to the bottom – a boggy marsh, with a stream half hidden by briars, alders, and osiers running through it. It was weary work plodding through the ice-covered slough and spongy snow; but neither the boy nor the dog minded this. The one had his small mind occupied with thoughts of rats, while the other was gleeful because of a few hours respite from the turnip cutter.

'Tom, you are certain there is a bird in there?' we dubiously asked.

'Yes, sir – ma'rm, I means – lots on 'em. Falfits (fieldfares), spinks (chaffinches), and once I seed a water-hen, but that was a month ago,' the lad replied, with a fatuous grin on his expressionless face.

Clearly no assistance was to be obtained from our ornithologically inexpert guide. So, determined to get down to business, we set to work; and our trials began. The dog discovered a hole, which, to all appearance, had not been occupied for a twelve-month, and scratched thereat with so much persistance that we turned our backs upon him with disgust. We ploughed our way up and down that bottom, now on one side of the stream, now on the other, occasionally making dives into the marsh; but all was to no purpose. Not a snipe was discoverable. The only feathered fowl in evidence was a robin which, disconsolately perched on a spray of hornbeam, strove to raise a winter song. Tom was beginning to cry with the cold, and we – I have been warmer in a blinding blizzard in Norwegian glens than I was in this beastly bottom. We were turning for the tenth time, when, half a mile downstream, and not a dozen yards from the place where the ratting dog was still carrying on his profitless pursuit, a snipe rose with that indescribable flight which has only to be seen once to be remembered for a lifetime.

It was useless to try further; and Alick suggested that we should send the boy and his useless companion home, and adjourn to the roadside hostelry. A shilling dried Tom's tears, and sent him on his way rejoicing; while we were soon absorbed in the mysteries of bread and cheese, and beer so small and weak that, as Alick pithily remarked, a syphon was needed to lift it out of the pewter.

By this time the wind had risen, and snow was falling heavily; but, disregarding the discomfort of drenched garments, soaked feet and benumbed fingers, we resolved to make one more bid for fortune. So we turned back into the marsh. It was in a nick of time. Alick had scarcely begun to poke in the bushes, when up rose our long-sought-for bird. Bang, bang! The first barrel missed; the second was more fortunate. The snipe fell – shot by a woman.

It was a magnificent creature, with a perfect bill, splendid wings, and fine plumage. As the farmer, whom we met on our return said, 'We might have gone down to the bottom for years, and not had such a chance.' The trophy lightened the toil of our homeward journey, and the subsequent 'trail' more than compensated for incipient influenza. – HELEN MACINTYRE.

RHEUMATISM CURE

WILDFOWLERS MAY now indulge in their favourite pursuit with extra zeal, as a new cure for rheumatism has been discovered. It is reported that at the town of Eden, a place in Australia which stands on the shores of Two-fold bay, there is a hotel, where rheumatic patients congregate. Whenever a whale has been taken the patients are rowed over to the works where the animals are cut up, the whalers dig a narrow grave in the body, and in this the patients in turn lie for two hours as in a Turkish bath, the decomposing blubber of the whale closing around the body and acting as a huge poultice. We almost think that the cure would be worse than the disease.

SHOOTING LADIES

IF I AM old-fashioned enough to think the fair sex much more in their place by the fireside on our return from hunting than scratching their faces, spoiling their complexions, and risking limb, if not life, by our sides in the field, I am just enough to admit that there is something to be said on each side in that case. Against the participation by women in the sport of fishing, it is difficult to say more than that they may be better employed. When we come to the gun, however, I must say I cannot be so moderate.

The lady shooter on Bradford Moor.

There is one form of it which especially raises my bile. I refer to deer-stalking. Every autumn, we read in the papers how Lady A., Mrs. B., or Miss C. has 'bagged a royal', or 'grassed a nine-pointer'.

Now I consider a man but half a sportsman whose joy is not tempered with regret as he leans on his rifle beside the monarch of the glen, and it seems to me that a feminine (as distinguished from female) mind should feel the regret but not the joy. And then the butchery details. I suppose the 'fair rifle woman' does not assist in the gralloch; but are there no such things as the life blood running from the wounds caused by both bullet and stalker's knife – the painful last contractions, the dying limb, the glazing eye? I think that such sights are not for women; and to show that I am not alone in my opinion, I will quote one scene from memory. It is nearly 10 years ago and the Devon and Somerset Staghounds have set up their stag in a small pond, traversed by a flight of rails, at Barnsworthy Farm, near Fairfield, on the Quantock Hills. A rope is quickly thrown over the animal's horns, with which he is drawn up to the rails, and Arthur's ready knife is thrust into his broad chest. The blood rushes out in a great stream, but the poor stag makes no sign except a moaning bellow of pain. Silently most of the sportsmen turn their horses round in the lane, and move off to empty flasks and light cigars further off. For several minutes, I am told, the poor beast stood so, his legs gradually beginning to shake, till he fell down with a crash. Throughout this time, a young woman remained quietly sitting on her horse, and looking on, within five yards of the animal.

'Did you ever see anything so sickening as that girl's conduct?' said one sportsman

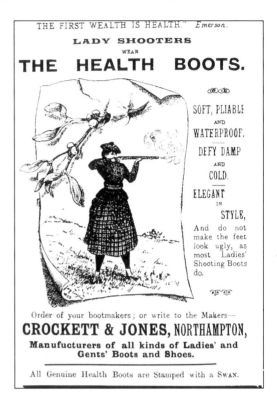
to another in my hearing.

'Never in my life,' replied no. 2. And every man present agreed with him.

Women of England, think of this before you submit yourselves to like criticism. – 'SNAFFLE'

SICK STAG

THE PRINCE of a small German state had invited a number of gentlemen to go on a deer-stalking expedition. Everything promised well. The weather was superb, and the company was in the best of spirits, when the head keeper approached the petty monarch, and, lifting his green cap, said in faltering tones. 'Your Highness, there can be no hunting today.' 'Why not?' was the stern rejoinder. 'Alas! Your Highness, one of the stags took fright at all the people and escaped into the adjoining territory and the other has been ill since yesterday. But your Highness must not be angry – it is most likely nothing but a bad cold. We have given it some herb tea and hope to get it on its legs in a few days!'

Ask your host before you bring a dog

1898

CAPTURED TIGER

A YOUNG TIGER was recently captured by Malays at Tanjong Basar. It was caught in a trap, from which it was transferred to a packing case and presented to the Acting Superintendent of Police. The tiger is now quartered in a large cage, which has been specially built for it, and is doing well; its chief food being unregistered dogs, which are run in by the police.

ELEPHANT HUNTING

THE RUSSIAN painter Poljakoff, who has just returned from Africa, has made a very singular communication about the expedition of Prince Henry of Orleans and M. Leontieff. To him its main purpose seemed to be the killing of elephants. The expedition consists of the two Chiefs, a French Vicomte, a representative of the Moscow syndicate, which entrusted goods worth about a 100,000 roubles to the expedition, two French sergeants, three Cossacks, two French servants, 10 Arabs and a 100 Senegalese. The sale of the rather worthless Moscow goods, which cannot for a moment compete with the much better and cheaper British and Indian goods, is the only ostensible purpose of the expedition. They have 20 rifles of the largest calibre and two Maxims, and hope to kill 1,500 elephants annually. Two rival expeditions of elephant hunters are about to be organised at Jibuti.

VERMIN LIST

IN HIS INTERESTING little sketch of Glengarry and Glenquoich, Mr. Edward Ellis gives the following list of vermin trapped in the first named glen between 1837 and 1840:- 11 foxes, 198 wild cats, 78 house cats (going wild), 246 martens, 106 pole cats, 301 stoats and weasels, 67 badgers, 48 otters, 15 golden eagles, 27 white-tailed eagles, 18 ospreys, 98 sparrow hawks, 7 peregrine falcons, 11 hobbies, 275 kites, 5 marsh harriers, 63 goshawks, 285 common buzzards, 371 rough-legged buzzards, 3 honey buzzards, 462 kestrels, 78 merlins, 63 hen harriers, 6 gyr falcons, 9 Montagu's harriers, 1,431 hooded crows, 475 ravens, 35 horned owls, 71 night jars, 3 barn owls, 8 magpies.

DUCKING BULLETS

IS IT ETIQUETTE to bob when bullets are flying? The question is interesting just now to our gallant little army in the Soudan. There is an amusing passage in Gordon's journal, in which that redoubtable authority says: 'Certainly. For my part,' he says, 'I think judicious bobbing is not a fault, for I remember on two occasions seeing shells before my eyes which certainly, had I not bobbed, would have taken off my head.' He says that in the Crimea it was considered mean to bob, and they used to try to avoid it. One of his fellow officers used to say: 'It is all very well for you, but I am a family man.' And he used to bob at every report.

Elephant shooting.

REMINISCENCE OF THE FIRST

THE SHOOT was over a small farm in Essex, and a capital little shoot it was for two or three guns. It was only about 120 acres in extent, but nicely broken up and generally plenty of cover, the roots doing wonderfully well in that locality. Game was usually abundant, lots of birds and every bank holding rabbits. The day had been hot, and my friend the farmer and I had been round and round the boundaries, breaking up some good coveys of birds and driving them in towards the middle of the farm, where there was a beautiful piece of mangold of about seven acres, a perfect death-trap for tired young birds, but, and there is always a 'but' in these cases, it was a very dangerous place to shoot, a lane bounding it on one side, whilst four or five labourers' cottages were dotted round the border of the field.

However, we had put several coveys right into the middle of the field, and we decided that we simply must follow them, although it was with a good deal of nervousness that I, for one, commenced the first beat across, with a cottage right in front of me about a hundred yards away. Almost directly, up got some birds, and flew just right for us, and we promptly bagged three of them; this was encouraging, but soon after a bird rose wild to me and, just as I got to him and all looked safe ahead, he swerved low to the right and instinctively I swung round with him and fired, bringing him down winged; but imagine my horror when a quavering voice came from the cottage garden, 'Hi! You've shot me.' My blood ran cold, and I went up to the fence and looked over, expecting to see a mangled mass of humanity. However, out toddled a very old man, with no visible wounds upon him, and proceeded to explain matters. It appears that he was crouching down behind the garden hedge, eagerly looking on, hoping to see some sport when I fired. He managed to slew himself around, and just a stray shot or two hit him in the rear, and he was decidedly more frightened than hurt. After much investigation we found one shot mark on his enormously thick corduroys, which had actually acted as armour plating and flattened the shot. We made the old boy very happy by presenting him with half a crown, and my friend gave him some good advice, telling him how silly he was to be in his garden, and strongly advising him to go upstairs until the shooting was over. The old man was very penitent and evidently thought he was quite to blame in the matter and trotted off indoors.

Well, we beat round once more, and this time up got a regular crowd of birds, scattering all over the place. Bang! bang! went our guns; there was a tinkle of glass, and a despairing sort of yell. 'Hi! You've shot me again!' This time I was not the culprit. But my friend, who had just been talking to me very seriously about my 'carelessness', had sent a charge of shot right through the old man's window, most fortunately missing the man but shattering the glass and frightening the poor old fellow half to death. He came out again and in appealing accents said, 'Where am I to go? You shoot me in the garden and when I go upstairs you shoot me there too'. 'Go into the cellar!' roared my friend, who was very angry at my laughter. 'There is no cellar,' said the old man. 'Then go to _ _ _ _ _!' the rest is a blank. We once more 'squared' our old friend and left the birds in peace, deciding that the birds in that field were not worth the candle. – 'GOVERNOR'.

'CANNONITE'

The King of Smokeless Powders.

The German Emperor shooting with "CANNONITE" over the Wemmensgill Moors.

SAFETY SMOKELESS POWDER

IN TWO VARIETIES.

No. 1 FINE GRAIN. —A concentrated Powder for cone-base cases.

No. 2 COARSE GRAIN. —A Powder measure for measur with Black for loading int ordinary Nitro Cases.

SOLD by ALL THE PRINCIPAL GUNMAKERS & DEALERS IN AMMUNITION THROUGHOUT the COUNTRY.

Wholesale only

JOHN HALL & SON, LTD.

79 CANNON STREET, LONDON, E.C.

CHASED BY A LION

I RODE OUT ON my bicycle from Blantyre on Monday afternoon, August 22nd, and reached Mr. Stroud's before the sun went down, and after waiting a few minutes, started again just after sunset. By the time I got to the Namazi crossing it had got quite dark, except for a little light the new moon was giving. The road leading to the Gala estate from the main road has just been made, and is quite soft and lumpy, besides being very steep for at least half its length. When I left the main road I dismounted, and started pushing my bicycle up the hill, but before I had gone far I heard a heavy body pushing its way through the bush on my left. When I had gone a short distance up the slope I looked round, and almost had a fit when I saw a full-grown lion standing across the road, broadside on, with his head turned towards me, and, as I looked, he started in pursuit. I attempted to mount my machine, but, owing to the slope and my excitement, I failed twice. The third time I succeeded in getting away, and I did pedal for all I was worth, but the machine kept wobbling across the road, and I saw that the lion had lessened the distance between us by about a half, though I was still 50 yards from the top of the slope. He kept up a low growling all the time, and I could hear him more and more distinctly as he lessened the distance between us. At last I reached the crest and flew down the opposite slope. I then suddenly remembered that there was an open culvert across the road some 200 yards ahead, but there was no time to dismount, so I rode into it, and the shock flung me high out of the saddle, but I fell back on it without being knocked off. Fortunately the side of the drain next to the hill was high, and the opposite side low, so the machine was not stuck in the culvert, and although the front fork was twisted and the front wheel grated against it, it was not quite jammed and I was able to ride on. When I reached the smooth part of the road near my plantation I was able to get up a good rate of speed, but I no longer heard the growl in the rear. – D.C. ROBERTSON.

ROTHSCHILD BEREAVEMENT

NOTWITHSTANDING the bereavement of the Rothschild family, caused by the death of Baron Ferdinand de Rothschild, the London omnibus drivers and conductors yesterday received their customary Christmas gift of a brace of pheasants each. The drivers, as usual, acknowledged the generous and thoughtful gift by sporting the Rothschild colours, and at the same time showing their sympathy with the bereaved family by tying them to the whip handle with a knot of crape. That the men are grateful for the handsome present each year goes without saying, but if anything their gratitude on this occasion is all the more marked, seeing that their benefactors have not forgotten them even in their hour of affliction.

1899

BULL V. LIONS

AN EXCITING fight between a bull and two lionesses took place in Madrid a few days ago, when, contrary to public expectations, the brave toro certainly got the best of the encounter. The bull promptly dashed at his antagonists who reared on their hind feet to receive him. One of them dealt him a heavy, tearing blow with the forepaw, and was promptly hurled into the air. The other lioness then crouched as for a spring, but the bull gave no time, driving his horns into the beast's side with terrific force. This drove the lioness into headlong flight, with the bull in furious pursuit, and the fight was virtually over. The bull's vengeance, however, was terrible. He was severely lacerated about the head, but the lionesses were in a pitiably gored and gory condition, and one has since succumbed.

PRECIOUS SPANIEL

WE ARE TOLD that the famous ruby spaniel, Fantine, which the Duchess of Marlborough has presented to Mrs. George Vanderbilt, is valued at £1,500. Fantine has a jewelled collar valued at £500, and every morning and night her coat is brushed and perfumed. For this purpose there are two perfume bottles in gun-metal with gold screw tops, two gold-backed brushes with an 'F' engraved, with the inevitable crest upon the same, tortoiseshell combs, crested gun-metal soap box, and innumerable satin sponges.

WHERE TO EMIGRATE

SIR, PERHAPS in your next issue you could kindly give me advice and information on the following subject. I am very fond of fishing and shooting, but find my income too small to enable me to have really good sport in this country. Where, in your opinion, would be the best place for me to go and settle, where I could have really

first-rate fishing for salmon, trout etc., and also fair shooting? I am a married man and do not wish to go right into the wilds, but to be within reach of ordinary and necessary supplies. I should like to buy a small amount of land to begin with, build a house etc., and gradually open up an estate on which I could rear livestock. I should like it to be in a place where living is inexpensive, and where sufficient labour can be had at a reasonable price; in fact, my idea is to begin on quite a small scale in some healthy climate, so that in 10 years time, say, I would be the owner of a nice little sporting property with livestock rear-ing as an occupation. Any information and advice you may kindly give me I shall be very grateful for.

Yrs., 'WOULD-BE
COLONIST', Cornwall.

[Personally, we think that either British Columbia or Vancouver would be the most suitable place. The climate is very healthy and severe weather rare. The fishing, both salmon and trout, cannot be beaten, and good sport can be had with a gun at deer, wildfowl, grouse, partridge, quail, etc. Hired labour is certainly expensive, but living is cheap if you raise your own stock and vegetables. – Ed.]

EXCITING ADVENTURE

FIVE YOUNG ladies, while taking an afternoon walk by the river a few miles from Colchester recently, met with an exciting adventure, being attacked by some swans which had nested on the river bank. Two of the ladies got behind a haystack, and three climbed up a willow tree. In descending, one of their number, a Miss Dalton, became entangled in the branches by her petticoats and hung head downwards. Fortunately, the Rev. H. Anson, curate of Coggleshall, and a lady friend, happened to come up, and soon released Miss Dalton from her perilous position. The swans were beaten off.

TRAP PIGEON TRADE

SOME INTERESTING details of his business have been supplied by Mr. Roberts, the well-known pigeon purveyor. It appears that from 3,000 to 4,000 pigeons are, as a rule, kept at the aviaries in Great Dover Street, and these include all descriptions of 'rock' birds, from the cheapest pigeon at half a guinea or 12s. a dozen to the Lincolnshire blues at 30s. a dozen. These last are small birds, and mostly come from the fen country, although some are bred in Cambridgeshire and Yorkshire. Some idea of the extent of the business may be gained from the statement that 20,000 of the birds were ordered at one time for Monte Carlo and delivered within lots in a very short period. In England alone it is said that over one million pigeons constituted a year's supply, whilst Monte Carlo, it is estimated, disposed of 150,000 in a year. This is without counting such minor Continental pigeon shooting centres as Aix-le Bains, Ostend, and Spa, which also take nearly as many in the season. These enormous numbers will give some idea of the importance of pigeon-shooting to the gun makers and powder manufacturers in this country, as these birds, it must be understood, are not reared to supply poultry dealers, but solely to afford sport with the gun.

NOTES FROM WESTMEATH

SIR, IN YOUR interesting notes I see a mention of hedgehogs. I always kill every one I meet, as I am sure they are very injurious to game eggs and chicks. Once, when visiting a trap that I set in the middle of a bog for a moor buzzard, I caught a hedgehog that had grouse feathers sticking about him. Rooks and crows have been a terrible nuisance to me this spring. They smashed nearly every egg I poisoned for the magpies, and, of course, had to pay with their lives. Magpies, when sucking an egg, do not break it up, whilst a rook will smash it and spill its contents. I got a sample lot of cartridges of the new issue of Normal powder, and tried them at rabbits, and found them highly satisfactory, killing rabbits over 40 yards dead at the mouth of the holes. An impudent rook walked into my kitchen when I was at dinner and would have stolen a three-parts grown chicken but for the servant hustling him out. I ran out and slipped in the last cartridge of the sample. Mr. Rook was well away, nevertheless I banged at him, and he collapsed into the middle of my early potatoes, where he was badly wanted to hang up as a warning to his brethren. The distance was over 83 good paces. Going over to a

Ptarmigan, a good all-round Irish sportsman.

friend's place to shoot the rabbits, his keeper asked me to bring home his setter, which had been staying with me whilst his master was away, so I gave Jerry a gallop over the bog. Never had I seen heather in a worse condition, and not a vestige of water; yet Jerry found two splendid packs of grouse, all well forward considering the small piece we hunted. There is a marked absence of magpies and co., round here now, which amply consoles me for the loss of the fishing. To revert to that impudent rook, fancy the beggar walking into the kitchen; the chicken is a cripple, and is a pet of the servant; she is delighted at my shooting what she, in her simple language, calls 'the d_ _ _ _ _d impudent old crow'.

Yrs., PTARMIGAN.

P.S. – What is a chough? I have never heard of one in Ireland. I have never seen a moor buzzard since I killed six on the bog of Allen in 1885 – they were a terrible scourge to the grouse.

[The chough is a member of the crow family, met with on rocky western coasts of these islands. It has decreased in numbers lately owing to the insatiable greed of that ubiquitous animal the 'collector'. – Ed.]

MOOR RENTAL

A TYPICAL five-hundred-brace driving moor in Yorkshire, without house accommodation was for seven years leased by a friend of the writer at £250 per annum, to include the wages of a keeper and the sporting rights over a few hundred acres of rough shooting adjoining the moor, consisting chiefly of rough pasture, with a few acres of cultivated land and a large straggling wood. The yearly expenditure did not exceed £310, inclusive of all costs except purely personal items; the total bag for seven years was 3,410 brace of grouse, 86 pheasants, 263 brace of partridges, 12 couple of snipe, 10 couple of woodcock, a few hares and over 1,000 rabbits.

RESOURCEFUL RAT

IT IS REPORTED that a rat that was caught alive on board a British naval vessel was thrown into the sea. A large gull swooped several times, endeavouring to pick up the unfortunate beast. At length the bird came too near the rat's jaws, and was grabbed by the neck. A fight ensued, and ended with the death of the gull. Then the rat, with wonderful presence of mind, scrambled upon the bird's body, and, hoisting one wing as a sail and using the other as a rudder, steered for the shore.

1901

DEATH OF THE QUEEN

THE WAVE OF sorrow caused by the death of our beloved Queen has swept round the world and depressed the hearts of all our kith and kin with the sadness of a sincere and profound regret. She was the embodiment of all that is good and sweet in womankind, and she was venerated almost as a goddess by millions of dusky subjects. It is difficult to realise the enormous changes that have taken place in the lifetime of our late Queen. Muzzle loaders and percussion caps were the order of the day, and that worry to present-day sportsmen, the Ground Game Act, was undreamed of.

Those were not smokeless days but good old black powder reigned supreme, with its accompaniment of powder-flask and shot-belt. Then the enthusiastic shooter sallied out at ungodly hours of the morning and disdained the pleasure of a sit-down, hot luncheon and unlimited liquid refreshments. The art of driving grouse and partridges had not been invented, and the routes to the moors and manors were travelled in tedious stages by coach instead of lightning expresses fitted up in the height of luxury.

FREE BARKERS

THE FAMOUS gunmaker, Joe Manton, was stopped one day by a highwayman while crossing Hounslow Heath. On hearing the summons to 'Stand and Deliver', Manton looked hastily out of the window and recognised a pistol of his own make levelled at his head. 'Why damn it, you rascal!' cried the indignant gunmaker, 'I'm Joe Manton, and that's one of my pistols you've got. How dare you try to rob me!' 'Oh! you're Joe Manton, are you?' said the highwayman coolly. 'Well you charged me 10 guineas for this brace of pistols, which I

call a damned swindle, though I admit they're a good pair of barkers. Now I mean to be quits with you. Hand me over 10 guineas and I'll let you go because you're Joe Manton, though I know you've got £50 at least about you!' Joseph swallowed his wrath, and promptly paid the 10 guineas. But he never forgave the highwayman for getting a brace of his best pistols for nix, and he made himself a special double gun, with barrels barely two feet long, which he always carried about with him afterwards when travelling and christened 'The Highwayman's Master'. With this weapon, I have heard, he subsequently shot a high-wayman who stopped his chaise and mortally wounded him.

BULLET MUSIC

MR. PREVOST BATTERSBY, who was a war correspondent in South Africa, describes the sound of a Mauser bullet passing through the air as 'resembling the note of a little brown bird like a brambling; the Lee-Metford's note is nearly a third lower; and the Martini has the dull buzz of a loaded bee. The Mauser's most melodious period is from eight to 1,800 yards. Over that distance its note is the most exquisitely lovely of single sounds. "The silky breath of the Mauser" – no phrase has described it better. But there is something more than beauty – something strange and baleful about it. It goes by like the sighing of a wandering soul that can only rest by bringing death to another. A sighing so indescribably tender and sweet and sad that every sound of human lips seems without charm beside it. One may be expressing a purely personal sensation, but after lying for any time under that silky breath I have consciously to resist a desire to lift my head and take the next puff in the face.' The note of a Mauser spinning the wrong way after a ricochet, Mr. Battersby says, 'is like the coughing of a sick ghost.'

OK, IF TAME

SIR, PLEASE let me know in your next issue if it is legal to use live pigeons at matches here during the months of April, May, June, July, and August.

Yrs., 'SNAP SHOT', Cork.

[Yes, if they are tame pigeons. – Ed.]

MADAME BERNHARDT

WHILST MADAME Sarah Bernhardt was in Florida a short time ago, she determined to try and bag an alligator, and with this object she put on men's clothing including a huge pair of waterproof leather boots. An alligator about 10 feet long was driven out of some reeds, and Sarah Bernhardt promptly fired and missed it. At the second shot, however, the bullet landed between the eyes of the brute and crumpled him up, and his skin was brought back to Paris as a trophy.

DEATHS IN INDIA

SOME CURIOUS figures with regard to the depredations of wild animals in India are given in a Blue Book just published. From 23,851 human beings who perished by them in 1890, we get to 27,585 in 1899, which is the highest figure on record. In 1897, tigers, leopards and wolves were the most destructive. Snakes in 1899 accounted for 24,619 human beings. In 1899, the tigers killed amounted to 899, whilst in the same year wild beasts destroyed 98,687 cattle. In 1899, 18,887 wild beasts were slain, and in addition no fewer than 93,921 snakes.

Remember the ferrets when rabbiting

1902

SPORTING PRIMATE

WHEN Primate Marcus G. Beresford was first appointed to an Irish living he proceeded to tramp over his glebe lands with a dog and gun; on his return he met a sour Presbyterian, tenant of some of the lands, who accosted him thus: 'We never read, your reverence, that the apostles went shooting this way with their dogs and their guns.' 'Ah! very true, my friend,' replied the rector, with a humorous twinkle in his eye, 'but, you know, they were so busy with their fishing, and they could not attend to more than one thing at a time.'

FRENCH SPORTSMEN

THE ORTHODOX French sportsman is described in the following and, we should hope, none too accurate terms:- Every Frenchman is a sportsman – or so he thinks he is. He dresses himself like a Corsican bandit, arms himself to the teeth with guns and hunting knives, and, with three or four fierce dogs – often bloodhounds – tugging at him, makes for the suburbs. At night he returns triumphant and in seventh heaven with two unfortunate sparrows. He is the hero of the neighbourhood for a week. Ten thousand Parisians take out shooting licences every year, and swear to have the blood of some doomed sparrow. They register these oaths at the licence bureau, where the right to blaze away in any part of France for the whole year costs only 22s. Sunday is the great shooting day. Soon after daybreak you can see at the Paris railway stations groups of men dressed as if for a lion hunt. They wear large picture hats like Fra Diavolo, and fierce, merciless scowls. They talk of the dangers of the chase as if they were nothing at all. They swagger up and down, almost bursting with excitement, elbowing out of the way mere men in ordinary attire. They are objects of great and admiring solicitude on the part of young women. 'There is the brave Alphonse. My heaven, regard him! Regard his face! He has no fear whatever as to danger. Ah! the hero who goes to shoot the desperate sparrow in his lair!' Then there is the dog, which looks up into his brave countenance with undisguised hero worship. His master afraid? Well, he'd like to see the sparrow that could frighten him! – The Parisian sportsman, before aiming at the bird, aims at the picturesque. He must look the part. It is a question of posing. The hat is the thing. It must be Tyrolean or sombrero type, recklessly turned up at the sides in a devil-may-care Three Musketeers kind of way. There must be a feather in it, too, and a big one. The true-born sportsman will not sell the game that falls to his gun, although the market price of a partridge is twenty pence, of a pheasant 3s. 6d., and a hare 4s. The middle-class sportsman distributes his sparrows and larks among his friends, imitating in this the sportsman of noble blood. Often he will donate one sparrow to a hospital in emulation of the seigneur who sends his pheasants there. For are they not bound by the common tie of sport?

LOST FEET

WE LEARN THAT Lord Francis Hope is slowly recovering from his gun accident, which was due to the carelessness of his loader, it is a curious coincidence that both he and his brother, the Duke of Newcastle, have lost their left feet as the result of accidents.

JACKAL HUNTING

A CURIOUS method of hunting jackals is said to be practised in India. In an open space in the jungle a number of bamboos are driven into the earth and the tops bent down and attached to the base by a peculiar fastening. To the end of each bamboo is tied a clay pitcher, containing meat and water. All being readied, the jungle is set on fire and the jackals driven into their holes. These holes would, then, contain 500 or more jackals, and the object was to drive them out of their retreat by means of smoke and fire. The animals, driven out by the smoke and heat, were hunted towards the bent bamboos where, smelling the water, they plunged their heads into the clay pitchers to obtain relief. Upon attempting to withdraw their heads, the loop was released and the jackals sent flying into the air. An eye-witness to this extraordinary sight says:- 'Some never came down to the ground again, but rent the air with piercing wails, hanging on the top of the bamboo. Now and then a bamboo would send a jackal to such a height that it looked like a mere speck in the sky, and then fell on top of the highest palm tree. The jackal killers say that if the bamboos are strong enough to do their job properly the air is filled with flying jackals. Sometimes the jackals see through the stratagem, and, finding some companion with its head in a pitcher, try to drag him away, with the result that two or three are thrown into the air together. Two jackals were seen by me simultaneously thrown into the air from opposite bamboos, and they collided in mid air. The pitchers broke with a crash, and the two creatures fell to the ground fearfully stunned. Now and then the machinery of a bamboo was out of gear, and the rope snapped in twain, and the jackal would be sent skimming along so near the surface of the ground that it brushed against and struck another jackal that was running past.' It seems a tall story, but then we often hear remarkable hunting yarns from Indian sportsmen.

HOW TO EAT GROUSE

Willow grouse in winter dress.

THAT PRINCE of Chefs, Alexis Soyer, thus advises those who would thoroughly appreciate the flavour of well-conditioned grouse. 'To be well enjoyed, grouse should be eaten in secret, and take my experience as a guide. Do not let the bird you eat be too raw, but well roasted, and drink with it at intervals a little sweet champagne. Never mind your knife and fork; suck the bones and dwell on them. And take plenty of time, that is the true way to enjoy a game bird.' This is sound, honest advice, with the exception of the opening sentence which we do not agree with, and we consider all grouse and game birds are better enjoyed in the company of two or three friends.

SHAH OF PERSIA

THE SHAH OF PERSIA, like most eastern potentates is very fond of sport, particularly shooting. He possesses some very fine English guns, and it is expected that he will indulge in some grouse shooting during his visit to this country. When he was in France a couple of years ago he was invited to shoot a few miles from Contrexeville by some officers of the regiment temporarily stationed there, and he duly started off in a closed landau with a pair of breechloaders in front of him. When halfway there some birds got up in an adjoining meadow, and his Majesty at once took up his guns and let go at them from the landau with both barrels, much to the consternation of the driver, who imagined a terrible tragedy had taken place within the carriage. His suite comprised about 70 persons, including all his Ministers and also the leaders of the Opposition, so that no revolution could take place in his absence.

Common quail.

1903

FOR SALE

SALE 12-bore breechloader by Purdey, in brass-tipped leather case. Cost £80.

SALE Second season retriever dog, very tender mouth, splendid nose, good on runners, strong and active worker. 8gns.

ROYAL LUNCH

THE STANDING dish at all the King's shoots is Irish stew, and this is served punctually at one o'clock, when the Royal party and all the beaters, keepers, etc., participate in the savoury mess. As can be understood, the quantity required is very large, and the stew is conveyed in properly heated pans.

GEESE

24 January

SIR, I HAVE killed over 200 wild geese in the Island of Islay, Argyllshire. My best day was 27 geese, 16 of which were killed with one barrel of a 7½lb. gun, 2ft. 4in. barrels, 1½oz. of No. 3 shot, at 11 p.m. I often killed eight to 10 at a double shot.

Yrs., JOHN LEGGE, Kilbirnie.

31 January

SIR, SIXTEEN wild geese killed at one shot seems a rather incredible yarn. They must have been asleep, and huddled up close together. Such an account of a shot makes your mouth water.

Yrs., FRAZER, Westmeath.

14 February

SIR, I HAVE shot in all parts of the world, and at all kinds of game, and I am quite confident that it is impossible for anyone to have killed 16 geese with one barrel, 12-bore. Even if one tied them up in a bunch, or pegged them to the ground by the feet, in any position to suit oneself, you would still be lucky if you hit four or five. I do not say kill them even then; in fact I dare say the majority of the four or five would not be much hurt; but as to killing them, why, you would hardly kill 16 starlings.

Yrs., S. ELLIAG, Sheerness.

21 February

SIR, I MAY say, 'evil be to him who evil thinks.' I am sure that no gentleman ought to have written such a charge against a perfect stranger. The day I shot the 16 barnacle geese I was staying the night with Mr. A. McDonald, a gentleman farmer, whose grandfather, a Mr. Campbell, left him the farm and the celebrated stock of Highland cattle; and Mr. McDonald was a cousin of Lord McDonald. After dinner we were chatting and, hearing the geese calling from a field close to the house, we went out together, and Mr. McDonald stayed at a gate at the lower end of the field, while I

Well stopped!

went up behind the whin fence. There was a large flock of the geese, and I could aim at about 25 or 30 yards from the fence, as I had a wire cartridge in the other barrel. I did not fire till I met Mr. McDonald and a single goose flew over my head; but I missed it. Then we went up, and found the 16 all dead, as any winged or live geese had plenty of time to get away. No doubt many were wounded, and went to the 200 acre island in the sea, as nearly 60 skeletons were found in the following spring.

Yrs., JOHN LEGGE, Kilbirnie, Ayrshire.

7 March

SIR, AN OLD friend has sent me a cutting from February 1860, in which Mr. Legge reported, shortly after the occurrence, his having killed 16 geese at one shot – a fact about which one of your correspondents lately expressed some incredulity. My friend, who has been devoted to shooting for fully 50 years, says he has no doubt about it; but he adds: 'That was in the good old days when birds were plentiful.'

Yrs., J.J. MEYRICK, Budleigh Salterton.

LARKS

A CORRESPONDENT writes in reference to the strings of larks hanging in the poulterers' shops and laments the cruelty of killing such lovely song birds. The writer is evidently under a misapprehension, as these birds are not the English sky-lark but birds that have come over here from abroad. In the autumn thousands of these larks and other migrants arrive and stay with us through the winter, when they depart. A considerable business is done in trapping them for the London markets, and they form the chief ingredients in the savoury puddings which are so much in evidence at this time of the year.

COMMISSIONER'S RETIREMENT

WHILE IN India, Sir Edward Bradford, the retiring Chief Commissioner of Police, made a big reputation in tiger hunting, and it was in connection with this sport that he had the thrilling adventure which cost him the loss of his left arm. He was out shooting and was waiting at the riverside for a friend to beat up to him when a tiger appeared. At the moment he was standing behind a tree with a number of well-leafed sprigs near the ground. Sir Edward fired, but though he hit the animal and wounded it badly, it charged him furiously. He fired again, but, owing to the fact that a leaf got on to the cap – for it was the day of percussion caps – the shot missed its target. Sir Edward saw it was a case of bolt, and, as the furious beast came bounding towards the tree, the young officer ran as fast as his legs could carry him towards the river. He got to the bottom of the steep bank and had just reached the water's edge when the tiger overtook him. As the animal opened its mouth, Sir Edward thrust his left arm between the jaws. Fortunately, the beast was badly wounded, and, after lacerating the arm terribly, let it go. For some moments man and beast lay watching each other, and then Sir Edward's companion arrived and put an end to the tiger's career. Of course Sir Edward's arm had to be amputated, but his life was saved.

ENGLAND'S GREATEST SPARROW SHOT

MR. G. HANNAY, England's greatest sparrow shot, is 29 years of age. At the age of 15 he had a rage for sparrow shooting and shot splendidly till he was 23, when he was termed England's finest sparrow shot. On four occasions Mr. Hannay has killed 15 in succession, one barrel, gun below elbow, till bird was on wing. In 1900 Hannay defeated A. Murray at pigeons, after killing seven trained birds in succession. The champion could always be found in his flight picking out the very best birds for practice, where he keeps four or five hundred. He is booked to perform at Tudor's Circus, Blyth, before he goes to Canada.

GREAT EGG COLLECTION

LORD WINCHILSEA is said to have the most valuable collection of eagles' eggs in England.

CAT SCARER

A FEARSOME automaton tom-cat has been invented, made up of a tin frame and covered with a fur coat. The general principle of construction is based upon powerful clockwork, released by a lever when the tail of the animal is moved. The clock works a pair of bellows, with two loud, screeching reeds, at the same time forming

W.G. Grace at a shooting party in 1903–4 in
Hertfordshire. He preferred rough shooting to any
organised drives and was undoubtedly a good shot.
His 'eye' was just as keen at shooting as at cricket.

a contact to light the lamps in the eyes, and forcing outwards a dozen long needle points, which come up through the skin of the back. The tail also acts as a trigger, and releases a hammer formed of the lower jaw of the cat, which explodes two percussion caps in the mouth.

IMPERIAL SHOOT

THE GERMAN EMPEROR had some wild boar shooting in the Sau Park, near Hanover, one day last week, immediately after his arrival at his hunting box of Springe. It is said that in 50 minutes 103 boars had been shot by the Imperial party, of which 35 fell to the Emperor's gun. The method of shooting wild boars by Royal sportsmen on the Continent is from stands placed in the forest. An enormous number of beaters gets in line and drive in converging lines on the stands. The result is that a horde of hogs are driven up to the guns, and a tremendous fusillade takes place, and hundreds of boars fall in a very short space of time.

BUZZARDS

SIR, I PROTECT the buzzards in every way I can, as they are becoming scarcer than ever, owing to the man with the gun who shoots every rare bird that is seen; but if I found anyone interfering with them, I should make it fairly warm for him. I may mention that I breed pheasants in the same wood; but I do not think the buzzards do much harm to them – anyhow, if they do, it is easier to raise pheasants than buzzards. I hear that a so-called sportsman in this district killed a gyr-falcon not long ago, and was quite proud of the performance. Six months hard labour would be a good correction.

Yrs., 'KATERFELTO'.

SPORTING PONTIFF

HIS HOLINESS the late Pope was at one time an ardent sportsman, and extremely fond of shooting. In the old Pecci home at Carpineto the favourite gun of the Pope is still to be seen. Of late years the infirmities of age prevented the Pope indulging in his favourite occupation, but up to two or three years ago he took a great delight in the netting of birds in the Vatican gardens which are of great extent.

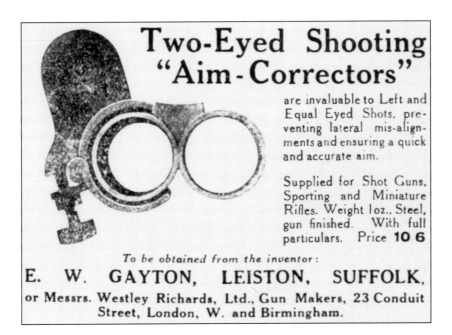

SHORT-SIGHTED SHOT

A STORY IS told of a short-sighted gentleman who went shooting on the moors. On occasion he astonished his companions by blazing off with both barrels at no animate object which they could see, and afterwards shouting, 'Mark that bird! He's hard hit and can't go far. There, he's falling. He's down.' For some time the mystery was inexplicable, but ultimately it was discovered that a spider, which had got on his cap at lunchtime, had depended itself from the peak of his cap right before his eye, and he had mistaken it for a grouse.

BOUQUETS OF GAME

MISS NELLIE FARREN relates how, on a certain 12th of August, a bouquet was thrown at her from a box which was found to be a brace of grouse with floral trimmings. This exploit became all the rage, and the ballet girls were fairly bombarded with grouse, but the birds were not appreciated, and the exponents of the art of the light fantastic toe spoke of roast grouse as 'nasty dry little things' and disposed of them at the poulterers round the corner. A story was current in the Lobby on the 13th that one of the Government Whips received a brace of grouse from Sir Harry Bullard bearing a card inscribed, 'I return my pair'.

CHARGING BUFFALO

SIR SAMUEL BAKER placed the elephant, the hippopotamus, and the African or Asian buffalo before the lion in courage, and doubts whether the tiger is a more courageous creature. But, in his opinion, the buffalo is the most dangerous of all animals. He had seen a wounded lion put to flight by one of his native hunters, and himself tracked one to its lair, and killed it at five paces. It is a different matter in tackling a buffalo once it has decided to charge. In the shallows of a small lake, Baker discovered a bull and put a couple of bullets into him. Neither took effect, and the animal charged. Sir Samuel had no ammunition left, but luckily the bull halted to stare at him. 'Suddenly a bright thought flashed through my mind. Without taking my eyes off the animal in front of me, I put a double charge of powder into the right-hand barrel of my gun, and, tearing off a piece of my shirt, I took all the money from my pouch, three shillings in sixpences and two anna pieces. Making them into a rouleau with the piece of rag, I rammed them down the barrel. They were hardly home before the bull charged forward . . . The horns were lowered, their points on either side of me, and the muzzle barely touching his forehead when I pulled the trigger, and three shillings of small change rattled into his hard head. Down he went, and rolled over with the checked momentum of his charge.' Baker and his companion put out for a tree half a mile away. The bull regained his feet and charged after them, and, though he fell exhausted two hundred yards from the tree, he revived and got away. The story sounds Munchausen-like, but its truth is undoubted.

OMNIVOROUS CROCODILE

On the banks of the Teluga River, in Cutch, there was recently killed a crocodile and the following inventory was made of the contents of the brute's stomach:- A half-digested little calf, a human skull, a silver bangle, some brass ornaments, a little tin box containing tobacco, a lime case, a nutcracker, a railway ticket, a horn case containing 12 annas, six pies in copper and a soda-water bottle containing some mustard oil.

SEED SHOT

The Duke of Atholl has devised a highly original method of sowing seeds on the inaccessible rocks which tower above a portion of his property, and have been guiltless of even a green leaf so long as the oldest inhabitant can remember. Some antiquated cannons lying idle in the neighbourhood were charged with canisters filled with seeds of hardy plants and little shrubs, and fired at the cracks in the rocks. A little soil had collected there, and as some, at all events, of these novel charges alighted upon it, the experiment is expected to be successful.

COMBAT WITH A LION

One of the most extraordinary lion stories ever told is the adventure of Game ranger Wolhunter, in the service of the Transvaal Government. So extraordinary is it that it is attested by the certificate of a magistrate, less unbelievers should scoff. The story is wonderful, and told in the words of Wolhunter himself: 'I was riding along a Kaffir path about an hour after sunset; it had been a long march, and I had pushed on ahead of the boys in order to get to the kraal at Metzi Metz as soon as possible. My dog barked at something which I took to be reedbucks, but a moment later I saw a lion crouched close to me on the offside. I turned my horse sharply in the opposite direction, and this no doubt caused the lion to miss his spring, as, though the horse had some nasty claw marks on the quarters, the bound which he gave saved him. I was unseated, and simultaneously I saw another lion coming at me from the opposite direction; the horse rushed off with the first lion in pursuit, and the second, no doubt considering me easier prey, picked me up almost before I had touched the ground, and gripping me by the right shoulder in such a position that I was face up, with my legs and body dragging beneath his belly, proceeded to trot off down the path at the same time uttering a growling purring noise. The lion took me nearly two hun-

dred yards, my spurs all the time catching the ground until the leathers broke. Suddenly I bethought me of my sheath knife, which I carry on my belt behind my right hip; as the lion had hold of my right arm and shoulder, I had to reach behind with my left hand, a matter of some difficulty; but at last I succeeded, and I am sure no one ever gripped anything so tight as I did that knife after I had got it out. On reaching a large tree with overhanging roots the lion stopped, and then I stabbed him twice in the right side with my left hand, near where I judged the heart to be. I found afterwards that the first stab touched the bottom of the heart, and the second one slit it down for some distance. The lion immediately dropped me, and I again struck him in the throat with all my force, evidently severing some large artery or vein, as the blood poured over me. He jumped back, and stood two or three yards away facing me and growling. I scrambled to my feet, not knowing that I had mortally wounded him, but after a few moments he turned and went slowly away still growling; soon the growls turned to moans and then ceased, and I felt he was dead. Before this,

however, I had got up the tree as fast as my injured arm and shoulder would allow me, and I was hardly securely seated when the other lion which had returned from unsuccessfully chasing my horse, came back to the spot where I had been seized, and coursed along on my blood spoor to the foot of the tree. He had been pursued throughout by my dog, a large, rough, and very courageous animal, with whom I had often hunted lions previously; he, no doubt, was of assistance to the horse in his escape.

'I now shouted to my dog, and set him on the lion; he came up barking furiously and the lion retreated, but came back again and made a rush for the dog, who dodged him and continued to bark all round him, until presently the lion went off. After a time I heard the boys coming along the road, shouted to them, and they came up and rescued me from my position. The horse was found next morning, not much injured, and the boys found and skinned the lion, an old male, with the canines worn flat at the points. He must have been hungry as his stomach was absolutely empty.'

1904

SEA RESCUE

AFTER A LONG course of stories of dogs which have plunged into seas after drowning babies, the tale of the Scarborough greyhound will come as a refreshing antidote. A labourer and his dog were blown off the West Pier into the sea. But did the dog seize his master by the collar and battle his way to shore through the surging waves? Did he hold him up with one paw and call for assistance with the other? No. He scrambled in a business-like way on the man's head, and sat there waiting for happier times. When the rescue party arrived, the master was filling rapidly, but the dog, with the exception of a few drops of spray on his coat was getting along quite nicely.

TALL SHOTS

SPEAKING OF tall shots – we are now referring to height, not veracity – most sportsmen are quite unable to accurately measure with their eyes the height at which a bird is flying overhead. In nearly every instance a man over-estimates the altitude. The Duke of York's column is just 120 feet, or 40 yards, high, and, of course, this is by no means an excessive distance at which to crumple up a bird; yet, if some of our readers went and watched the pigeons flying about the summit of this column, we would undertake to say they would swear that a bird was quite out of shot at the top of the shaft. Many a partridge and pheasant is allowed to pass overhead because he is considered to be out of shot, whereas probably the bird is not more than 40 yards away, if that.

JAPANESE GUN

ADMIRAL MORESBY relates an incident showing the practical intelligence of our friends the Japs. He says: 'In January, 1865, just two months after the action of Simo-

nosaki, where the Japanese were partly armed with bows and arrows, and clad in chain armour, I happened to be senior naval officer at Nagasaki, and became on very friendly terms with the Governor of the city. On my departure for England, on promotion, he gave me a farewell banquet in the old Japanese style, and at its close he caused a Winchester breech-loading rifle to be put into my hands. I guessed there was an ulterior object in view, and, observing that the name "Winchester" had evidently been engraved by a hand unaccustomed to Latin characters, I remarked, "Your Excellency has done well to manufacture so perfect a lock." With huge delight he informed me that lock, stock, and barrel, all had been made by Japanese workmen, and begged me to tell my Queen what I had seen.'

KAISER'S MEMORIAL

WE PREVIOUSLY stated that a monument, weighing 50 tons, is being raised in the Schorfielde, near Zehdenick, Germany, on the spot where the Emperor stood when he killed his one-thousandth stag; and we now learn that the stone will bear the inscription: 'Our most illustrious margrave, and lord, Emperor William II, stood here on September 20th, Anno Domini 1898, when slaying his 1000th stag of 20 tines.'

MUSCLE BOUND

PREMATURE OLD age is, of course, produced by a thousand and one other agencies besides over-indulgence in strong drink; but the case of a certain Scottish shooting gentleman, high up in the social scale, who has reduced himself to the condition of a physical wreck by the undue exercise of his muscles is, perhaps, uncommon. From his boyhood, gymnastics and athletic games possessed a peculiar fascination for him, and nothing afforded him such genuine and perfect delight as to find himself applauded for some surprising deed demonstrating extraordinary strength. Five in the morning always found him at his dumb-bells and Indian clubs, and in the evening twilight his brow was still bathed in perspiration, the result of ceaseless exertion to break some vaunted 'record' or other. As he advanced in age he devoted more and more attention to his baneful hobbies. He studied his diet like a boxer training for the ring, and ardent liquors never passed his lips. Yet today, at the age of 45, he is bent, shrunk, and wrinkled, and easily mistaken for a person who has reached his allotted span. While recently attempting to raise two 56lb. weights above his head – one in each hand – the overstrained muscles in each arm suddenly became paralysed, and he is since unable to raise them from his side. All this was told to me (continues our correspondent) by his aggrieved father, who added that his son's curious and egregious infatuation had proved quite as ineradicable as the most insinuating and noxious forms of vice.

THE HOME OF SIR PARTRIDGE

I CANNOT remember the day when I first clapped eyes on Sir Partridge. It must have been before I had even learned to walk, and when I was certainly far too young to understand what a bird really was. Be that as it may, almost the whole of my life has been spent in close intercourse with 'the sportsman's darling', as the partridge is sometimes called.

More than the best part of my boyhood I

spent roaming over the famous Grange estate, Arlesford, which, as every sportsman worthy of the name knows, is owned by Lord Ashburton. His Lordship is generally acknowledged to be the most graceful partridge shot England can boast, whilst his estate has not unjustly been eulogised as the home of the partridge in England, just as Sandringham, in Norfolk, is sometimes spoken of as the home of the pheasant. More than 10 thousand acres are given up to 'the little brown bird', and including Marlow, the head, there are eleven keepers to look after it.

Go where you will on the grand estate, excepting the depth of the dark, mysterious woods, partridges you will find everywhere, cackling and playing, and hurrying to and fro, and all seeming as gay as little princes. No partridges are hand-reared at the Grange, Arlesford, nor are any imported; all are hatched in the thick, widespreading hazel hedgerow beneath the breasts of their parents of their own flesh and blood. Incubators and foster-mothers alike their noble owner will have none of. He detests the hand-reared bird with a vehemence almost incredible. From the day of their first coming into the world to the day that they fall victim to the gunner's deadly powder and shot, the Grange partridges are as free to roam where they like as Robinson Crusoe was on his desert island. Moreover, not only a few hundreds are hatched each springtime, but thousands – nay, exaggerating slightly, tens of thousands.

Who requires reminding that on the gigantic shoot in November 1897, six guns in three days made the enormous bag of 3,350 odd birds, and that without any undue preparation or great exertion? All one day, two days and three days' existing partridge-shooting records in England were broken on the occasion, and the records then established still remain to be beaten. No imported birds were especially turned down a day or so beforehand for the great event, I can positively state, as some people affirm must have been the case. Every partridge that was laid low was hatched on the estate, or the immediate neighbourhood.

It had happened that Lord Gray de Wilton, as he then was, in the October of the same year, at Houghton, in Norfolk, had beaten the Grange's best three-day bag, and such an intolerable offence Lord Ashburton, naturally, could not pardon, or allow to pass by but slightly reprimanded. On the first day 1,374 birds were shot, on the second 1,461, and on the third, 701. Lord Gray de Wilton's bag for the three days had been some 300 partridges less than the 3,536, which number was the exact total of Lord Ashburton's bag.

Yet, be it remembered that the Grange has not always been a great estate for partridges. Some years before his death the late Lord Ashburton boasted that ere his life had outrun its course he would have made Hampshire as great a partridge county as Norfolk. He did more; first he made the county as great, and then greater. It was about the year 1868 that he commenced the gigantic task. He had just secured the services of Marlow, who is, perhaps, as great an authority on partridge rearing as one can find, and certainly a great head-keeper. He is an old man now, but as keen and alert as ever.

In the year 1868 on the whole estate of 17,000 acres only 177 partridges were shot. But from that year the shooting began to improve rapidly. In the following year a bag of 468 birds was made, in 1870 one of 1,521, and in 1873 one of 2,334. Again in 1884, 3,253 partridges were killed, in 1885 a few over 4,000, and in 1887 the huge total of 8,707.

Up to the end of the year 1902, from the

beginning of the season 1868, 93,039 partridges had been shot on the Grange estate. Truly a wonderful number. Last year very little shooting took place on the estate, first on account of the prolonged and painful illness of Lady Ashburton, which lasted through almost the whole of the winter, and eventually ending with her Ladyship dying towards the end of January; and second on account of the scanty supply of game of any description; for, needless to mention, the heavy rains of last year played dreadful havoc not only amongst the partridges, but also amongst the pheasants and hares.

It is, therefore, likely that good bags of partridges will again be made during the present season. There certainly seemed to be no lack of stockbirds in the springtime, and at present there are more youngsters on the Grange estates than the writer has seen elsewhere this summer.

Pains are always taken at the Grange to leave a sufficient number of stock birds to assume a good season next year. The shooting does not open up on the First, but seldom, if ever, before the last week in October, and frequently not before the middle of November. The system is excellent, for who will not tell you that part-

ridges always provide the best sport in November, and on the First no sport at all?

The pheasants are shot in December, or thereabouts. One need hardly mention that all the game is driven, the best partridge drive being the so-called New House drive. The birds are driven over a fence which is some 350 yards in length, and composed for the most part of hazel bushes and small oak trees. The guns are placed behind this fence 60 yards apart, and, as they can rarely see the birds approaching, a most exciting time they invariably have, as covey after covey, from, seemingly, nowhere come suddenly streaming over the high, thick screen with incredible swiftness. There is one famous wood on the estate. It is Thorney Down, which is about a mile long and three-quarters of a mile broad, and which is planted entirely with nut bushes and oak trees. It is in this wood that the bulk of the pheasants and hares are shot. Generally two days are spent 'shooting' it, the guns standing in the 'sides'.

Happily, the egg-stealer and the poacher proper are both almost unknown to the Grange gamekeepers. Still, they have enemies to contend with, the most formidable being but a slightly decreasing army of rats. It seems next to impossible to expel the pests from the estate. Needless to say, the skulking vermin destroy hundreds of partridge eggs, and in addition to other extensive damage. Naturally, a continual warfare is being waged against them. For instance, only last winter a few thousands in all were killed on the estate. Five hundred were accounted for in one afternoon during the threshing of a wheat stack.

But the day may arrive when the Grange rats, plentiful as they are now, will no longer hold sway. Then no doubt more record bags will be made, and the home of the little brown bird become more famous and better known, and the best of good sportsmen, Lord Ashburton, and the admirable old man, Marlow, who, everybody must confess have, both of them, done much indeed to improve the partridge shooting, will be gratefully remembered all the country over. – J. C. BRISTOW-NOBLE.

1905

ARMOURED DOGS

AN ARMOURED coat for dogs, to serve as a protection against motor-cars, has been invented by a New Yorker. The coat is studded with sharp steel points, like a steel hedgehog. If the armoured dog is run into by a motor-car, the sharp points puncture the tyre, and the consequent rush of released air blows the dog out of danger.

COOKED RHINO

IN FULFILMENT of his promise to send the society of Canadian Campers 'a rare and unique animal for their next banquet at New York', Prince Henry of Prussia sent, the other day, a two-horned rhinoceros, weighing 2,000lb., which was brought into the banqueting hall on a wagon amid a great flourish of trumpets. The creature was served roasted on an immense wooden platter holding huge portions, the alleged delicacy being garnished with horns, hoofs, and hide. We are sorry to hear that the cook – wretched woman! – was a little low-spirited because few of the gentlemen took kindly to the crackling.

DEATH OF 'BLUCHER'

A CORRESPONDENT writes: 'Poor old Lattimore Lee – or, to call him by his nickname, "Blucher" – the notorious Lincolnshire poacher, has been run to ground for the last time. A few days ago, death came to the keepers' aid, and grimly and tragically laid his hands on "Blucher" when he was in the very act of following his lawless avocation. The old man – he was over 60 years of age – left his home with a comrade for, to all appearances, an aimless walk in the green fields, which he loved so dearly. But on his way, entering a dilapidated hovel, he took a gunstock and a barrel from a hiding-place under some hay. "Blucher", it seems, had made up his mind to try and get a rabbit for the following day's dinner. He secreted the stock in one trouser leg, and the barrel and ramrod in the other. Then, a few minutes later, as the men were approaching some coverts near Barrowby, with appalling suddenness there came a report, and he reeled to the earth with a gaping wound in his side. The poacher's faithful dog – the silent dog, as he was generally called – lay down by the dying man's side; his friend covered "Blucher" with an overcoat, and then quickly, and weeping, hurried in to Grantham, and informed the police of the accident. Apart from his record of over 50 convictions for poaching, Lee was known the county over as an absolutely honest and upright man. An incident characteristic of him is worth relating. He was seen early one morning coming down one of the streets on the

The old order – 'velveteens'.

outskirts of Grantham, and, in company with him a man who had a bag of onions on his back. A constable met the pair, and promptly took them into custody. "Blucher" was charged, jointly with the other man with theft. The old man's look and speech to the bench convinced them of his innocence. "Stealing onions!" he gasped; "why, gentlemen, I'd scorn to do such a thing. You know what my business is – it's only poaching." Keepers and police knew both man and dog well and it is said that, out of kindness and admiration for their cunning, they avoided them as much as possible. The dog instinctively knew when danger was ahead, and would go quietly up to his master and lay its nose in his open hand.'

FEROCIOUS MANGOLD

THE FOLLOWING communication has been received from a correspondent who is evidently labouring under the stress of a great mental excitement – 'On the banks of the little tributary of the Medway, named the Len, near Maidstone, a fierce fight was witnessed yesterday between a mangold-wurzel and a stoat. The latter animal, which is the most vicious of England's wild animals, attacked the mangold by the root of the tail, nibbling furiously. The man-

gold, worked up into a wild passion, turned and seized the stoat by the throat, and then a battle royal ensued. Eventually, after a fight lasting 20 minutes, the stoat gave up the struggle and died, the mangold still having a firm hold of the throat.' We should imagine it would be a bit risky taking a stroll through the fields in Kent where such ferocious vegetables are at large.

CONSUMED BY BEAR

A GERMAN millionaire named Johann Kugler, residing at Tiflis, has been killed and partly devoured by a bear. Kugler, who was an ardent sportsman, had trapped a number of bears in the Caucasus. These he placed in an improvised menagerie on his estate, and plied them with liquor. When the bears were in a sufficiently intoxicated state, Kugler was in the habit of having wrestling bouts with them, in which, owing to the helplessness of the animals, he always was the victor. On the last occasion, however, a bear of more formidable strength than the rest, and rendered more savage by the spirits which Kugler had given it to drink, flung itself upon him and crushed him to death. The body of Kugler, who, as a rule, would not permit spectators to witness his wrestling matches, was afterwards found in the bear's den, terribly mutilated, one of his limbs being partly gnawed away.

FALLING GAME

NOT THE LEAST risk to a man shooting is the danger of game falling upon him, and this very often occurs if he is preoccupied with sport, and quick in turning on a bird with the second barrel. A cock pheasant which has had a good start and the wind behind it is soon flying at a rate of not far short of 60 miles an hour; if shot dead its impetus is not much lessened till it reaches the ground and the further it has to fall the greater the violence thereof. At Elvesden, in Suffolk, some years ago, a loader was hit upon the head by a bird the sportsman he was attending upon had shot, felled to the ground and picked up with blood flowing from ears, nose, and mouth. He was insensible for several hours and laid up for weeks with concussion of the brain. The blow he received must have been most severe for the effects were those resulting from a terrible fall.

A large proportion of grouse are shot flying straight at the sportsman, slightly higher than his head, and he often is forced to duck to avoid being struck by a bird he has killed. We have known a grouse to knock down the front of a butt, and that butt one substantially built with solid sods of peat. On the Deeside moors, a keeper engaged in picking up wounded grouse

The new order – 'mister keeper'.

after a drive was struck by another in full flight, and bowled over as if hit with a heavy fist. He was thoroughly dazed when picked up, bleeding freely from the mouth, and several days elapsed before he entirely recovered. We have known a shot and falling duck to knock a man backwards into the pond from which it had in the first instance been flushed. For all this, a pheasant is the bird of which one must be careful, especially at a place where they come thick and fast, and two guns or more are in constant use. Also, do not forget to warn the loader if one is falling perilously near, as his duty precludes his looking up. –'HOVERER'.

FIGHT WITH OTTER

WHEN MR. JAMES WISEMAN, Seatown, Gardenstown, was taking a short cut to the west end of the village, through the sands, on Tuesday, last week, he had a curious adventure with an otter, which appeared from the rocky promontory, and endeavoured to make for the sea. Mr. Wiseman, who carried no weapon of any kind at once conceived the idea of endeavouring to secure the animal by seizing it with his hands. Nothing daunted, he gave chase, and, just as the otter was on the point of dipping into the water, threw himself full length upon it, at the same time seizing it firmly by the throat. The otter did not succumb without a struggle and, seizing a favourable opportunity, caught Mr. Wiseman by the hand inflicting a somewhat severe wound. Mr. Wiseman's blood was now up and after a fierce struggle, he managed to strangle the vicious beast, which showed great game. Mr. Wiseman brought the otter home with him and is having it set up as a momento of the occasion.

TIGER ATTACK

LUAK, A SAKI, was digging for potatoes with a wooden spade at Ulu Juk, Perak, in the Malay States, when a tiger seized his left leg below the knee. He turned and hit the animal on the head with a big chopper, which was lying close at hand, killing it with one blow. Subsequently he had to force open the brute's mouth with his wooden spade, to release his leg.

1906

THE VALUE OF A GUN

HUNDREDS OF sportsmen ask and will continue to ask, 'where is the difference in a double-barrelled sporting gun at £3 and one at £30?'

Many men believe that, because a gunmaker can command £30 to £70 for a gun, it is because they are fashionable gunmakers and old-established, and are patronised by the nobility; but this is certainly not the case. It is because this high priced gun is worth the money, being an article containing the very best of materials and mechanism known to the gunsmith's art.

The barrels of the expensive gun are made of the very best of steel and welded into barrels by competent men, who draw a bigger wage than the ordinary welder, and spend more time and trouble in their work. Many of the cheaper barrels are welded by means of a tilt hammer. Again, the boring and grinding of the cheaper barrels is not done so perfect and true as that of the more expensive. The good class gunmaker tests his barrels in the rough, as well as in the finished state; but the cheap man omits this altogether. The common barrels are soldered together and to the rib (that is, the strip of steel extending from breech to muzzle of the gun) with soft solder and sal ammoniac, instead of solder and resin; the latter prevents rusting beneath the rib and between the barrels. The lumps underneath the breech are simply 'let in', instead of nicely dovetailed in. The rib on a cheap gun is seldom straight, and generally laps right on one barrel, and scarcely touches the other, and is made of some soft iron or steel that is only fit for 'scrap'.

The locks or trigger mechanism on the expensive gun are made from the best hard steel, and the side plates are perfectly levelled, thus giving the sears and tumblers free and even play, and preventing the 'pull off' varying. Locks can be made or bought from 4s. to £4 per set, or pair, but, of course, the standard of the metal and the workmanship is entirely different. Again, ordinary cheap gun breech actions can be bought for a few shillings, whereas in the best hammerless guns they cost anything from £10 to £14. Gunstocks can be bought from 5s. to 30s. apiece and the difference in price between a good workman's and a poor workman's work on it varies as much as the cost of the stocks in the rough. A gun today can be engraved from muzzle to stock for a few shillings, such engraving as it is; but take a high grade gun and notice the difference – beautiful, clear cut engraving (in many cases costing £2 to £4 to produce), whereas the cheap gun's engraving is no regular pattern, and put on any way but the right. These cheap guns are known as 'export guns', and are generally made in Belgium, Germany and America, and turned out at a cost of about 26s. each. Every sportsman has seen them advertised by the retailer at 35s. to 45s. each. Their true specification is: common iron or steel barrels, soft, spongy, highly varnished and polished stock, fore-end fastener (called hand-chequered), gashed into deep ugly grooves by a file, which either falls off when the gun is fired, or else has to be wrenched off with the aid of a screwdriver or similar instrument. One hammer rests on the striker and the other is right off; the striker in one nipple protrudes through the breech body, and when the gun is fired, is driven right into the cartridge and prevents the gun being opened; the other striker, however, is shorter, and causes a misfire. The hammers are by no means a pair; one of them when cocked 'shouts out loud', and the others won't speak, or complains in a soft whisper. Again, the barrels scarcely fit against the breech body or else have to be driven into place by violence. The lovely horn heel-plate (as advertised) is a composition of rubber stamped by the thousands, and ornamented by a stag's head or some other sporting figure.

Always remember that a gun at £10 will last fifty times as long as one at £3, and if you do not feel that your means will allow you to sport a good new gun, buy a second-hand one which cost a good figure originally. These cheap Belgian guns are dear at any price, and very dangerous. Never buy a gun without a maker's name on it. I hope by this article I have clearly pointed out to my brother sportsmen how the difference in gun prices arises.
– LEONARD A. CUSTON

DROLL KAISER

If accounts be true, the Kaiser's humour takes a curious twist sometimes. It is said that at the first big shoot of the season, when his guests were both numerous and distinguished, he suddenly discovered that he possessed no licence to shoot game; but he said nothing about it until after luncheon. Then he announced his infringement of the law and fined himself £5. He also directed a representative of the law to demand the licences of every one of his guests, and, as they were nearly all defaulters, he fined each of them £5. As William dearly loves to score off his intimates, this coup afforded him immense delight.

HIBERNATING SWALLOWS

APROPOS THE question whether swallows hibernate under water, Major-General R. Owen-Jones, R.R. states that in his house in Wales there is, in the cellar, which is separated by iron bars from the outer air, a small cistern built around a spring. Some alterations having to be made to the house a few years ago, an old door was placed over this cistern in the month of December. When the workmen had completed their job, in June, the doors were removed from the cistern and the cistern cleared out. In the mud was apparently a dead bird black with mud. The General examined it, and detected a slight movement in the claws. He brought it into the light and found it evidently had life in it. He had to leave it while he went in to lunch, and on his return it flew off with apparently the strength of an ordinary swallow. The General suggests that if some of our ponds were covered over with netting in the month of December, many other instances would be discovered of swallows (either too old or too young to migrate) having hibernated in our climate.

HARE STORY

SIR, A FARMER and his son were trying to pen some sheep, but, after five hours ineffectual effort were about to give it up as a bad job. Up comes a sailor and says to the farmer 'Can you give me a job?' 'Yes,' said the farmer. 'You pen these sheep for me, and I'll give you a couple of bob. My son and I have been trying for five hours and can't manage it.' 'All right,' says the sailor, 'I'll have a try.' So the farmer and his son go off to their dinner, and return in an hour's time to see what had happened. They find the sheep all penned and the sailor sitting down smoking his pipe. They go up to look at the sheep, and find a hare in amongst them. 'Why, you've got a hare in with them!' says the farmer. 'Hare?' says the sailor – 'Hare?' scratching his head. 'What, that little brown one? Why that was the one that gave me all the trouble.'

Yrs., H.A.J., Edenbridge.

BIRDS IN TREE

A BISHOP ONCE asked a class of boys some questions in mental arithmetic, and received an unsolicited let down. Said he: 'Now, my little man, you there. If I were to shoot at a tree with five birds in it, and kill three, how many would be left?' 'Three, sir.' 'No, no, my boy, there would only be two left.' 'Please sir, you said you shot three; only they would be left; th'other two would be flied away.' 'Yes,' replied the bishop; 'You are quite right; you may sit down.' And he passed on to another classroom.

KING'S PARTY

HIS MAJESTY the King had very good sport on the Castle Grant Moors, belonging to the Countess Dowager of Seafield on Wednesday and Thursday last week, motoring to the Moors and passing close to Grantown. The shooting party with His Majesty comprised Mr. A.D. Sassoon, Sir Edward Sassoon, Sir Arthur Davidson, Col. Legge, and Mr. Willie James. On Wednesday 160 brace of grouse were shot, His Majesty shooting very well. The ladies joined the guns at lunchtime, viz., Madame Sassoon, Lady Sarah Wilson, Lady Sassoon, The Hon. Mrs. Derek Keppel, and Mrs. James. The party returned by motor to Tulshan Lodge. On Friday 130 were bagged. The King motored to Balmoral on Monday.

COQ AU ROI

IN THE OLD days, in France, if Royalty attended the shooting parties at Rambouillet, when a cock pheasant passed within reach of the Royal gun, the guards and beaters raised a cry of 'Coq au Roi!' when no one was to fire except the King. The practice fell out when the monarchy ceased. President Felix Faure, a great lover of ceremony and etiquette, had it restored. When democratic M. Lubet was president, he was a bit surprised at the monarchical cry, and he substituted for it the formula of 'Coq à President!' M. Fallières, who is still more simple in his manners, has now had the usage abolished entirely.

1907

GUN HEADACHE

SIR, FOR MANY years I suffered from what I thought was a gun headache, but found it was simply a case of getting hungry and eating too much lunch. Now I always take a small lunch at eleven, and eat and drink sparingly at lunch, and never suffer. I cannot help thinking that many people have a headache from the same cause; anyway, it is worth trying.

Yrs., H.R.H. Stafford.

WOMEN POACHERS

WOMEN ARE rarely found actually poaching, but more frequently as confederates and 'accessories after or before the fact', as legal gentlemen say. For this they are very well adapted, both physically and because of their wit. A keen woman may be of the greatest use to a poacher, and, if she is given to babbling, and not sharp on his behalf, a veritable danger. A woman's tongue has brought many a criminal well-merited punishment, and a very simple action on the part of the poacher's wife may prove her husband's undoing. A poacher's wet clothes hung on the garden hedge to dry, after he has returned from his nightly excursions, and retired to rest, has placed many a keeper in possession of the man's real profession, and caused him to be closely watched till captured; and the sale of a hare skin to a supposed pedlar has also given the game away. More than one poacher has suffered 'three weeks' hard' because of his wife's yearning for the threepence a hare's skin realises.

As before stated, it is as confederates to poaching that women shine, for they are able to penetrate anywhere in search of information. An old woman will venture into the most sacred covert, avowedly in search of sticks for her fire, or some other errand, for she is nothing if not ready with an excuse where necessary. She will carry nets, snares, or a gun through the area upon which a suspected man bearing either would be searched; and her clothing is far more adapted than that of a man to the concealment of such material. 'All the world loves a lover', and who would suspect a courting couple resting on a stile of having designs against the game? However, the courting may be but a blind, and, perhaps, if the pair are watched, the girl will be found sitting alone while her swain sets snares close by. Many a young poacher, afraid that his nightly excursions from the village just at dark would attract attention, has sauntered forth with a girl on his arm, and she has returned home later. There are, indeed, many ways in which women are able to assist poachers without actually sharing their work. –'HOVERER'.

TIPS

SIR, I HAVE often wondered why men – business men of moderate means – do not go in more for shooting. There is no pleasure like it, no exercise more healthy, no pastime more invigorating and, shall I say, more rejuvenating. The reason is that they are staggered at the alleged expense, the tips, and the social obligations. The other day I chanced to be in the house of a friend who mingles with business men. The topic was shooting, and there I got an insight into the ideas which prevail relative to the cost of shooting, not only as a host, but as a guest. Conversation turned on keepers' tips. 'I would like to shoot,' said one of the company, 'and often get invitations, but I dare not accept them.' 'Why?' said I. 'Well,' he replied, 'what will it cost? There are my fare and other little expenses which, with tips, will not cost me less than £3 or £4 per day. The headkeeper will want a couple of pounds, the underkeeper half a sovereign, and all the attendants something.' Surely there never was a greater delusion. I have been a guest a hundred times, but never did I give a keeper more than half a sovereign when I had had a good day, and right well was he satisfied. My many years' experience of keepers is not that they want tips so much as good shots, who help to make up the bag, which to an honest keeper is everything. The tip is a casual thing, his situation everything, and he knows that it is sure so long as the bag is good and the sport and enjoyment maintained as it should be. A duffing shot may endeavour to cover up his bad shooting with big tips, but my experience is that a keeper would rather meet the guest who can shoot well and take his simple tip of a few shillings than see a man who cannot shoot for nuts and receive his golden guineas.

Yrs., 'A FREQUENT GUEST'.

SOLE IN DRAWERS

A BOY BATHING at Walcot, near Yarmouth, was heard screaming, and it was thought he was seized with cramp; but on being helped ashore, it was found that a large sole had got into his bathing drawers.

ACCIDENTS AND NEAR ACCIDENTS

THE TWELTH Lord Saye and Sele was in the habit, at Belvedere, in Kent, of providing night shooting as an amusement for his guests most evenings before they retired to rest. After supper, Croker, his lordship's head keeper, would come up to the room and say, 'My lord, the game hall be ready.' The plan was to fasten white paper collars round the rabbits' necks, and let them out one at a time from a trap. The gentlemen, guns in hand, stood round in a semi-circle, and blazed away at each bunny as it appeared; yet the hits were few. On the occasion I refer to, only six rabbits were killed out of the two dozen, but how near the sportsmen were to shooting each other may be gathered from what Croker said in the morning. One of the guests was congratulating the keeper on providing such good sport, when the latter broke in with, 'Well, I was never so thankful to see his lordship's friends going to their beds as I was last night, for some of you gentlemen – I mean no offence – would have better have gone there to recover from your dinner before you came to shoot.'

Some notable accidents in the shooting field occur to me. The father of the late Marquess of Queensberry was said to have accidently shot himself when out rabbit shooting in 1858, but there were those who doubted that the accident was not intentional. Captain Speke, the famous African explorer, was the victim of a gun accident just the day before he was to have confronted Captain Richard Burton in public and explained his conduct in appropriating to himself the credit which Burton alleged due to him. Frederic Gye, the once well-known manager of the Royal Italian Opera at Covent Garden, was shot dead by accident whilst pheasant-shooting on Lord

Dillon's estate at Dytchley on the same day on which Major Whyte-Melville was killed out hunting. The late Professor Fawcett was shot by his father when partridge shooting; only two pellets struck him, but they penetrated both eyeballs and left him stone-blind for life. Mr. F. P. Delme-Ratcliffe, a celebrated 'King of the Hunting Field' and a brilliant writer to boot, was also the victim of a gun accident, which, however, was attended with less tragic results than any of those I have mentioned. When out with a shooting party on his own estate he got somewhat out of line, and consequently received the contents of one of his guest's guns in the head and face. He fell senseless, and for the moment it was thought he was killed. But in a few moments he recovered consciousness, and as soon as he did so exclaimed earnestly, 'I call you to witness it was my own fault.' The sight of his left eye was completely destroyed, but his other injuries were not serious. Even after the loss of his eye, Joe Manton, the famous gunmaker, said he would not advise anyone to offer Mr. Delme-Ratcliffe many dead birds in a pigeon match.

A remarkable recovery from a terrible gun accident was that of Mr. Thomas Smith, of Hambledon, who was as great a Master of Hounds as his celebrated namesake, Thomas Assheton Smith. When he was a boy his head got in the way of a sportsman aiming at a rabbit, and down went Tom, apparently dead. He recovered, however, but his escape from death was marvellous, for a full charge of shot was taken out of his head, and afterwards shown to him in a wine glass.
– THORMANBY.

TIGER MAYHEM

THE INDIAN mail brings the following account of an encounter with a tiger:- The animal appeared in one of the ravine villages near Agra, and a villager, seeing it lurking among the bushes, threw a brick at it. The tiger charged and killed the villager. The latter's son then came to the rescue, armed with a 'lathi' and was also killed. An alarm was raised by the villagers, and the police arrived, some armed with guns, and a fusillade opened on the animal, which was seated by the remains of his victims, one of whom he had partially devoured. After being fired at, the tiger retreated into the thick bush. Thinking he was mortally wounded, two armed policemen fixed their bayonets and approached the bush. A villager also accompanied them. Suddenly the tiger charged and smashed the jaw of one of the constables. Indiscriminate firing now took place by all those who had firearms, with the result that the villager who accompanied the constables was, unfortunately, shot, while the tiger made off towards Gwalior territory, and has not been since located, although several officers have been out after the brute.

PRESIDENTIAL WRANGLE

AN UNSEEMLY wrangle between President Roosevelt and Parson Lang has broken out.

The President charges the parson, who is an assumed authority on natural history, with faking, and says that he does not know a bull from a bear. The parson, on the other hand, says the President is no sportsman, and avers that the last time Mr. Roosevelt went hunting bears it was in the spring, when the mother bears had cubs, and were weakened by the long winter's fast. According to his own boastful account, he and his heroic band killed 11 bears, all mother bears, and their little cubs, after the pack of dogs had driven the poor creatures into trees, and they were absolutely helpless. Then Mr. Roosevelt preached on the heroism of hunting, and urged all sportsmen to unite in saving the few remaining bears and other game animals from destruction. 'This time I hope,' says the parson, 'he will omit either the killing or the preaching.'

POWER OF A BITE

THE STRENGTH of a dog's jaws and teeth were never better exemplified than in the case of a Ross-shire gamekeeper, whose dog was unfortunate enough to be caught in a steel vermin trap. The gamekeeper, gun in hand, was soon on the scene, but in the short time the dog had become quite infuriated by the pain. Having nothing suitable to muzzle the animal, and fearing to place his foot upon the trap-spring with the dog's jaws free, the gamekeeper placed the gun barrels in the dog's mouth and held them while easing the spring. With a vicious snap the teeth closed on the cold steel ere he regained his freedom. The barrels, which are of steel, were holed through – an incredible performance – and were examined by our Northern Correspondent, and can be seen at any time. The dog was an ordinary black-and-tan collie.

£1,000 FOR A BRITISH BULLDOG.

Read late Owner's Testimony:—

The Limes, Uxbridge, 2nd September, 1904.

To Spratt's Patent, Ltd.

"Gentlemen, - I am pleased to say that my celebrated Bulldog, Champion Heath Baronet (sold by me to Mr. George Gould for £1,000), has been fed on

SPRATT'S PATENT DOG FOODS,

which I find

EXCELLENT FOR BULLDOGS.

Yours faithfully, E. A. MILLS."

Doggie Pamphlet and List of Foods Post Free of

SPRATT'S PATENT, Limited,

Manufacturers of Dog Kennels, Chains, Collars, Poultry Houses, and all Dog and Poultry Appliances

SHOW ROOMS - 24 & 25 FENCHURCH STREET, LONDON, E.C.

AMERICAN SQUIRREL

SOME ARDENT naturalist, desirous of adding to the fauna of his native country, released some of the American grey squirrels in Bedfordshire, and these have increased and spread to the surrounding county of Hampshire. So far we have heard little of them, but gamekeepers are beginning to complain that they are, or have developed into, arrant robbers, and are very carnivorous in habit. Eggs the grey squirrel lives on while they can be had, and although our British variety eats an occasional egg, it does not search for them. Nests are denuded of their young by this squirrel, and a curious fact about it is that it becomes unwieldily fat from superabundance of food, and is very different in appearance from what it is in the States. This is a very heavy charge against the new importation, but the one source of gratification is that the creature is easily cleared off, as it has no suspicion regarding traps. The native introduction and the new variety do not appear to agree, and it would be a pity were our own sprightly little variety dispossessed by the stranger.

SINISTER SWAMP

NEAR MBEGA (one of my favourite hunting resorts, some 20 miles from Cape Lopez), there is a dense stretch of jungle known as Iga Volo ('the broad jungle'). It is more than a mile in width and some 40 miles in length. Across it is a tortuous trail leading from one great plain to another, the only trail between them for many miles. At intervals along this route are small sections of open forest on low belts of solid ground; but most of the way is through a series of mere tunnels, made by elephants, through huge masses of matted bush and vines, through which no human being could ever creep, and in these narrow, winding tunnels, the foul marshes are in many places more than waist deep. A hundred times, perhaps, I have paused in these grim culverts to contemplate their novel structure and weird aspect, and, in all my wanderings through the wilds in both hemispheres I have long regarded this place as the most dismal spot on earth that I have ever seen. Several times I have passed alone through this dreary place, but never without feeling a timidity verging on fear; for this is not only the solitary highway of all the savage beasts that dwell within leagues of it, but it is also the abode of huge pythons and diverse kinds of venomous serpents that lie concealed beneath the slimy surface of the water, and many natives have paid their lives as the penalty for passing it.

On one occasion I was passing through this dreary jungle, in company with an expert guide, and while we were near the middle of the longest of these gloomy tunnels, the guide (who was about three paces in front of me) suddenly halted, raised his hand, and hissed at me as a warning of danger; at the same instant I heard a loud splashing of water and the crackling of brush in the trail a few yards beyond him. I glanced at him and then at the impenetrable walls of brush and vines on either side of us; for I realised the danger of meeting a buffalo bull or any other ferocious creature in that howling dungeon, from which there was no quick retreat and in which there was no possible refuge. We had no time to formulate a plan of action, for the moment of action was at hand. Swash! swash! swash! echoed from every crevice of that silent jungle and whack! whack! whack! (like the breaking of a thousand sticks) rang out as the accompaniment. The author of these sounds was certainly approaching, though not yet in sight. It was not a moment of suspense, it was one of action – one that demanded calmness and decision. Fight! was the only watchword that could be uttered; Fight on! was the only counter-sign; and I prepared to make the best of a slim chance. There was no choice in making that decision, and it required no courage to back it. The enemy was approaching, doubtless with like intent, and it was simply a question of whose life would be snuffed out in that charnel house of a jungle. The guide was yet between me and the source of the danger; but that only made the situation more embarrassing, because he was an obstacle in the way of my shooting. Having no refuge, he stood waist-deep in the mud and slime, facing the foe, and with his slender spear poised above his shoulder looked like the bronzed torso of a warrior.

In a few seconds I saw the grim face of a surly bull suddenly appear at the angle of an abrupt turn in the trail. His head was just above the water, and his eyes glared like two discs of greenish glass. He was within 10 feet of the guide. He paused for an instant, and then with a desperate plunge rushed at the man. Fortunately, the water was so deep that the bull could not bring his sharp horns to the proper angle without submerging his head, and the water broke the force of his assault and impeded his progress. With a strong, steady arm, the guide made a bold and sturdy thrust of his frail spear, aimed at the right nostril of his assailant. The aim was accurate, and the cold blade went home. The pain infuriated the bull, and with a loud snort and a violent toss of his head he broke the slender shaft. With his firm grip of the spear, the impact threw the guide off his balance. Headlong he fell, and for an instant all except his head disappeared. As he fell to the left, clinging to the broken shaft, the head of the bull was drawn around, so that the curve of his neck presented a fair target within three yards of me. On the impulse I fired, and luck, rather than skill, guided the fatal ball to a vital spot. The brute fell like a stone, and, as the guide struggled to rise from the murky water, the bull fell across his legs; but the weight was relieved by the water, and the man emerged unharmed, save for his viscid bath and blood-curdling fright. This was the crowning incident of all my experiences of hunting African buffalo, and I confess that I have never since passed through that place without shuddering at the thought of what I had witnessed there.
– ROBERT L. GARNER.

1908

LICENCED TO KILL

THE BIG-GAME hunter who takes out a £50 game licence at Nairobi, in British East Africa, can scarcely complain that he does not get good value – on paper – for his money. Once furnished with this document, he may shoot two elephants, two rhinos, two hippos, two zebras, two gemsboks, one eland, one sable hippotrage, one roan hippotrage, two koodoes, two tapirs, two hartebeeste, one bongo, two aardvarks, two cheetahs, two marabouts, two egrets, ten antelopes of various species, and ten chevrotains. All these he may slay and capture – if he can find them. A confirmed grumbler might perhaps kick at the shorter allowance of bongos and hippotrages, but the supply of chevrotains seems princely.

THE KING'S SHOOTING

1 February

WE READ IN the 'London Letter' of a local newspaper that 'the meeting of Parliament closes one prominent part of the King's existence – namely, his shooting.' We greatly dislike these printed remarks about Royalty in general and our Sovereign in particular, especially when they are malignant and inaccurate. As a matter of fact, the opening of Parliament has nothing to do with the closing of his Majesty's shooting, except in so far as it synchronises with the end of the shooting season. Nor is it correct to speak about 'a prominent part of the King's existence'. The King shoots less than any other landowner – far less than the majority of sportsmen. A day or two with the grouse, a few hours' deer-stalking, and, perhaps, half a dozen pheasant battues. That is about all the season's shooting for the busiest man in the land. Good Heavens! Think of what the King does in the way of national business, and then think of the malicious libeller who insinuates that his Majesty virtually devotes his time to carrying a gun. – C.C.

15 February

Our readers will be interested to learn that his Majesty the King has been graciously pleased to take notice of the issue of the *Shooting Times* containing C.C.'s remarks on the Sovereign as an ardent, skilled, yet after all necessarily casual sportsman and gunner.

RAT BAG

An amusing incident took place at Mitcham the other day. The police arrested a man on suspicion of being a poacher, being confirmed in their suspicions by a sack which he carried, in the depths of which there was something which lived and struggled. The man refused to answer questions, and he and his bag were taken to the police station. There he protested that the bag contained his own property, and, as he refused to give any further explanation, the sergeant of the police cut the string that closed the bag. To the horror of the assembled police, two dozen huge rats rushed out. The rodents scampered about, resisting all attempts at capture, and fairly 'held up' the police station, the police being powerless in the presence of these lively rats. Finally the police gave the suspected poacher a sum of money to catch the rats again and put them in his sack, which he did successfully.

DYNAMITING THE LOCH

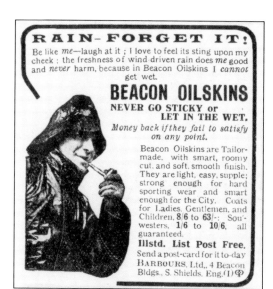

Thousands of pike and other fish were killed in one of the Bute lochs last week by the order of Lord Bute, who wishes to stock the water with trout. The loch, which is 14 acres in extent, was mined with dynamite at points 100 yards apart. Cones of water were thrown 100 feet into the air by the explosions. We doubt, however, if this plan has been completely successful, as lots of the pike will have been merely stunned. The worst of using dynamite is that it destroys not only the fish, but much of the natural live fish-food in the water.

BAGS OF TIGERS

HIS HIGHNESS Nawab Mohamed Nasrullah Khan Bahadur, heir-apparent of Bhopal, is reported to have recently killed nine tigers in two days. Once in a single beat of a jungle four tigers appeared and were shot dead in five minutes, and on the second occasion five tigers fell to his Highness's rifle in one night over one kill.

BITE OF A LION

THOSE WHO HAVE had the misfortune to have had a tussle with a lion and have been bitten by one agree that they have to a great extent been paralysed by the bite, and, in fact, have felt little or no pain. Mr. Selous states that it is not nearly so painful to be bitten by a lion as it is to suffer the same thing at the teeth of lesser beasts. The well-known hunter says: 'All the first-class evidence I have been able to gather goes to prove that the bite of a lion or tiger is practically painless. I imagine that the reason for this is that the tremendous energy exerted by a lion in biting is the equivalent to a heavy blow – which produces such a shock to the nervous system that all sensation is for the time being deadened, as it would be by a heavy blow from a sledgehammer.' The results of the bite are, however, quite a different matter, as the teeth of a lion or tiger are poisonous, and inflammation is set up which is often fatal and in the best conditions slow to heal.

ARTFUL TOM-CATS

SIR, IN YOUR current issue you evince some scepticism as to a cat imitating the call of a corncrake as a lure to assist in stalking its game. Old cats become very artful as well as ingenious in their methods of securing game. A friend of mine was the owner of a wily old feline who was in the habit of secreting herself in a haystack near some rabbit burrows. She would then make a noise like a turnip, and when the rabbit came out would have no difficulty in securing the nucleus of a good meal.

Yrs., W. MITCHELL.
Grosvenor-square, W.

THE FUNNIEST THINGS SEEN

SIR, IT STRUCK me that it would be interesting to read the funniest things known and seen, relating to sport, by your numerous readers. When I was a very young chap, my brother, who was 12 years older than I, one day was very annoyed at our father asking a friend – a legal luminary – to shoot partridges; so he withdrew the shot from the guest's cartridges the night before and filled them with sand. Next day the friend came home with an empty bag, having missed, as he thought, every shot. He was so disgusted with his breechloader (pinfire) that he made a present of it to our steward. On another occasion a fellow praised his dogs so much that my brother and a friend got fairly sick of it. One day, when out shooting, our friend rubbed the noses of the bragger's dogs with oil of aniseed, which utterly deprived them of scent, so that they put up bird after bird. A policeman visited our kennels one day to take down the number of harriers (for taxing) that my brother was master of. My brother got the kennelman to anoint the boots of the policeman with oil of aniseed, and when he was about a quarter of a mile on his way,

the hounds were let out. They went full cry after him, being well used to drags with oil of aniseed, and it was highly amusing to see, with the aid of glasses, the 'peeler' swarming up a tree. A gentleman, long deceased, after a ball went with others to shoot ducks in the early morning on the islands on Lough Derravaigh. He was 'half seas over' and armed with a heavy single-bore muzzle-loading duck gun. On being left on the island he proceeded to load the gun, and, being semi-intoxicated, either forgot to put the cap on the nipple or dropped it. Ducks came over. Taking aim, he pulled, but a click was the only result. Thereupon he loaded the gun again and went through the process of putting the cap on the nipple. A brave lot of ducks came over; he pulled, but, lo! another click. Again he charged the gun. This time the cap was on the nipple. One duck alighted on the shore of the island and he pulled – earthquake! Over went the gun into the lake, and he sprawled about till found by his friends.

Yrs., 'PTARMIGAN'.

1909

KINGFISHERMAN

Sir, It is some time since I have come across anything in bird life out of the ordinary, but the following incident, which occurred at 12.45 p.m., one day in December last, after a storm, is, I think, worth recording. At the time mentioned I was taking advantage of the sunshine to clear out the snow, etc., from the punt. Having just placed a bag or two on the post close by, I caught sight of a kingfisher heading straight towards me. Instinctively I kept perfectly still, though fully facing the oncoming tide, just to see how near it would come before noticing me, when, to my utter astonishment, about a foot away from me, it turned

Kingfisher trap.

upwards and alighted on the top of my cap. Such moments as these are difficult to calculate, but I should say I remained in that unique position for fully 30 seconds – possibly longer – but on gradually raising my left hand to the level of my head the bird continued its flight with alarm. All nature-lovers, particularly those acquainted with the habits of this bird will, I think, agree that this is a very rare occurrence. At the time I was in fowling rig – blanket coat etc., so that I might take it as a great compliment to my get-up.

Yrs., 'A SUBSCRIBER',
Duddingston, N.B.

WILDFOWL BAGS ON FORTH

The following is a list of the total number of fowl etc., secured by wildfowlers, shore-shooters etc., in and around the neighbourhood of Portobello on the Firth of Forth, compiled from reports sent into us:- Geese, 48, the majority being pink-footed; wild duck, including mallard, scaup, pochard, golden-eye, teal, tufted, eider, long-tailed etc., 720; divers, including great northern (three examples), red-throated, great crested grebes (five), little grebes (nine), scoters, guillemots, razorbills, puffins etc., 940 (many of these are shot for food on various parts of the coast);

golden plover 966; curlew 187; other shore-birds, oyster-catchers, turnstones, godwits, lapwings etc., 1,123.

PURDEY WILL

MR. JAMES PURDEY, of Devonshire-place, W., the well-known gunmaker, carrying on business in South Audley-street, died on March 13th, leaving £200,289 gross and £178,248 net. He gives his business of a gunmaker, with the goodwill, stock-in-trade, plant, and the capital and book debts, as to two-thirds to his son Athol Stuart and one-third to his son Cecil Onslow, but neither is to take any interest in the residue of his estate without bringing into account, as to Athol Stuart £60,000 and Cecil Onslow £30,000, as the value of such business.

SHOTS TO KILL

COLONEL WELFORD relates that in the war against the Kaffirs the English burned 80,000 cartridges to put 25 of their adversaries out of action. This was when the English were operating under excellent conditions, as they were opposed to a poorly armed, undisciplined enemy. At the combat of Zaribrod, November 24th, 1885, the Serbians used 200,000 bullets to hit 58 Bulgarians – 3,400 shots to make a hit. General Kuropatkin said of the Japanese that the effect of their fire was relatively small, even with the greatest consumption of ammunition. In January 1907, a detachment of Moroccan troops attacked the bandit Raisouli with 65 men in his party, in an entrenched position. The troops fired 80,000 cartridges, 800 Maxim projectiles, and 120 shells without hitting a single man. At Colenso the Boers, whose reputation as marksmen is universally admitted, fired 600 cartridges for every Englishman put out of action. This is the best battle shooting on record – 600 shots to one hit. This result was obtained by extraordinary marksmen, descended from the most phlegmatic race, most difficult to excite or unnerve. The Boer united in the highest degree all the characteristics of the ideal marksman. He was undoubtedly the best battle-shot that has appeared in action since the invention of gunpowder. But he was wanting in organisation and discipline. These examples confirm the old saying that it takes a man's weight in powder and lead to kill him in war. In reviewing these results it does not seem that the improved rifles and ammunition had done anything to make rifle-fire more deadly in the last 100 years. After all, it rests with the man behind the gun. – Lieut-col. EVANS, U.S.A. Army.

CORNCRAKE SIMULATING DEATH

SIR, MANY YEARS ago, in the dim remoteness of early childhood, when returning from a hayfield where mowing operations were in progress, a bird of bright brownish plumage ran out of a tuft of grass I was passing by, and on my instantly starting in pursuit it at once collapsed on the ground and lay there – dead. I picked it up and carried it home, where my mother informed me it was a corncrake, but as to my story of how I came by it she seemed rather incredulous, and was not prepared with any explanation. Meantime the bird lay on the kitchen table, outstretched and limp, and as I stood there, silent and wondering, watching it, my mother having moved off meantime to another department on domestic business of some kind, to my intense astonishment I saw the bird's eye open, on which I at once called out what I had observed, when the eye was immediately closed again at the sound of my voice. Then followed quite a flutter of excitement in the kitchen; the bird was placed under observation on the ground, and I stood quietly at a distance with my eye upon it. In less than a minute the eyes opened again, the bird instantly pulled itself together, and started for the open door, with me in loud and shouting pursuit; but it made its escape and got clean off through the back-yard and into the garden and we saw it no more. My father was from home at the time, and on his return, when informed of the occurrence, spoke of it as something with which he was quite familiar. But the corncrake was, to my thinking, much more common in Westmeath in those days than it is now.

Yrs., W.F.

IRISH SHOOTING

IT IS THE greatest mistake not to take advantage of the rough shooting which most Irish estates afford, for the peasantry like a sportsman who will come freely among them. If the sport is confined to covert-shooting, little will be seen of the people about the place, but the man who shoulders his gun and tramps over the rough ground will soon earn the good opinion of the peasantry if he is pleasant towards them. Go into their cabins and have a talk with 'herself', and she will never forget the honour conferred as long as she lives. The Irish peasantry are the nicest people in the world if treated properly, and are generous to a fault, and it is only with the greatest difficulty that the majority of them can be made to accept any return for favours shown. The gaining of backsheesh is far from the uppermost thought in their mind, and that can hardly be said of their *confrères* on this side of the channel. For all this, a shilling means a great deal to them. Most of the troubles which arise in connection with preservation in Ireland might be avoided if the proprietor of the shooting would take a little more trouble to ingratiate himself

with the peasantry and drop the patronising manner he so often assumes. It is the rarest thing in the world for an Irish peasant, particularly those of the west, to be bold, disrespectful, or discourteous, and the writer openly confesses that he sees much to admire in their frank, independent manners. It is the easiest thing in the world to get oneself disliked in Ireland, and just as simple a matter to earn the people's good opinion, and the position a man occupies in their esteem depends entirely upon the course he follows. There are some men who would never get on among the poor Irish, and they would do well to keep away. These good folk never respect mere wealth, but love 'the free and aisy manner'. – 'WEST GALWAY'.

TRAVELLING TROUT

A TROUT WHICH for about 10 years was the mascot of the Inverness railwaymen is dead, and is being preserved by Messrs. McLeay and Sons, taxidermists, Inverness. The following is the history of the fish. Upwards of 10 years ago a son of Mr. McDonald, engine driver, caught a brown trout at Millburn and took it home. The driver transferred it to the engine tank, and since that period it has passed a curious existence in the tanks of three separate railway engines. In the course of time the fish became very tame, and came up to peck crumbs from the engine-driver's hand. So intelligent did it eventually become, that when a pail was dropped into the tank to take it out the trout would swim round and round the pail until it could drop into it. Occasionally the driver took his pet home with him, and on the last occasion of his so doing an accident happened – a box of matches fell into the tank, and the trout was poisoned. The tame trout is lamented by all the railwaymen. It travelled during its stay in the engine tanks over thousands of miles, and once narrowly escaped being the victim of a snow-block. The water on that occasion ran down, and the tank was empty, but the trout was kept alive by having the occasional pailful of water put in with it. The fish is beautifully spotted, and in the bottle of formalin in which he reposes looks intelligent and well nourished.

EXTRAORDINARY PLUCK OF DACHSHUNDS

SIR, THIS AFTERNOON, at the Sachzenwald, my pack of six small dachshunden kept a wild boar weighing some 230lb. fighting for two hours, till the largest of the dogs, who only weighed some 20lb. was killed, another disembowelled and carried off on the boar's tusks, a third crippled in the shoulder, and the remaining three dogs so exhausted that two of them had to be carried home. I was posted at a pass, but the boar refused to break cover, and I did not know of the tragedy going on. I have sent men out with lanterns to look for the wounded dogs and telegraphed for more dogs, and as soon as it is light tomorrow will go into the cover with the dogs and try to get a shot at the boar, as he refuses to break cover.

Yrs., WALTER WINANS,
Hamburg, December 10th.

P.S. The two smallest members of the pack weigh some nine pounds each.

SIR, THE MEN with lanterns were unable to find any trace of the dog we were afraid was killed by the boar, and there seems no doubt now that the dog is lying dead in the thicket where it is too dense to find him. The little bitch who was carried off on the boar's tusks had a narrow escape, but she has only a flesh wound. The dogs we have got as reinforcements are of no use. One, a Welsh foxhound, turned tail as soon as he was put into cover; the others are dachshunds who have never hunted a boar before. As soon as we put the pack into the thicket where the boar was left last night they began giving tongue. I found it impossible to follow them inside, as I could not see a yard in front of me. First a sow came close to me, on the outside, and then a three-year-old boar, very close. This was obviously not the boar we were after, so I did not shoot at him. We therefore called the dogs off and drew the next covert. A big boar broke, within half an hour, about 180 yards from me, galloping hard. I broke his shoulder with the first barrel, and hit him in the brain with the second barrel. I did not go up to him, as I wanted the little dogs to think they had killed him amongst them. Little Hexie, the mother of three of the pack, hunted up to him first, and as soon as she had made sure he was dead she began dancing round him, giving tongue. The rest of the pack straggled up as fast as their crippled condition would let them, all except the little bitch who had been on the boar's nose yesterday. I am afraid she must be dead. The boar is not yesterday's boar, the men say.

Yrs., WALTER WINANS,
Hamburg, December 11th.

SIR, THE little bitch we lost yesterday came home this morning, very tired, but her wounds are doing well. She has been shut up with the other wounded dogs and I expect they will all recover. The one killed has not been found.

Yrs., WALTER WINANS,
Hamburg, December 12th.

P.S. – Evening – We have just killed the boar who has done all the damage to my pack. He fought three-quarters of an hour, charging each of us in turn, and was finally killed by a friend who got within three yards of him and was charged so viciously that the boar nearly succeeded in reaching him.

A PROPHETIC PEEP

AH, WELL! The day is over – another Christmas Day – Christmas Day, 1959, and my 129th birthday – and I, a tough, hale old boy, feeling, save for the periodical twinge of rheumatism and a certain slight flabbiness of muscle which none of us can avoid after reaching the age of 120 or so, as fit as a dozen fiddles, and good for all a man of 50 could do before those magic million-microbed chocolates were given into the hands of a disease stricken world just over 50 years ago.

What a blessing to the individual the discovery has proved! One lives on and on and on; one goes through life knowing he has only two possible forms of death before him – accident or painless senile decay – instead of the possible, nay probable, torture of disease which would have been his in earlier years. One does not now begin to think of the end till over twice three score years and ten.

Sitting with my port and walnuts before me, I find my thoughts flowing pleasantly outwards. What changes come about in this world of ours! It seems strange to think that less than 50 years ago it was actually illegal to kill game on Christmas Day. Now, of course, it is one of the most important days in the sportsman's year – the opening day of the pheasant shooting season – the day equivalent in Nature to what was October 1st before Halley's Comet came along and knocked our seasons out of tune with the calendar to the extent of 86 days. Our hoary old earth seems to fare just as well under her new conditions, however, as she did under the old ones.

I have had a delightful day's sport this Christmas Day. While my latest million microbes are gaily seeking out their prey in every hole and corner of my system, while the pleasant process of digesting a heavy Christmas dinner is taking place – a process filling me with feelings of unutterable calm and contentment – I will jot down a brief account of it for whose who may care to read.

Yes, I have had a delightful day's sport – not a heavy bag, truly, but sport fine enough for the gods themselves. The days of heavy bags are over. I, for one, do not regret them. I would rather have an hour in the 'plane with my gun and kill a single woodpigeon after an exciting course than stand for a whole day beside the coverts, as one did 50 years ago, and fire a hundred cartridges at birds driven unerringly within shot. And such poor, tame, grandmotherly shots one had then! Extremes of age met in my gun 'plane at 9.30 this morning – on the one hand, dear old Colonel Blazer, a year my senior, and myself; on the other hand my great-great-great grandson, Tommy, aged 13. In a weak moment, a few days ago, I had promised that I would give him his first experience in a gun 'plane on Christmas Day. A wilder, more mischievous young devil never sucked a million-microbes chocolate. Tommy's first act when we were well on the wing was to give my planeur's elbow a punch, which jerked his hand clean off the free compensating wheel, the 'plane taking a tilt that would have ended our careers for ever if Wolf, the planeur, had not succeeded in clutching the wheel in time and righting our keel almost by a miracle. Colonel Blazer took him by the collar and, in spite of vigorous remonstrance, hauled him to the stern of the 'plane and planted him down by the vacuum retriever.

Then our sport began. Peering through

the high-power eye-piece of the prismatic camera obscura, without which no gun 'plane is more than half complete, I detected a cock pheasant sprinting across a stubble towards the shelter of a small copse about a mile and a half away. The course of the 'plane was set in the direction of the copse. In a minute or two we were circling over it.

'Now for a smoke-ball, Colonel', I said. 'If we don't have him out in less than three minutes, I'm a Dutchman. One ball to windward ought to do the trick.'

The Colonel took a smoke-ball from the box beside him, and dropped it just clear of the windward side of the copse. A single whiff of the dense black cloud of fetid smoke liberated by an exploded ball is enough to make anything from a tomtit to a fox clear out of cover as though the very Old Gentleman himself were after it.

The bird rose with a loud whirr, and began to climb the air, up, up, up, as pheasants always do when a dose of smoke gets into their heads. Quick as thought, Wolf had touched lever and wheel, and at the same moment saw us swooping at terrific speed towards the earth, placing our quarry between ourselves and the blue. A pheasant is at all times a comparatively poor subject for a course. A snipe or a woodcock is the bird to make your hair rise.

A clumsy, perspiring-looking wretch, the pheasant appeared as he struggled vainly to outdistance us in his upward efforts. Tommy clamoured loudly for a shot, his first shot from a 'plane. I yielded, handing him the full-choked 28-bore. He took a really sporting shot, just as the bird swooped, and, somewhat to my surprise, killed it as dead as a stone.

Down went the 'plane in graceful circles after the bird. Tommy invented a new sporting law on the spur of the moment, viz., that the one who kills a bird has the sole right to retrieve it. I raised no objections as anyone can use a vacuum retriever when a bird is lying in the open as the pheasant was. Tommy released the clutch and let the tube of the retriever run out to its full length. With finished skill, Wolf brought the 'plane over the spot at the exact elevation, the mouth of the tube not a foot above the ground. Tommy pressed the push and the pheasant shot up the tube into the net beside him.

After a peaceful luncheon in a meadow where we had landed, the Colonel remembered a copse which had yielded a woodcock four seasons before. A second or two after the smoke-ball, a magnificent 'cock twisted forth like a 'cock gone mad. We were in for a course that could be called a course. While he streaked upwards, we swooped down, with the result that we were quickly beneath him. Then began what promised to be one of the toughest struggles ever engaged in between 'plane and bird. He twisted and dodged and broke away in a gloriously sporting manner, sometimes gaining as much as quarter of a mile before Wolf, at a tilt that made Tommy clutch the rail desperately, could bring the 'plane round in a straight line of chase again. During three-quarters of an hour we never got within three gunshots of our quarry. By this time we were a good five-and-twenty miles out to sea, and sometimes a mile and a half above the water. No one had spoken a word, so tense is the excitement of a good course. Not a sign of tiring did the 'cock show. It seemed an even money chance on his taking us over the coast-line of Holland before we bagged him, even if nightfall did not beat us. But Nature and fluke combined to bring matters to an abrupt conclusion by means of a sudden strong gust, which caught the 'cock as he twisted, while it barely touched the plane. Tommy seized the 28-bore and blazed at the bird as it dashed some 90 yards away and a stray pellet struck the skull and the stone-dead 'cock plunged through that mile and a half of space to the waves below.

Tommy once more asserted his right to retrieve and, as well as the 'cock, got two gallons of salt water in the face which nearly dashed him from the 'plane. The dear old Colonel laughed till he gasped for breath.

There – I think I have told everything worth telling. Life is a fine thing when you take it in big doses. Let me drink a toast to long, long life to all tough old boys who burn powder in their 'planes, and of unimpaired fecundity and voracity to the microbe hosts which enable them to do so.
– L.H. DE VISME SHAW.

1910

HOW GAME FALLS

SIR, IT IS CURIOUS the different positions game falls when it is shot. A deer crouches, stretches out its neck, and pitches forward. A wild boar falls sideways and flaps like a fish. A bear collapses in the attitude of a bearskin doormat. A buffalo drops to his knees and then rolls over.

Yrs., WALTER WINANS,
Zsolna.

Mr. Walter Winans.

PIGEON SHOOTING

TRAP SHOOTING or pigeon shooting seems to be the pet object of aversion to promoters of the Spurious Sports Bill. Well, a pigeon is hatched, reared and fed and looked after. On a certain date it is put in a basket with others of its kind and taken to a certain place; it has plenty of room in the basket, plenty of food, plenty of air and so on. No cruelty, so far, let us say. In its turn it is placed in a trap and, at a given signal it is released and fired at by some shooter, who in 99 cases out of a 100 kills it dead or misses it altogether. In either event where does the cruelty arise? If killed dead, it is put in a sack and for sixpence forms a meal for some poor person who never sees any other form of poultry. If clean missed, why it flies straight home! Wounded pigeons at a pigeon shoot are few and far between, because at 1s., 1s. 6d., 2s., or 2s. 6d. per pigeon very few novices care to compete. Men then don't shoot pigeons at pigeon matches until they are good shots, pigeon shooting being a specially expensive job for a bad one and, as good shots kill clean or miss altogether, but seldom if ever wound, why the element of cruelty needs looking for with a microscope! – D'ARCY I. HAMILTON.

FLYING FISHES

YESTERDAY A new sport was born; Waikiki Bay was the birthplace, and H.P. Wood, of the Hawaii Promotion Committee, was the *accoucheur*. For the first time in the history of the field and gun, flying fishes were flushed with a steam launch and shot on the wing. It was a brand-new experience in the hunting line that a party of local Nimrods and visitors indulged in yesterday morning – an experience that will undoubtedly be shared by many others in the future. The shots came fast and furious. Taking pot-shots at fish on the wing is sport of the first water, affording plenty of exercise in the good sea air, giving the opportunity for quick shooting, providing for the use of all the alertness contained in a man, and not being too hard upon the fish.

COVERT SHOOTING

UP GETS A sovereign, bang goes a penny, and down tumbles half-a-crown.

tional weight, and almost insurmountable difficulties were experienced in shooting the rapids and negotiating the falls in safety. However, the party got safely to the station, and eventually, via St. John's, Mr. Peel reached New York, where he embarked for home in the steamship "Lusitania."

At the conclusion of the lecture the moose and one of the caribou captured on the hunting trip were exhibited.

VARIOUS BIRD CALLS.
BY OUR SCOTTISH CORRESPONDENT.

The successful use of these calls mainly depends upon the operator's knowledge of the proper notes given by the different species in a wild state. The art of success-

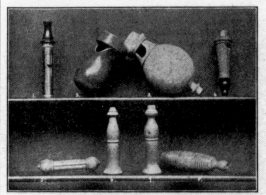

FIG. 1.
1. Curlew. 2. Cuckoo. 3. Woodpigeon. 4. Golden Plover.
5. Lapwing. 6. Rabbit. 7. Hare. 8. Wild Duck (Mallard).

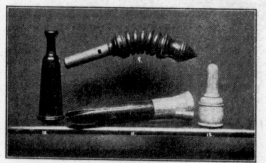

FIG. 2.
9. Pheasant. 10. Wigeon. 11. Heron. 12. Cormorant.

FIG. 3.
13. Partridge. 14. Blackbird. 15. Snipe. 16. Jay. 17. Teal. 18. Magpie.

ful bird-calling is little known, but it is a very fascinating subject, and well repays one for the time spent in acquiring the necessary knowledge. Since the formation of the Wildfowlers' Association I have received

many communications from fowlers desiring information as to the best calls, and particulars as to how to use them properly, and the illustrations may prove useful to other readers interested in this fascinating study. I shall be glad if I can be of any help to anyone desiring further particulars.

CLAY BIRD SHOOTING.
THE EALING GUN CLUB.

There was but a small muster of shooters at the above club's ground at Park Royal last Saturday, and consequently only practice shooting at driven birds was indulged in.

CLAY BIRD SHOOTING FIXTURES.
THE EALING GUN CLUB.

Saturday, November 26.—Shooting ground   off Coronation-road, midway between the G.W.R. Station and the D.R. Station.—2.30 p.m., Pool Shooting, five birds, scratch, centre trap, entrance fee 1s., the highest scores divide pool; 2.50 p.m., Handicap Sweepstakes; 3.15 p.m., Driven Birds; 3.30 p.m., Winter Handicap Silver Cup (2s. sweepstakes), 10 birds down the line, to become the property of the member winning it the greatest number of times during the season, September 3, 1910, to February 25, 1911; 3.45 p.m., Five Birds, single barrel, scratch; 4.0 p.m., Dr. W. Mitchell's Handicap Prize; 4.15 p.m., Five Birds, centre trap; 4.30 p.m., Silver Spoon (club prize), 10 birds, handicap, down the line.

THE BREEDING SNIPE.

In the marshes of West Somerset we are in the ancient land of Damnonia, the local kingdom of that name of the Britons before the coming of the English. It is the country of King Arthur and his knights of story and legend. It represents a corner of the earth where the Celt has struggled for ages with his compeers, where he has met the Roman and mingled with the Saxon and his kindred, and left a rich compost which has wonderfully fermented and fertilised the world. But the tides of history have flowed round these plains rather than over them. Yonder on the horizon, where the limestone hills climb upwards, the Romans came to the lead mines, and the road ran west and east to meet the fosse which crossed the country to the ancient Aquæ Solis—the modern city of Bath. On the slopes of the hills the Roman villas rose and flourished. But when the Roman soldiers looked out from the heights over this country they saw only a swamp and the waters of an inland lake, with the Tor, which is now Glastonbury, rising at one end. The inland lake has gone, and the swamp has been partly reclaimed. It is now a land of watercourses and deep rhines, which carry the drainage to the sea. But it is for this reason a country in which wild nature has remained in large part unchanged for centuries. The surface of rich land formed from mud covered by the sea at a previous time gives place to peat, marking the site of the swamp and lake of ancient days. Many parts are still covered with water, and are overgrown with deep sedge. In others, the heather has nearly extinguished the rival vegetation. This land is the retreat of vast numbers of waterfowl in winter—wild geese, mallard, shovellers, teal, curlew, coots, snipe, bitterns, moorhens, and various kinds of plover.

Many of the birds, including numbers of snipe, remain to breed. You walk far in the early summer noonday without encountering any human creature. It might be Nature in her primæval mood, so silent is the landscape. Yet in the prevailing stillness you become conscious of a peculiar ghostly sound which seems to haunt the footsteps. The cause of it must be the distant wood in front; but there is no one when you arrive. It must be in the open space beyond, and you expect to see figures in the fields and busy men at work; but you emerge again, and still there is no one. The sound is as difficult to define as it is to localise. It suggests now the hum of machinery; or, again, the distant bleating of goats or sheep; or, yet again, the subdued converse of people close at hand at work. But there is never any-

LOW SHOTS

A PARIS GAME dealer has in the basement of his shop a popgun and a supply of pellets, and unsuccessful sportsmen who wish to affirm that they have shot the birds they purchase may, on payment of a shilling, fire some small shot at their purchases. It must be understood that most of the game in Paris shops has been netted.

Look out for coveys directly you reach your butt

1911

TRAGIC DEATH

NEWS OF THE tragic death of Sir Wilfred Hepton whilst on a fishing excursion on a lake near Argeles, South of France, has just come to hand. Sir Wilfred, having reached the middle of the lake, decided to anchor there. In order to do so he tied a large stone to a rope, the other end of which he attached to his leg, and then threw the stone into the lake. Unfortunately the rope was too short, and did not reach the bottom, with the result that the boat capsized, and Sir Wilfred Hepton was dragged down by the rope fastened to his leg. The body was recovered later.

CUPID'S NEW WEAPON

When we first met 'twas love at first sight.
Even before I heard you speak
My heart was thumping with delight;
At once I pressed you to my cheek.

This bold caress you did not flout –
In fact you were even bolder;
You seemed to know your way about
For you nestled on my shoulder.

I looked at you from end to end.
You were indeed a pleasing sight;
Your waist is slim just where you bend.
Again I clasped you to me – tight.

Thought I, you've beauty, grace and charm;
You'd make my walks a dream of joy
If I could take you on my arm
Your company would never cloy.

The question then I had to pop,
My heart at last completely won –
And all this happening in the shop
When I was buying my new gun.

C.D. SMART.

A REEVE INLAND

SIR, DURING the rough weather experienced at the end of November last, a reeve was shot near here. The bird was in good condition, but, unfortunately, it was shot too badly for setting up. Do you consider it sport to shoot into a flock of green plover? I did so the other day and killed seven. But some of my friends seemed to look upon it as unsportsmanlike. I should like your opinion; also that of any other good sportsman.

Yrs., 'REDSHANK', Tenbury.

[It is by no means an unsportsmanlike act to shoot into a bunch of wildfowl, but no sportsman worthy of the name would 'brown' a covey of partridge or a nive of pheasants – Ed.]

EGGS TO THE PALACE

THE FIRST THREE plovers' eggs of the season were discovered on Salisbury Plain last Saturday. Later in the day two of the eggs were sent to the King at Buckingham Palace in accordance with the usual custom.

TROUSER SNAKE

AN ANGLER, having lunched, stretched himself out on the river-bank and was soon wrapped in slumber. He was awakened by feeling something cold and clammy gliding up the leg of his trousers. He soon realised it was an adder, having noticed several in the vicinity whilst crossing a boggy piece of land. He had the presence of mind to remain quiet for the moment and then to decide on operations. He took his handkerchief and cautiously introduced his hand under the waistband of his garment, and then by degrees worked his hand down until he reached the head of the snake. Making a sudden grip with his handkerchief, he had the viper by the neck, and after considerable wriggling he drew the reptile forth and slew him. This yarn reminds us of one related to us by a friend. He had been down to the Docks and after wandering through some bonded warehouses, he returned by train to London. On the journey he felt something making its way up his trouser leg. Turning cold with horror as he imagined a snake, he gave a terrified yell, much to the astonishment of his fellow passengers, and, grabbing the intruder through the cloth of his trousers, he squeezed the life out of it. Upon investigation a well-grown rat was found crushed to a jelly.

SHOT AT PECKHAM'S

SPORTSMAN (to Snobson who hasn't shot a single bird all day) 'Do you know Lord Peckham?'

'Oh dear, yes! I have often shot at his house.'

'Did you ever hit it?'

SHOOTING SPARROWS

ALL OVER ENGLAND, sparrow clubs are in full swing from beginning to end of the close time. Get out round the thick hedges and round the outer margins of the plantations, or about the ricks and outhouses, and shoot them as they come in to roost. They will be nearly all oncoming or approaching shots; therefore, take them singly, bird by bird. Don't risk extravagant shots nor shirk merely difficult ones; don't pick your shots, in fact, but take all fair offers. After each half dozen shots, using, say, one ounce of No. 8, see then how you stand in the way of kills to cartridges fired, and I will wager three pence farthing you will have run up against a bit of a surprise! Or, if your cousin happens to be staying with you who fancies himself as a driven-game shot, you can bet him he won't kill three 'rights and lefts' in 12 attempts, and unless he is nine miles above the average, you will win your money hands down. No, my friend, an oncoming sparrow fairly high up, with a bit of breeze behind him, calls for some shooting, take it from me.

– D'ARCY I. HAMILTON. M.D.

YOUR 'OLINESS

A GAMEKEEPER who was in the habit of looking after parties of shots when they came for sport on his rich master's preserve was fairly well up in the suitable styles of address. He understood that a duke was to be addressed as 'Your Grace' and a common baron as 'My Lord'. One day a bishop arrived, and this was a bit of a puzzle to him. A bird rose, and the prelate seemed a trifle slow and confused. 'Fire, fire, you silly old fool!' exclaimed the gamekeeper excitedly – 'Go on! 'It 'im! 'It 'im! Dot 'im on the nut, your 'Oliness!' To quote his own words. 'And then I knew I 'ad addressed him wrong by the way he looked at me.'

[117]

RIPE GAME

A POULTRY DEALER had been paying a holiday visit to his district and, by way of combining business with pleasure, collected a considerable quantity of fur and feather from surrounding farmers for disposal at his shop when he returned home. Unfortunately the dealer found it impossible to obtain hampers locally in which to pack the game, which had in some instances been killed some days and was beginning to advertise. After a couple of days' delay, the dealer, as the best available substitute for hampers, at last succeeded in bargaining with the village joiner and undertaker for a boy's coffin that had been a misfit and had been lying on his hands, and in this the game was packed and hauled away to the station, where, covered with a cloth, the dealer stowed it on the luggage rack of the carriage and proceeded to make himself comfortable. Shortly afterwards a chatty old farmer entered the compartment.

'Phew!' exclaimed the farmer, mopping his brow, as he sank into the corner seat. 'Hot day!'

'Yes,' assented the poultry dealer.

'Bit close and . . . er . . . sort of stuffy in here, ain't it?' went on the farmer and the other agreed that it was. Very soon the farmer was sniffing curiously.

'Any objection to having the window open?' he asked, and the other had none whatever.

'Any objection to having the other window open as well?' was the farmer's next question. Even the gratification of this last request did not produce the desired result, and the atmosphere remained decidedly rich. At last the old fellow peeped under the seat, and then peeped up at the rack, where he spied the distinct outline of the coffin through its coverings.

Assuming a suitably sympathetic pattern of expression, he murmured inquiringly 'Relative of yours?'

'Humph . . . er . . . yes, in a way.'

'Oh, I see. Taking him home to bury, eh?'

'Yes.'

'Been dead long?'

'A day or two.'

'I thought so,' said the old farmer. 'Well, these 'ere things will happen, and – sniff, sniff – we've got to bear 'em. But you've got one blessed consolation in that you can bury him as soon as ever you get home without any misgivings because you can take it from me – sniff, sniff – he ain't in no blooming trance.'

AUTOMOBILISM IN SPORT

THE SPORTSMAN IN this present hustling age must 'Git thar' and the motor 'gits him thar' – generally. With the car things are easily practicable that without it are utterly impossible in the rural world where the only train that would be convenient only runs on the days you don't want it, and the timetables are so ingeniously arranged for cross-country travel that if there was a spot to which you could get expeditiously, it is a dead certainty that you can't get back. Moreover the ultimate sporting destination of the traveller is usually a considerable distance from any railway station whatever and the last 10 or 12 miles of the journey may have to be done in a country bus that averages six m.p.h. when actually running, but stops for 20 minutes every three miles outside the village inn while the driver tries to sell a few rabbits to its customers or discuss the sensational news, which has just reached the district that Queen Anne is dead.

Let me illustrate. The other day my son and I determined to have a day on the water of a dear old friend of mine – a fine trout stretch not quite 40 miles away. Waiting until the morning's mail had arrived, and the morning's mail in Arcadia does not come in until the morning has got well aired, we glanced through our correspondence, flung an assortment of waders, rods and creels into the car and were away over hill and dale. By 11 o'clock we were on the river, had six solid hours of fishing, left a dish of fish at the Hall, had tea and a leisurely chat with our host and got back home well before nine o'clock. Now there is nothing remarkable about that; the noteworthy part of the affair is the fact that had we been compelled to undertake the trip by public conveyance – bus and train – we should have had to start the day before six, stayed two nights and returned home on the third day.

Of course in the early days of the petrol engine, the element of uncertainty that flavours sport so fascinatingly was simply cocksureness compared with the deluge of uncertainty with which early motoring was saturated. It was all very well to start out for the coverts with your bosom gently tingling with a delicious doubt about whether you were going to kill a brace of birds or a barrow load; but it was quite another emotion that bulged in your breast when you stepped into your motor in the heyday of glorious summer and you knew it was about even chance whether you arrived at the other end of the journey in time to take a hand in the grouse-shooting on the Twelfth, or just scrambled in as the party were drawing for places on the first pheasant shoot of October. Today the efficiency of the petrol engine is such that it is the rarest thing to miss a sporting appointment on that account. Some minor mishaps may occur, but that they are such that it is seldom a matter of more than a few minutes delay, with, perhaps a more thorough adjustment on the completion of the journey.

The subject is interesting, particularly at this time of year, not merely for the man who is anxious to get from place to place, but to the owner of the grouse-moor who has to provide means to carry his guests to and fro from the butts – which often necessitates journeys of considerable distances – as well as to and from the railway station; and it is here that the motor is each year being more and more relied upon. Nor is it necessary to buy the latest big-powered cars for this purpose – cars which are only to be obtained at prices prohibitive to all save the wealthy. During the last half dozen years fashions in motors have changed materially, and there are a lot of high-powered engines and chassis on the market to be had for the proverbial old song, which are the very thing for conversion into sporting brakes. The cars I have in my mind run to 40 or 50 horse-power, and were built when the petrol engine had attained practical efficiency, but before the low-bodied car of the present fashion had come into vogue. Some of them, built before the 12 m.p.h. speed limit was abolished, and the rest before the mania for excessive speed on the roads had developed. They are not overgeared, as so many of the latest cars are, and consequently, are well up to the task of tackling stiff hills and rough roads. They have simply been ruled out of use by the present trend of fashion, and it is possible to pick up several, which, while cheap, are practically as good as when turned out. The thing to do is to buy these effective patterns and chassis and have built on them bodies on brake lines with removable seats, so that, besides carrying the guns to and from the shoot, they may be utilised for luggage.

It is astonishing over what moorland roads these high-powered cars will travel. I know one man possessing one such 40 horse power car which, in the shooting season, is constantly on some of the most rudimentary moorland roads in the North of England, who is jestingly wont to boast that his car will do anything – including climbing over stone walls. It is certainly not only the comparatively level main roads that petrol is ousting the pony. The King largely uses the motor when grouse-shooting, and when in the North of England, on the Duke of Devonshire's moors, cars may be seen conveying the Royal party over rough moorland tracks through a sea of purple heather, right to the shooting huts from which the actual start is made. – W. CARTER PLATTS.

GREAT FIELDING

WE ARE TOLD that the 'clou' of Lord Ripon's shooting is to hit a rocketing pheasant at such an angle that he can catch its falling body without moving from his post. This is the sort of story we like, and are proud of, as it will serve to show those bragging fishermen that they are not going to have it all their own way.

GREATER LOVE HATH NO DOG THAN THIS

WE REMEMBER once having in hand a youngster who was careful enough during the process of learning how to shoot, but directly he got in the field he lost his head through excitement. Such a novice is the greatest danger of all, and requires very close watching. We were out shooting grouse over dogs one day, and the inevit- able occurred, for he killed one of our best setters. I well remember his trembling figure and white face as the many warnings I had given him coursed rapidly through his mind. Our first words to him were 'That dog has died to save a man from a like fate, for you appeared determined not to listen to me. What would you have done if it had

On the marshes.

been me or the keeper instead?' The lad did not go out again for some weeks, and when he did once more take gun in hand, the lesson had not been lost. Many a dog dies in the shooting field to save a man.

– 'HOVERER'.

HOLLOW BULLETS

MR. J.J. MEYRICK is a strong advocate of the use of hollow bullets for antelope shooting. He says that years ago in India it was common practice to shoot at deer with solid bullets, with the result that many were wounded and went off to eventually become the prey of wolves or jackals. He relates an instance of the danger of solid bullets where a colonel in the native army fired at a deer with an Enfield rifle. The bullet struck the top of an old mud hut, ricocheted for a long distance, and passed through the brain of a villager. The colonel was so horrified that, although a keen sportsman, he gave up rifle shooting for many years.

SLEEPING DOG

MR. WALTER WINANS told us this curious incident a few days ago:- 'I had the most curious thing happen to one of my retrievers during the hot days lately. I sent him after a partridge 'runner' and the dog hunted the line through a gap in the hedge. He did not come back for some time and my man went to look for him and found him lying asleep, snoring in the ditch. He is a nice, quiet young dog, bred by myself, and never runs in. But this was being a little too quiet!'

RABBIT PLAGUE

IT IS REPORTED that in some districts on the east coast of Scotland that rabbits are suffering from a most insidious and distressing disease. Its gravity may be apprehended when one reads the list of symptoms exhibited by the stricken animals. It includes inflammation of the mucous membranes, the ulceration of lips and other parts of the mouth, the swelling of the head, and a general woebegone appearance. The diminutive patients are reduced to a state of much weakness, and they are almost wholly bereft of their running powers. What adds to the direfulness of the disease is that it is extremely contagious. If it is to be successfully eradicated it must be dealt with on lines somewhat similar to those followed in respect of foot-and-mouth disease in cattle. All the affected rabbits must be killed down as closely as possible and also all which by any chance they could have come in contact.

SHOOTING FLYING

FOR SOME TIME negotiations had been made with owners of certain tracts of land on the Yorkshire Wolds, where the grey geese annually resort, with a view to gratifying the desire of an airman friend (a keen wildfowler) to procure wild geese by the aid of his machinery. After considerable searching over the countryside I was able to locate on October 15th, a field to which the geese had resorted to feed. All being kept quiet by the keeper, the birds were allowed to feed unmolested. No large numbers came, however, and more than 24 birds were never counted on the fields together. On the 21st, my friend had all the preparations made and had flown a few trials over the ground on the afternoons of October 17th and 18th. His idea was not to shoot, but to mount quickly over the hedge from an adjoining field above the birds, and keep them low to two flanking guns on foot, which would approach from either side of the field simultaneously with the rise of the aeroplane. The first attempt was an absolute failure. The flock of 24 geese were on the field. Undoubtedly they heard the 'whiz' of the machine. As the aeroplane approached, the geese, gaggling loudly, towered high, and with one swing swept to the left suddenly and winged from the scene with remarkable swiftness. This was at about 8 a.m. At 10 a.m., a gaggle of 16 came high, and after some reconnoitring settled in the centre of the field. Preparation for the attack was duly made. A fairly stiff breeze had then sprung up, and as the fields being worked were some 150 acres each the sound of the machine, on this occasion, due to the rising wind after the fog, was evidently not audible to the birds. So little success had attended the first attempt, all of the party seemed disappointed, and had not much confidence in the arrangements.

Rapidly the monoplane rushed forward, and in a few seconds was passing 60 feet high over the geese, which seemed taken absolutely unawares, for they did not attempt to rise, but crouched or squatted like partridges. By this time the guns were up to them, and the first shot at a bird on the ground put them on the wing. Quickly they tossed themselves into the air and fled downwind, but the airman had quickly circled, and, sweeping down with the breeze, was soon above them. At this moment they rushed to the ground, and some fluttered to the hedge-bottom, and others sought the shelter in the long grass of a dry ditch in a narrow plantation. Meanwhile, and for some time after, the flying machine wheeled overhead, and though three or four geese were hidden unbagged, the airman alighted. These 'kited' birds, after being flushed by the retriever, the airman had the pleasure of shooting, excepting one, which the dog caught in the hedge-bottom. The result was the total annihilation of the whole flock of 16, for all were bagged.

– STANLEY DUNCAN.

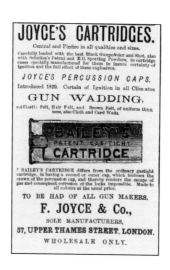

1913

PREPARING SPARROWS

To kill mercifully a sparrow that has been trapped, place the thumbnail at the base of its skull and dislocate its neck by hard and quick pressure. To dress it, cut off the legs, the wings at the outer joint, and the neck close to the body; strip off the skin, beginning at the neck; make a cut through the body wall extending from the neck along the backbone until the ribs are severed, then around between its legs to the tail, and remove the viscera. If sparrows are to be broiled, save only the breasts, as this method of cooking shrivels and parches the lesser parts as to render them worthless. In this case tear off a strip of skin from wing to wing across the back; grasp the wings, in front of the body, in one hand and the neck in the other, and by a quick pull separate the breast from the ribs; turn the breast out of the skin that covers it, and sever the wings at the second joint. The whole operation requires but a fraction of a minute, and it can be done by the fingers alone. Sparrows may be cooked by any of the methods required for reed-birds or quails. When boned, broiled, buttered, and served on toast, they are particularly good and compare favourably with the best kinds of small game. English sparrows are good to eat, and their use as food is recommended because of their nutritive value and as a means of reducing their numbers.

COWARDLY POACHERS

For all his boasting and occasional serious crimes, the poacher cannot be said to possess great courage. He will put up a very good fight sometimes, but that only occurs when it is the only way of escaping arrest. Under such conditions, he has been known to fight severely, but it is a conflict of desperation and not of courage. The average poacher is full of nerves, and it would be hard to find one who will not take freely to his legs if by that means exists the slightest chance of getting away. Once the risk of losing liberty confronts a poacher, he is transformed either into a supreme coward or a desperate maniac, and it is the latter condition responsible for the serious affrays which occasionally startle society and give rise to ideas that such crimes would be better prevented by rendering the preservation of game impossible.

One day last winter we visited with a keeper, a well-stocked rabbit warren. During the season a night never passes that alarm guns are not set in this warren, and another favourite precaution is barbed wire extended at a height of a foot from the ground. The night previous a poacher had evidently sprung one of the guns and, imagining he had been shot at, dashed away in fright. He was intercepted by the wire and, judging from the remnants of clothing attached thereto, had suffered an experience likely to do more good in preventing further attempt at poaching than half a dozen small fines.

A keeper's ingenuity is supposed to stop at sawing a plank half through when he wishes to play a trick on a poacher and immerse him in a brook running beneath; but a poacher we know would hardly agree to that infertility of resource. He was seeking a pheasant at roost to shoot it, when the contents of a bucket of tar were emptied all over him, being dislodged by a wire touched beneath. The keeper tracked him to his home by the drippings of the tar and smears on gates and stiles, and instead of prosecuting added insult to injury by sending him a pound of tallow.
– 'HOVERER'.

OFFICIOUS CONSTABLE

A YORKSHIRE shooting man was entertaining a party of friends on land adjoining a lonely lane. It was practically an occupation lane; there was no traffic on it, and one might stand in it for hours without seeing a soul. The local constable happened to come along the lane and pause by the hedge to watch the sport. The landowner, seeing him, came over to the hedge to have a friendly chat. While they were talking, a hare suddenly burst into view from behind a tussock. Up went the gun, just inside the hedgerow, and over went the hare, and the policeman summoned the gunner for discharging a firearm within 50 feet of a highway etc. When the case came before the court and had been outlined, the defendant turned to the bench and asked:

'If you had been in my place, what would you have done?'

'Well,' murmured the sympathetic chairman, 'If I had been in your place, I think I should have let the policeman have the second barrel.'

[125]

COLONEL'S PARTY

THE COLONEL came down to breakfast, the morning after the party, with a bandaged hand. 'Why, colonel, what's the matter with your hand?' they asked him. 'Confound it all,' the colonel answered, 'we had a little party last night, and one of the younger men got intoxicated and trod on my hand as he was walking across the room.'

MOTORISED STALK

OUR SOVEREIGN'S august cousin, the Emperor of Germany, was perhaps the first person to engage in deer stalking by motor. He shot a stag one day before breakfast in the forest of Romingten. A report was received later that a 'High-grade stag, with irregular 16-pointed antlers' was roaming in another section of the preserve. The Kaiser jumped into his swiftest motor-car, and, a little after two o'clock, got within range of his quarry. With 'a splendidly aimed shot through the vitals', the noble quadruped, which weighed 389lb., was brought to earth. Stalking on wheels is a form of sport which has not yet been witnessed in British forests.

MISC FOR SALE

FIVE YOUNG Merlins on sale. £1 the lot. Apply, LLOYD, Keeper, Llangynog, Oswestry.

FRANZ FERDINAND

ARCHDUKE FRANZ FERDINAND, the Austro-Hungarian Heir Apparent, will visit Windsor for the pheasant-shooting some time in November. The prince is one of the best shots on the Continent, and is noted especially for his skill with the rifle. A wonderful bag of wild boar, deer and chamois stands to his credit.

STALKING

Sir, Stalking as it used to be has entirely died out. We used to try to get within 60 yards, or even less, of a stag; if he was 120 yards off, it was a very long long-shot, and 200 yards was out of range, practically. We used to, in consequence, have to stalk very well to get within range. Now, with .275 rifles and telescopic sights, 200 yards is a very easy, sure shot, and 300 yards no more difficult than 120 yards used to be. Stalking is, therefore, rendered very easy; it used to be the last 50 yards or so which were so difficult to cover without being seen. Now one need not trouble about that at all; in fact stalking, as an art, has died out.

As to running shots, I find I get nearly double the number of beasts I should if I confined myself only to shooting an animal standing still, without counting the satisfaction of making a good running shot and turning the stag over like a rabbit. It is curious how some people, because rifles were so clumsy and innaccurate formerly that only standing shots were tried, cannot realise that with modern rifles one should shoot running shots, in preference, just as one does not shoot at sitting birds with shotguns since the old wheel-lock days.

Yrs., WALTER WINANS.

A successful shot from behind a stalking horse.

FLAMINGO

SIR, I THOUGHT perhaps it might interest you to know that on the 23rd, while shore shooting on Bridgemarsh Island, in the Crouch, I shot a fine specimen of the flamingo in splendid plumage and condition, height 5ft. 8ins.; length from tip to tip of wing, 5ft. 8½ins.; wings and legs, bright salmon colour, black points on wings.

Yrs., J. PARKER,
Burnham on Crouch, Essex.

P.S. I also shot a perfect specimen of albino wild duck (mallard).

1914

SHOOTING A PONY

SIR, A FRIEND of mine, together with another man had finished what had been a poor day's sport, and to show his feelings to his chum my friend said to him, 'Look here old man, I'm sick of the day. I'm going to have a plug at that pony in the paddock and damn the consequences!' At the same time looking as fierce as he could. Stalking carefully up to the pony, my friend shot him dead. Turning round with a smile, he saw his friend bolting the other side of the field like the wind, go through the gate, and nearly collide with the old roadman at work on the road to whom he said, 'Run, man, for God's sake! That chap's gone mad in the field, he's killed a pony, and one of us may be next!' However, the roadman's wife had been in the habit of getting my friend a cup of tea, and on the last occasion had asked him to mercifully shoot their old pony, about 35 years old, when he could find time. Thinking it a good finish after a poor day's sport, he carried out his commission in as dramatic a manner as possible. He had to suffer for it by spending three hours waiting for the train alone, his friend having gone down to the junction some three miles down the line and caught the earlier train for home in record time.

Yrs., R.E. PEACH.

SHOOTING IN BURMA

THERE IS ONE sentence of the Burmese lingo (and about the only one I've ever learnt that I shall never forget). It was, or sounded like, *Na milla boo, takin* – (I don't know, sir). For whenever I asked any question in Hindustani it was only natural that they could have no other answer, accompanied as it invariably was with a good natured grin. What jolly fellows the Burmese are! No cringing about them like the natives of southern India. More like Ghurkas, always ready to enjoy a joke or a bit of fun. Several of them – men and women – were recently squatted, plaiting matting in the anteroom of our mess. Being in charge thereof, seeing them idling and gossiping, I approached one of the offenders and, lightly boxing his ears, pointed to his neglected work. Up he jumped, grinning from ear to ear, and, sparring up, caught me – one, two – playfully on either side of the head. At this girls and men laughed heartily so entering into the fun of the thing, I retaliated and we had a friendly bout, all the workers stopping work together, clapping hands and thoroughly enjoying the show. When we cried Pax! they all returned cheerfully to their jobs. Imagine natives of India doing this!

But to return to our sport, several more were added to the bag and then an (at first sight) unpleasant incident occurred. There were a lot of men and women working in the rice fields we were trudging through. As we got near them snipe rose between us and them. I was much to blame, but, only thinking of the bird, fired. Down he dropped. At the same time a scream told me I had bagged something else! One of the girls, dropping her basket, collapsed. All her companions rushed to her, and, of course, we went to see what had happened. There was much palaver, gesticulation, and many scowling faces to meet us, and one of the men pointed to a little blue mark on her leg. Seeing it was but a flesh wound, I whipped out my knife and quickly picked out the cause of alarm – a tiny No. 10 shot. Laying it in the palm of my hand, I showed it to them. At this their innate sense of humour betrayed itself. An exclamation, a laugh, then many laughs, and when, to wind up matters, I put a rupee in the girl's hand and gave her a slap on the back, I believe all of them would gladly have received a similar peppering – and the same cure! – 'KIL-KOLA'.

BEAR SHOOTING

SIR, I HAVE just arrived here this afternoon from a fortnight's bear shooting trip to north Russia – almost as far north as Archangel. I found that the usual way of shooting bear was to let some hundred to two hundred beaters drive the forests, the guns being posted at likely passes. This method, besides being very expensive, is most uncertain. The bears may not only get missed in the thick brushwood, but they often break back, indeed, the beaters sometimes purposely let them break back so as to be able to sell the bears to other shooters. I shot 10 bears in 10 days in the professional skin hunter's way. You go with the man who has found a bear's winter den, stand with the man 10 yards from the mouth of the den. 'Are you ready? Pull!'

Mr. Winans' exhibit at Vienna.

(i.e., tell the dog to go in). Out comes the bear and you plug him in the head. The last day a bear came out, I dropped her with a bullet in the forehead at seven yards distance. Directly after three young bears (three-year olds) came out after her. I got a right and left, and my gun loader (there was no time to change rifles) shot the third. Four bears, all shot in the head, in less than a minute. We were in rather a rough country, got lost in a snow blizzard once, and on another occasion when at dinner were shot at out of the darkness with what sounded like an automatic pistol. I am writing for news of more bears, but it is thawing. Until it freezes again, we cannot locate bears.

Yrs. WALTER WINANS,
St Petersburg.

OUTBREAK OF WAR

THE OUTBREAK of war will alter the plans of many sportsmen who had made engagements for shooting in Austro-Hungary. Two or three friends, including Mr. Walter Winans had intended going to the country named for chamois and mouflon shooting, but now they are all in a state of uncertainty. A good many English sportsmen now go regularly to Hungary for the partridge shooting which is first class.

CARRIER PIGEONS

A LONDON correspondent suggests that farmers and others in the Eastern Counties should be advised to shoot outgoing pigeons, which, he considers, the only means of communication between England and Germany. The events of the past few weeks have shown that the country is honeycombed with spies armed with bombs and rifles, and, considering the elaborate system of espionage which has been set up, it would be a singular thing if the use of the pigeon had been omitted. Any official orders given to shoot carrier pigeons on sight would have to be safeguarded, or it might happen that the birds in the service of the Fleet might become the victims of slaughter.

SPORTING OFFER

SIR, I SEE in the Notes dated August 15th, that, on account of the war, numbers of preserves will not be shot over. As I am not going on holiday, I would give my services to the shooting of game and give up all the birds. If you know any keeper requiring the assistance of a gun in the shooting of game I would be obliged if you would let me know.

Yrs., W.H. FITZMAURICE,
Dunmanway, Co. Cork.

[There are doubtless many who would like a shoot on the above terms. –Ed.]

FIELD GLASSES

SIR, THERE ARE many sportsmen in Great Britain who, for various reasons, are unable to take to the field for their country. I appeal to those who possess field glasses, race glasses or stalking glasses to render a real service to those who are going to the front by giving them the use of good glasses. If the owner's name is engraved upon the glasses, every effort will be made to restore them at the conclusion of the war. Great care will be taken over the distribution of these glasses to the troops.

Yrs., ROBERTS, Field-Marshal.

LEASE DISPUTE

SIR, IN JUNE last my son, who is an officer in the Territorials, entered into an agreement to take a grouse moor in Scotland, and at the time he never anticipated not being able to shoot on the Twelfth, and he made all arrangements for doing so. On the outbreak of war he was called up, and he is now doing his duty to his country, having abandoned all idea of shooting. He wrote to the lessor of the shooting, informing him of the position in which he was placed, and resigning the shooting; but the lessor insists upon the bargain being kept, and says he will have to bring an action for the rent. I should be glad if you will inform me if the landlord is justified in his actions, and if he can recover any rent under the circumstances.

Yrs., A.M.

[We think your son could plead *force majeure* – that is to say, that overpowering circumstances prevented him from carrying out his contract. He was, of course, bound to obey the summons to join his regiment, and we think if the landlord insisted no jury would give him a verdict. It is unfortunate, and both parties are entitled to sympathy. – Ed.]

DRIVE TRIALS

WE HEAR THAT keepers who have been authorised to kill grouse because of the war are making good use of their somewhat unique opportunities. On one moor especially they have provided themselves with screens made of net, into which sprays of heather were drawn and these have been utilised instead of the ordinary butts. With the assistance of these screens the moor has been driven in every possible direction, with a view to improving sport, and a great deal learned. A great fear exists of trying a fresh system of driving for it may lead to failure, and no one cares for that to occur when esteemed guests are present. However, the keepers have had their chance to see what alterations are possible, and the result should be apparent next season.

IRISH PROSPECTS

THE COURSE OF shooting appears to be more affected in Ireland by the war than it is even elsewhere. So many officers spring from the Irish families, and there is scarcely one of the latter which has not several members at the Front. Irish country houses are also to a great degree deserted, for everyone prefers to be in London where the first news is to be heard. On one estate which boasted of 8,000 pheasants released in a covert hardly a shot will be fired, and the same conditions apply to hundreds of smaller estates. The peasantry keenly look forward to the shoots, and the good wages that they earn as beaters, and they freely curse the Kaiser for depriving them of both sport and cash.

SPIES

SIR, ONE WONDERS if, after the recent events on the NE Coast anything will be done to limit the actions of naturalised Germans of both sexes. Daily here I come into close touch with such. To all seeming, everything is quite all right, but it does not seem reasonable to believe that the womenfolk are devoid of all power to work mischief. We know what the male naturalised Hun has done. A civilian officer told me a few days since that he was far from satisfied with the lax precautions of the day.

Yrs., 'SOUTH SUSSEX'.

[We think that some of our East Coast wildfowlers might be of great assistance in detecting signals at night. Whilst out on the sea in their punts or motor boats, they could more easily distinguish flashlights on the shore than those who were engaged in patrolling the land. – Ed.]

1915

GAME TO FRANCE

A LOT OF GAME, estimated to weigh more than a ton, has been despatched from the Royal preserves by order of the King to hospitals in France where wounded British soldiers are being treated. As there has been little or no shooting at Windsor this season, the game there has had to be thinned by netting.

KILLER ALBATROSS

SIR, I SAW the note in last week's *Shooting Times* stating that some of the German sailors in the late battle of the Falkland Islands were attacked by the albatrosses and killed. I have heard some old sailors who used to go round the Cape in the days of sailing ships say that if a man fell overboard where one of these birds was in sight, the chances of saving that man's life was small indeed, as by the time the ship was brought to, if she were going fast, the albatross would kill the man by one or two strokes of his powerful beak on the man's head. An albatross is even a more powerful bird than an eagle, or even a vulture, and I can well believe the tales one hears of danger from them. I shot a gannet once breaking his wing, and after some trouble, got the bird on board the boat I was sculling in. This was an old-time Thames wager boat, and the place was a mile or more off the sea coast, where such a boat was not safe in any jump of the water. The gannet is, of course, very small in comparison with an albatross, but the beak of the gannet is a very formidable weapon and I was glad enough to get this creature over the side when he offered me battle when I had resumed rowing. I made stems for my pipes out of the bones of its wings. It looks as if even the animal world is fighting the German tyrants also, and they may help to chain the Mad Dog.

Yrs., 'OLD HEAD'.

SHOOTING AEROPLANES

SIR, I NOTE IN last week's issue 'Colonel' states that Westley Richards (rifles) .450 can be obtained cheap for shooting aeroplanes. Could you tell me where? Could you also say whether it would be best to purchase a cordite rifle, with the intention of resale at the end of the war, or to buy a black powder rifle and be prepared to scrap it?

Yrs., ARTHUR E. BROWN,
Newcastle on Tyne.

[Try Westley Richards and Co. We should say a long range rifle is what you require if you are out after aeroplanes or Zeppelins. – Ed.]

ESTATE COTTAGES

OVER EVERY gentleman's estate, houses are scattered to accommodate his retainers. First comes the rather palatial residence of his agent, the man responsible for the smooth working of the whole staff. Then the head gardener's cottage is to be found adjacent to his glass house, as it should be. Alas! The coachman's cottage is too often occupied by a chauffeur, and the loose boxes turned into a garage. There may be several entrance lodges, and in these assistant gardeners generally reside. Their selection as occupants being governed by the fact that they are considered able to keep the surroundings in nice order. The lodges are all many people see of an estate, and they are apt to judge regarding its upkeep by the appearance they bear. The lodges also convey first impression to those entering, and we all know what is said concerning first impressions.

The most difficult cottage of all to find, and albeit the most interesting, is the head keeper's, as this is invariably located in some secluded spot, out of sight, so that it does not attract every passerby. Those in the know are always guided to it by the barking of dogs kennelled near. The keeper's cottage is the continual resort of the male members of the family of the owner of the estate, from the small as yet only interested in ferrets, ratting, and birds' nesting, to the grey-haired sportsman who has taken out a game certificate for 50 years. If they have an idle moment, off they go to see Jones the keeper, and very often Jones would far rather they allowed him to get about his work. However, he is not always at home, and is never easy to find if abroad, for he goes about so secretively, and turns a deaf ear to loud whistling.

As the gentle people are so fond of calling at the keeper's cottage, he makes a worthy endeavour to keep it as nice outside as his wife does the interior, but that is not an easy task. He is generally a decent gardener, and his efforts at producing flowers are supplemented with gifts from the big gardens when the bedding out has been completed, but he has to keep poultry, and occasionally an energetic old hen utterly destroys some group of cherished plants. The romping dogs, too, are sinners in that respect, and cock pheasants are inclined to investigate the flower beds at early dawn. So if the keeper does manage a floral display, it is only with considerable difficulty.

Usually the keeper's house is so prettily situated among a bower of greenery that a very little bloom is sufficient to make a grand display. He is always able to cover the walls of his cottage with creepers and the porch in front is invariably a bower. Old-fashioned roses, gorgeous and sweet-scented, vie with clematis and jasmine, and grow rampantly, in glorious but agree-able disorder, all over it from earth to roof. Indeed, one has to be a bit of a gymnast sometimes to secure entry without beoming ensnared in trails of sweet fragrance. The keeper's wife occasionally ties in a more than usually wilful branch, but neither he nor she believes in too much tying and pruning so we have to dodge our way in at the porch.

The keeper's wife does her best to encourage the flowers, and often their presence is attributed to her skill and energy alone, for the season of flowers is about the busiest period of her good hus-band's year. She does not have much to say when the gentlemen come down, but the flowers and the pretty appearance of the cottage brings ladies there as visitors, and then she is delighted and in her own element. Seldom do they escape unless bearing sheaves of sweet blooms, for amidst such profusion she is able to gratify her desire to give without despoiling her plants. The children go to school each summer morning bearing big posies for the teachers and, at the harvest festival, beg-gars for trails of her flowering creepers are never scarce.

Tea at the keeper's house is ever a great event with his employer's children, and a dainty tea the keeper's wife is always able to provide. Cream and butter from her own small dairy of one cow, honey from her husband's hives, crisp radishes and lettuces from his garden. Perhaps she is Scotch, and in that case there will be heaps of delicious scones and other small cakes dear to the digestions of her enthusiastic visitors. Attached to the keeper's house there is generally an airy luncheon room used by the shooting parties when they are engaged nearby, and that is where these teas are laid out for the youngsters.

The luncheon room is often a kind of sporting museum. Its walls are decorated with Leach's sporting pictures depicting shooting episodes, and big glass cases con-taining rare birds and other creatures obtained on the estate are placed there. We see the first partridge or pheasant killed by the heir with a plate beneath giving his age and the date. Old weapons hung in groups – flint locks and Joe Mantons used by sportsmen long since gone to happier hunting grounds. The spotless appearance of these bespeak the loving care of the keeper and both he and his wife take the keenest of delight in having this room as attractive as possible. In one corner is a hot plate, pristine with polish, to keep the food warm while the guns decide to have just one more beat before lunch.

Even in winter the keeper's house is an attractive place, for the green pine trees around give it an aspect of cheerfulness, and the blue smoke from his wood-fire curls cheerily upwards among the branches. Storms scatter leaves and twigs over the walks leading to it, but these are scrupu-lously and regularly swept away. There are always some fine old cock pheasants close by, usually late ones which were brought there from the rearing field to receive extra and prolonged care. They feed with the fowls and the keeper's children have invested each one with a pet name. After each covert shoot, great is their anxiety to see if these pet birds turn up safely, which strangely to say, is usually the case because the birds cleverly hide away.

WHISTLING PIGEONS

A MAN WHO IS much interested in the use of pigeons by our land and sea forces informed us the other day that when pigeons fail to reach their destination it was generally due to attacks by birds of prey, the pigeons used by ships being more liable to attack in consequence of the large number of hawks which frequent the cliffs on our coasts. Since the conversation, we turned up a description of how the Chinese attach whistles to their pigeons, and a contrivance of this kind would serve to scare off any hawks making an attack on our war pigeons. The whistles are made of very light bamboo tubes and are attached to the tail of the pigeons by fine copper wire.

When the bird is flying, the air rushes through the tubes and produces a loud whistling. Some of the whistles consist of two, three or five tubes, and there are some made of a tiny gourd which has a mouthpiece attached and is pierced by a number of holes to the number of perhaps half a dozen or more. The whistles are attached to the tails of pigeons when quite young, in order that the birds may get accustomed to them. Travellers who have visited China state that in some of the cities the sound of the whistles on the pigeons is quite melodious, and effectively scares the rapacious birds which abound in the Happy Land.

EXPLODING PEAT

A PERTHSHIRE keeper tells us of an ingenious plan which he recently formed to rid himself of the plundering attentions of some gypsies. In every stack he deposited a large peat which he had dug hollow, charged liberally with gunpowder, and closed up with a peaty plug. Shortly afterwards, a startling explosion occurred in the gypsy camp fire. Peats and glowing embers radiated to an immense distance, and pots and pans were flung high into the air. The hint was taken. Horses were hitched to wagons and the whole party were immediately on the trek to some more hospitable retreat.

SHOOTING ZEPPELINS

SIR, I AM afraid the theory of using 4-bores against Zeppelins will not hold water. Catch those white-livered curs, the Huns, descending to 2,000 or 3,000 feet! Nine thousand feet is about the lowest they ever come, and when picked out by searchlights they rise to 12,000 feet and over. Also, we have found that shrapnel shell is of little use against them. What we want is a high explosive, charged with some gas or a chemical that will give an intense flame on bursting. Now, then, chemists, buck up!

By the way, any sportsman or other reader of the *Shooting Times* who has any idea for killing Huns or preserving our men should send said idea to Assistant Director of Trench Warfare, Trench Warfare Department c/o the Board of Education, Whitehall, SW, where the said idea will be duly considered by experts.

Yrs., W.H. BRADISH,
Strandfield, Wexford.

SHOOTING ROMANCE

THE DINNER gong had gone ere the black tie had consented to behave. I had forgotten all about X, but traversing the corridor, I heard his roar – he calls it 'laugh' – and knew it meant a specially merry dinner, and bucked along. I have said before I am deucedly shy, and never felt a bigger fool in my life than when, diving into the hall, I found not only X but a woman. This flurried me. Beyond the fact that her frock was blue, and that she was just terribly at ease, all was chaos.

This, as the days went along, wore off some, and pretty often I found myself trying to contrive to be next to her in line, and so on. One day, shooting some outlying coverts, we were paired. It had looked pretty threatening all morning; now a regular buster of a thunderstorm came up. Heavens! How it rained! It was as dark as a hedge, save for the flashes of wicked lightning. We had drawn together for shelter, and during one of the illuminations I saw

something akin to fear in her eyes. Wild things herd together during a storm, and I guess humans feel the same. It seemed unwise to keep near the trees. I knew of a lean-to sort of shelter, and proposed a bolt for it. We bolted, leaving our guns behind. Fortunately, I had a flask and I insisted on a peg apiece. She suggested I should smoke. I did, and, somehow, the things I felt came out. Goodness knows how; I don't.

I've had reason to bless that thunderstorm. The glimpse of those frightened eyes gave me a sort of superior feeling. Otherwise, I imagine – well, I'd rather not imagine. I didn't care a cockle for the chaff of the others, and it is my firm belief that the two good fellows had an idea how things were with me long before.

The next New Year that ever was, once more it was my pleasure to escort the girl – this time up an aisle – not by request of a very irreverent brother! She forbids me to say more! – 'SHIKARI'.

PROPORTION OF ROYALS

Sir, In making an entry in my game book today, I was struck by the small proportion of Royal stags (12 points or more) which I have. They work out at a fraction under one Royal or over to every 29 stags I shot. My list to date is: Two Imperials, 18 points; two of 17 points; three of 15 points; two of 14 points; five of 13 points; 18 of 12 points. – Total, 32 of 12 points or more. I count as a point anything long enough to 'hang your watch on', which is the usual definition of a point. Of course, I do not count fallow deer in the above.

Yrs., WALTER WINANS,
Claridge's Hotel, W.

Hawk trap.

1916

SIZE OF BULLET FOR BIG GAME

SIR, SPEAKING from my own experience, I think 'Garhwali' is right in recommending a .400 for big game, especially for dangerous game. The .280 may not always, if shot with a cross-cut or expanding bullet, stop an animal in time. I shot wild boar with the spitzen bullet – the military, not the copper-nosed, bullet. I found, if it hit a bone, it set up a whirling motion which caused fearful wounds. This was the .303, not the .280, and none of my bullets went through. They were shot at short range, however, 25 to 40 yards. I suppose at 300 or 400 yards, the velocity being less, they would be apt, if not hitting a bone, to go through. I like a big bullet, which knocks down at once and leaves a big blood trail; a .280 bullet or less leaves so little blood that if a wounded animal goes into a thick wood it is almost sure to be lost. I have given up anything smaller than a .400-bore even for such a small animal as mouflon. I think a good double is far better than a single; one can get in the second barrel instantly after the first, without having to fumble with the loading. I would not face a dangerous animal with a single barrel; one's life often depends on getting in instantly with the second.

Yrs., WALTER WINANS,
London W.

VARIOUS

SIR, TALKING to a man the other day who does a good deal of cushat-shooting over decoys, he told me that he pinned the eyes of shot pigeons on to those of the decoys, finding it a great help. Is it now illegal to shoot larks if one holds a game certificate in the proper season? If so, how long has this been the law? I recall how we used to pursue the dainty brown wee beggars, considering them well worth the powder and shot. Delicious they were, too, especially in lark pies.

During one of the recent air raids we met a poor fellow in the small hours of the morn carrying a poor wee bit bairn. Suggesting to him that it were better both should be at home in the warm, his reply was, 'My home is gone, sir, and I don't know where the wife is.' We found them shelter. With such things happening, yet we permit Huns to remain unmolested in houses on the sea front. It cannot but disgust the Britisher at the absurd policy of interning a certain number of Hun males, leaving all the females at liberty. Surely they are a potential menace; or think you they be all innocent sucking-doves? What must our allies think of some of the queer things we do? One hardly dares think.

I've wondered right from the first whether the uncovered watch worn on the left wrist was not a danger to its wearer. Under certain conditions it becomes a veritable helio. Probably I'm all wrong, but the position of the blade on the knuckle duster affair for close quarters seems to be out of place. Anyhow, I should not like to try on at tough togs – that is, not using a straight right. Glancing at various articles for sale, presumably intended for officers, it was impossible not to notice the fearful prices asked. Surely, if these things be necessary, which, fortunately, many are not, the fighting man should not be exploited? I think, Sir, you are to be congratulated on keeping our paper going, despite the shortage of paper and other things incidental to the war.

Yrs., '20–BORE'.

ROYAL EXAMPLE

EVERYBODY REMEMBERS the lead given by the King in the matter of abstinence from alcohol during the war. It was a very fine act on the part of His Majesty, who hoped it might influence men who had previously indulged too freely and thereby lessened their own efficiency, and consequently that of the country. In the interests of economy, about which so much has been written of late, it is now stated that pheasants' eggs are being eaten by the Royal Family instead of plovers' eggs.

GUN NEST

A BLACKBIRD has built her nest on a seige gun which is in daily use at the Front. The bird has four eggs in it and is 'as saucy as she is confident of our protection'.

INSTANT OF DEATH

SIR, I ONCE HEARD a curious case, where a doctor asked a Chinaman who was to be beheaded if he would answer the question whether he felt pain after his head was cut off. The doctor was an Englishman who had known the Chinaman for some time as his coolie, to carry the game-bag on the trips he made up the Yangtse etc., and he promised to give the friends of the Chinaman a sum of money if he answered the questions. The doctor was present at the execution, and his servant took up the head when it had rolled from the body. The doctor put his question as to whether the poor man felt pain, but, though the Chinaman's face worked and his eyes moved as if in answer to the words spoken, yet was there no word uttered by the head. I was told by an M.D. that the organ of speech is in the chest, and that, therefore, the man's head could not answer the question; but that the man still lived there was no doubt, as he looked from one speaker to another, as if he understood what was said. I do not think there is absolute sudden death in our present existence; there may be rapid extinction or quick death, but no more.

Yrs., 'OLD HEAD'.

FROM THE FRONT

SIR, SINCE I last wrote to you I have succeeded in knocking over a couple of brace of hares with the aid of a rifle. 'Pot shots', of course, sounds rather unsportsmanlike in the eyes of our sportsmen at home, but I think if one takes the circumstances into consideration it is to a certain degree pardonable. For example, after daybreak one morning you hear a couple of pheasants crowing behind the front-line trenches. You carefully look over the parados, bearing in mind the proverbial German sniper in the opposite trench is lying in his lair, with his accurate telescopic rifle, awaiting his chance at bigger and more important game. The average German sniper is not to be despised. Sometimes you find your bird to be in range from the trench, but usually a little stalk via shell-holes is necessary before you get within easy range. This must generally be accomplished to a certain degree in view of the wily Hun, should he chance to be watching that particular part of the line.

After a crawl in these conditions across wet, muddy ground, you generally find the pheasant moving about, and your object is to hit him in the head, if possible as our bullets cut a bird up somewhat. Partridges are very plentiful, but in their case shotguns are necessary, and I feel the loss of one very much out here. A large covey numbering about 14 birds fly over a certain part of our front line every morning, with clockwork precision, and drop into No-Man's Land to spend the day there between the two fires, and return again in the evening, presumably to feed during the night in some once-upon-a-time tillage fields behind our lines. Some mornings ago, just before 'stand down' I heard the unmistakable 'honk' of geese coming from our rear, flying towards the Hun trenches. I shouted at our men on the 'firing steps' to give them rapid fire, which they did as the geese passed overhead, and as they reached the Hun trenches they met with a similar reception, but in each case there were no

E. Galway Foley, an old contributor to the *Shooting Times* and an all-round sportsman.

the pigeons make a hurried exit. One morning, last week, just at breakfast time, I saw a pigeon pitch on one of these trees. Shortly afterwards there was a fusillade from the Hun trench and the pigeon tumbled down. Fritz had to wait that day to retrieve his bird, as we kept a good watch on the spot during the day, and we had a fixed rifle kept going that night, so whoever went for the bird ran a sporting chance. Hawks are very numerous in this part of the country. We often get a nice shot at them as they quiver over our lines. One of my men brought down two in one morning, both birds being shot through the head. We get excellent practice with our revolvers at rats, which may be counted in thousands, some of them being as big as the average cat. In fact, the few cats we have in trenches and billets seem anxious to keep out of their way. Some time ago I saw a cat meet a large rat in a disused trench. The cat paused for a few seconds and then beat a hasty retreat. I hear from home that 'cock and snipe are plentiful in old Tipperary, but I fear I will not get back for any shooting this season. Possibly we will be back for the opening of the pheasant-shooting next year – but one never knows!

casualties, both sides being taken unawares, and the light at the time was not too good. There is the remains of a shell-battered wood, some 60 yards in the rear of the enemy line on our front. In the early morning I often see pigeons pitching on the few surrounding hapless trees. They do not rest there for long as, invariably you hear the sharp crack of a German rifle, and

Yrs., E. GALWEY-FOLEY,
Somewhere in France.

THE SPORT

He's known for a Sport, of truth, honour, and grit,
With cheer and good-fellowship ready and fit
To greet the whole world with a smile;
   He's a pal! On the strength of his hand sincere
   Sorrows and troubles all vanish – dark fear
Nor worry seem no more worth while.

Now he's settling the Huns with zeal and zest
Heartening his comrades, by deed and jest
Lightening the horrors of war.
   In the glad future of peace we've got to thank
   Not ships, ammunition, or mighty tank
'Tis by him and his like we score.

He's British! – real English! – the stuff that stands
Home, honour, freedom, rest in his strong hands.
   Right up to the standard, whate'er befall,
   He'll answer the challenge, salute the call,
Die, as he lived – A SPORT.

CLARISSA ALCOCK.

Mrs. Clarissa Alcock and her spaniel Jess.

[The writer of these lines is a charming, all-round sportswoman. – Ed.]

1917

RABBITS AND TRAINS

Sir, If a hare or rabbit is placed with two front feet on an ordinary railway line, and the train is travelling on the line a mile away, is it possible for the animal to get away before the train reaches it? A friend says it cannot move owing to the vibration, and a man can walk up and pick up the animal before the train has run over it. Can you contradict his statement?

Yrs., 'SHOT', Bolton.
[Why not bet your friend, say, five shillings, that he is wrong, and then try the experiment and rake in the shekels? It is too easy! – Ed.]

SNIPING FREAK

The following is an account of a remarkable incident at the front related by a German sniper: 'From one of the trenches I aimed at my adversary. At a distance of 70 yards, the outline of a cap allowed remarkably good aim. I pointed my rifle and was already sure of success. I was just pulling the trigger. The aim was clear; my bullet could not fail. Suddenly I staggered back, and when I recovered, I found my rifle damaged at the lock and the chamber. I had a very ugly wound in the forehead. I examined the rifle, and I found in the barrel, a French and a German bullet, both flattened. What had happened? After closer examination I saw that the muzzle of my rifle was only slightly damaged. What had happened was this: a French bullet had entered my rifle at the muzzle and had followed the course of the barrel; had caused the explosion of my cartridge, and the butt of my rifle had wounded me.' This sounds very much like a story related by another German, Baron Munchausen, but in his case the weapons were cannons. Still, it is quite possible that the yarn is true, as a bullet must go somewhere, and there are millions flying about. It is interesting to note that the calibre of the German military rifle is .315, whilst that of the French is .311.

THE LATE MR. JOHN RIGBY

SIR, IN LAST week's *Shooting Times*, referring to the late well-known rifle shot, you state: 'We believe this is the same John Rigby who took part in the first international rifle match between America and Ireland in 1874 at Creedmoor.' You are quite correct in believing so. I knew Mr. Rigby well, and I recollect that he competed at that match. In 1867, when six friends of mine were in his rifle range, he was kneeling beside me while I was firing. My first shot was on the right side of the bull's eye, and with the next three shots I got three bull's eyes, when Mr. John remarked 'That is tall shooting'. I gave my half dozen friends an eye opener. Next time I used a rifle was at rabbits, and killed two with one bullet, and the time after a major and a captain (now a lieutenant-colonel at the front,) both used my rifle for a number of shots at rabbits without killing any. After the rifle was handed to me, I saw a rabbit running down a path about 900 yards away. I put up the rifle in the way I would a shot gun, the rabbit sat up, and I knocked him over.

Yrs., AENEAS FALKINER NUTTAL.

WAR DOGS

A CONTEMPORARY, referring to the dogs employed by us at the Front, says it is believed that their canine intellect is able to scent danger in the difference between the gutteral Boche and the softer accents of their native masters. From what we have been told, we believe it is the overpowering personal odour of the Boches that they scent.

SPORT IN FRANCE

THE NESTING season is now in full swing out here. Of late I have come across a good number of pheasants' and partridges' nests containing eggs within a couple of hundred yards of the front-line trenches, and the shooting prospects for next season out here are decidedly good. It is remarkable with what contempt pheasants, partridges and hares treat the constant shelling. How often have I seen pheasants perched on trees and ruined cocks of hay, while whizbangs and 5.9's were bursting all round them, and our 18-pounders barking from gun emplacements only a couple of hundred yards from them. The same applies to partridges. One can see them running along, feeding among the shell-holes, during a bombardment, just as if they were in some big preserve in the Old Country, guarded on all sides by gamekeepers. Frequently I have disturbed hares on their forms close up to the firing lines. This may be accounted for by the fact that the nearer the front line, the better the feeding, the earth being tossed up daily by numerous shells.

Circumstances considering, I had quite good sport out here during the season. Sport was always best when my company was in supports. There I was in the midst of the best shooting ground, and with, in most cases, plenty of spare time. Provided the day was dark, with little visibility, I could beat about with a certain degree of safety. On a certain night last January, when in supports, I had wandered into a dugout and met an old acquaintance and countryman, whom I shall call M. – a well-known sportsman in the South of Ireland, being breeder and owner of many race horses. That night, over a bottle of 'Johnny Walker' in the absence of Irish, we arranged for a little shoot the following day. Accordingly, the following morning I called round at his dugout at the appointed hour, where I found him in readiness for the fray. Our armament consisted of two walking-stick guns (28-bore), and M.'s batman, who accompanied us in the dual capacity as beater and game carrier, carring his Service rifle and two ever-useful sandbags.

It was an ideal day, being dark, with a certain amount of mist, which protected us from being observed by the wily Huns in their O.P.'s. In any case we had little to fear, as most of the ground we had arranged to shoot over was 'dead ground'. After a short tramp through some trenches and barbed wire entanglements we reached our destination. The first field we decided to beat was a large tobacco field with good cover, considering the time of year, and studded all over with shell holes and Hun shells which had failed to explode – known as 'duds' out here. Having placed our beater we took up our position some 20 yards on each side of him, and started off. The first rise was a brace of partridges well out of range. Approaching the centre of the field, two cock pheasants rose to M., who accounted for one of them. The other flew to the end of the field, ran into some bushes, and, in spite of a close search, we failed to rise him again. We made another beat of the field, picking up two more pheasants, and I had a shot at a snipe, failing to bring him down. Snipe are very scarce in these parts except during the severe frost, when they were fairly plentiful round the springs. We had now to make a right wheel and miss some good looking ground which was on too much of a rise to be safe. Four partridges rose in the next field. One fell to M.'s gun, and I accounted for another – a crossing shot.

At this point the shelling began to whistle overhead, and shrapnel burst over a point some thousand yards away – the Huns searching for a battery which, as usual, does not happen to be there. After nine or ten shots, peace reigned again. We next searched a bit of cover near a stream – a likely looking place for a 'cock; and, right enough, in a few minutes there was a whirr, and out broke a 'cock. I fired, knocking off a few feathers, and M. finished him off just as he was disappearing round a bush. In the next field M. accounted for a pheasant, three more going away wild. We picked up two very nice brass nose caps in this field – souvenirs. It was now lunch-time, and, selecting a sheltered spot, we sat down to enjoy our lunch, which consisted of bully-beef sandwiches, some biscuits, and a tot of ration rum each to wash it down. Away to our right Hun trench mortars started bursting. The usual afternoon 'Hymn of Hate' had commenced; but our chaps were not long in joining in the chorus with Stokes and mediums and the odd 'flying pig', and when we had sent them three for every one they sent over– our usual retaliation – things quietened down again.

A hare jumped up some 60 yards from us and made off at an easy pace. We whistled, and the hare sat up. M. seized the rifle from his batman, and the hare rolled over – a beautiful shot through the head at about 100 yards range. A little further on another hare rose. We again brought him to a sitting position by a whistle. This time M.'s shot was about a foot short, the bullet glancing off a stone about that distance away. He had another try at about 300 yards, and, though apparently dazed, it cleared off out of sight. In the next field we started three pheasants, out of which we bagged a brace, two fine cocks.

It was now getting dark, and we decided to make for home. Nearer our destination, we decided to try some grass-fields near the remains of a wood which usually held a couple of coveys of partridges. This spot was said to be under observation from a small hill in the Hun lines about 2,000 yards away; but, as the light was bad, we decided to risk it. A covey of eight rose in the first field, out of shot, and pitched in the next field. As we walked towards the spot in the hope of raising them again, a whiz-bang passed overhead and burst some 200 yards away. 'The usual afternoon blind shooting,' I remarked to M., and we carried on. Five seconds later another whistled over and fell within 100 yards. M.

said he thought we must be spotted, and I agreed with him, when a third shell burst within 40 yards, and a fragment from the same whistling past within a few yards of where I was standing – no luck for a blighty! Things were now getting too hot, and we ran for the wood at the end of the next field. As we ran three shrapnel burst over the field – one in front, and the other two to our left. Then within 20 yards of a gap, shrapnel burst 30 yards on the hedge, and the next within 10 yards of the gap. We ran through the opening and turned up sharp right. The next shot burst in the gap – a beauty – and at the same time M. rolled over, his steel helmet falling off with a crash. I felt for my field dressing in vain, and then shouted at the batman for his; but M. picked himself up, at the same time remarking, 'That d_ _ _ _ _d wire!'

We jumped into the drain that ran along the fence. The wily Hun registerd three more shrapnel in the hedge near the gap, but we now had good cover, crouching in two feet of water. Firing now ceased, but we waited 10 minutes and had a smoke before continuing our retreat. Our objective – the wood – was only some 30 yards away, and we decided to move on before breaking cover. We waded 40 yards or so up the drain, and then bolted for the wood. As soon as we broke cover, three more shrapnel burst over the field, but to our left. Once in the wood, we were safe, and we made our way to M.'s dug-out and turned out the contents of our sand bags. The bag consisted of five pheasants, two partridges, one hare, and a woodcock – not bad under such conditions.

Yrs., 'ROYAL IRISH',
Somewhere in France.

RECRUITS AND MORE RECRUITS WANTED

SIR, AS YOUR valuable paper has a large circulation among the sporting parsons, it may help one to persuade the bishops of the various dioceses to let their able-bodied vicars and curates of military age go to shoulder the rifle and help their King and country. It is surprising to see in these small towns, as you go through the country, the number of men, strong and hearty-looking, wearing the clerical collar. I believe many of them would be glad if their bishops told them to join up. There are plenty of retired clergymen who have still the energy to step into the breach if there were not so many services to attend to on a Sunday. Here, in some churches, you have services at 7 a.m., 8 a.m., 10.30 a.m. and 11 a.m., and at 4 p.m. and 6.30 p.m. We are at war, and in one church, especially in the evening, we get a dose of a sermon of 45 ½ minutes. The late King Edward VII often said a man who can't explain his subject in 10 or 12 minutes was not worth listening to. Look at our French allies – 20,000 of their clergy are in the ranks with rifles. I was told the other day that the Bishop of Winchester was 'making a move'. But the country requires more than making a move. It wants action; and that at once.

Yrs., EDMOND LLOYD (Col), Bournemouth.

1918

GERMAN PRISONERS

IF IT WERE generally announced to the German Army through leaflet balloons that, in addition to other comforts and luxuries, we provided German prisoners with most excellent sport with guns and ammunition, we feel sure there would be a great rush to surrender. Some of our readers may imagine we are joking, but it is a fact that two prisoners were caught by a game-keeper one night in July trespassing in pursuit of rabbits in a Midland preserve. We understand that the residents in the locality have protested against the farmer, who provided the firearms, having any more prisoners, but we are informed that he is still to have prisoners, but probably the sport will be curtailed. We were told that two German officer prisoners were seen at Reading station last week carrying tennis racquets.

MISC FOR SALE

Artificial Champagnes: Champagne Liqueur, Chandon et Moet, Schneider, Fleur de Sillery, Louis Roderer; Artificial cognac of very fine flavour, specific gravity .920; any of the above genuine recipes sent on receipt of 1s. – Box F08 *Shooting Times*.

VARIOUS

SIR, IT MAKES one's blood boil with rage to hear how those Hun demons treated our prisoners, cutting off tongues and drawing of finger nails. These fiends incarnate have been let off too easily. If I had my way I would hang every one of those Germans we have in our hands.

Lieut. Dawson, R.F.A., asks for my objection to ladies taking to sport. I dread seeing them come to grief in any sort of sport. I have seen one badly injured while hunting; one shot herself in the foot with a .380 rook rifle; and I once saw one nearly drowned in a swift flowing mountain river, and had it not been for the ghillie dashing down the bank and jumping into the river, catching her by the end of her skirt, she would have been assuredly swept out to sea. I read some years ago that a lady shot her husband accidentally. A lady angler who has lost a big fish is anything but a pleasant companion for the rest of the day. Will Lieut. Dawson tell us where the lady did her right and left at snipe? Was it on a soft bog? In all my years of bog trotting I have never seen a female cross a bog, be it ever so dry, not even by those born and bred by its side. The only parts of the bog they will go is where the turf clamps are. I have met scores of them tramping the road three to five miles from their homes on their way to and from the village, whilst by crossing the bog they would have less than a mile to walk – even in the driest summer.

The doctor was at a funeral the other day. He met a tailor with a parcel under his arm. The doctor asked the tailor where he was going? The reply was home with his work like the doctor was doing. Isn't it a damn good pun? I hope our good sporting Dr. Hamilton is on his pins again.

Yrs., 'PTARMIGAN'.

[Dr. D'Arcy Hamilton, we are sorry to say, is still in the nursing home, and kindly sends greetings to all old friends, who, we are sure, sincerely regret his illness and wish him a speedy recovery. – Ed.]

Otter trap.

1919

BOLSHEVIST'S SKILL WITH AUTOMATIC PISTOL

SIR, FROM THE half-tone blocks from photographs which appear in today's papers, one can see what extremely good shooting the Bolshevist Cottin made. What a misfortune he put his great skill to such an unpardonably disgraceful use! From the half-tones it is seen that the automatic pistol had a short three inch barrel (it looks like a Colt automatic pocket pistol). Of the 10 shots shown, all, except one, were within a fraction of an inch dead true vertically, and within an inch true horizontally, showing that the man was a very good judge of pace and swing. To get nine out of 10 bullets just where he meant them, and the other within four inches, shows exceptionally great skill with an automatic having such a short barrel.

Yrs., WALTER WINANS,
Carlton Hotel, London.

[Of course the picture referred to by Mr. Winans was a reconstructed scene, and therefore purely speculative. Evidently taken by a cinematograph camera. – Ed.]

EYE COLOUR

STATISTICS COMPILED by the War department of the United States show that proficiency in marksmanship usually runs according to the colour of the eyes, and in the following order; Grey, blue-grey, blue, hazel-brown, brown, black. Soldiers with eyes light brown to black could not shoot with accuracy at a distance greater than 500 yards according to the records, and at 800 yards they missed the target altogether. Mexicans – whose eyes as a rule are dark-brown to black – are the poorest shots in all the world with a rifle. These rifle statistics proved interesting and made 'Arms and the Man' curious to know how the eye-colour idea would work out in trap shooting, so they wrote to 100 leading trap shots and 93 made reply, with this result: Brown, 30; blue, 26; grey, 22; blue-grey, 11; hazel-brown, 4. Brown-eyed men may not be able to score a hit with a rifle at 500 yards or 800 yards, but it is quite evident from the above figures that they are most proficient with the scattergun. Grey-eyed men may be the best shooters, according to Government reports, but there are a lot of trap shooters willing to argue the point. Annie Oakley, who can handle a gun as well as anyone, said 'that with the exception of Dr. Carver, who had brown eyes, all, or early all, the good shots I ever came into contact with have grey eyes'. Miss Oakley's eyes are blue-grey. We wonder how billiard champions would show under similar tests.

LOWLY SPORT

THERE MAY BE foreigners content to shoot blackbirds, but I have known Englishmen do likewise. Without going into names, I have known a party of five guns who bore names to conjure with in shooting circles, get up an organised blackbird shoot, the locality being a fruit growing district. Perhaps they would have asserted they did it for the sake of the fruit, but one and all enjoyed it, and I heard more than one announce that driven blackbirds were as difficult to kill as partridges under similar conditions. I can easily understand any man fond of a shot trying his hand at an occasional blackird in the absence of other game. Many a one have I seen brought down at a covert shoot as a trial before the pheasants commence to come. And who is to blame but the blackbird which is so foolish as to fly high enough to tempt a shot. – 'HOVERER'.

ROYAL SHOT

IT IS NOW practically settled that the King will visit Balmoral in the early autumn, and that his stay will extend to about four or five weeks. As is well known, he is an accomplished angler and a first-rate game-shot. He has inherited in full the family dexterity and skill with the rifle, and has many splendid trophies to his credit. We remember being told of a curious experience which his Majesty, then Duke of York, had in the Forest of Mar. He had been stalking an apparently sleeping stag, when the animal rose and commenced lazily to scratch his right shoulder. The Duke had actually pulled the trigger when the deer happened to turn his head towards his assailant. The creature fell to the shot; but, on being examined, no wound could be anywhere discovered on his body. For a time the party were nonplussed and utterly unable to account for the creature's death. At length an ingenious ghillie inspected the stag's mouth. He found that the bullet had entered the slightly distended jaws and found a billet away deep in the skull.

SNIPING

AT THE COMMENCEMENT of hostilities our people were absolutely unprepared for sniping work. As proof of this, if proof other than the deaths of thousands of good fellows were needed, we may state that the German Army were the possessors of 20,000 telescopic sights, whilst we could only produce 500 in 1914.

Small wonder that it was unsafe to show one's head above a parapet, or loiter at exposed gaps and corners. Not only had the Boche a sufficiency of accurate sights, but he had the rifles and men who knew how to play the game and use their 'scopes and weapons to the very best advantage.

Sniping is essentially a waiting game. You can occupy a post for days and never get a chance to fire a shot, but the time always comes when a human target appears, and then you have to shoot quick. In order to be able to notch the stock of your rifle with a tally of 'kills', it is essential to possess a deadly accurate weapon, and a knowledge of how to hold it absolutely straight. One cannot afford to wait for a shot and then miss.

It is needless to say that both the telescopic sight and the rifle barrel should be kept spotlessly clean, and before firing the interior of the barrel should be dry. This is very important if you value your life. Although, contrary to public opinion, a bullet from an oily barrel does not fly wild, the oil causes a puff of smoke, and the latter gives your position away at once.

The average Tommy did not care a d--n whether his rifle was clean or not, so it was necessary for sniping to have men who were interested in shooting as well as the care of their rifles.

Pull-throughs were issued to the men for rifle cleaning on account of their porta-bility, but we invariably used a rod when we could get one. The life of a rifle barrel for deadly accurate shooting is about 500 rounds with a pull-through whereas you can say 1,000 rounds if a rod is used.

With a sight giving magnification of 2½ to 3, you get a clear view of your object, and can tell more or less accurately the result of your shot. Just as you know instinctively whether you are low or dead-on when you pull the trigger at a stag, so your experienced sniper can tell whether he has made a kill or only hit his Hun hard. If your Boche only shows his head and you get him square through the 'napper' there is an appreciable moment of time before the said head moves forward and then slides downwards out of sight. A man whom your bullet has grazed or come almighty close, ducks with a quick movement quite different from the target who is doing his last 'stunt' in the great game.

We had an excellent chance during a certain afternoon's shooting towards the end of the war, to gain a few ideas of how men fall when fatally hit with a bullet or otherwise.

The night previous we had gone into the line with the battalion, and a certain number of men were required to hold a gap in the said line. There were no regular snipers' posts so we joined a gap party. There was a short length of trench, 30 yards in front of which was a road running parallel to the trench. Beyond the road lay a wide flat, with scattered bushes, long grasses and the like, while across the flat the ground rose to a high ridge some 500 yards distant. The Boche was massing for a local attack, but his men continually showed themselves on the top and near the sides of the ridge, as well as at the end of some trenches running vertically up the ridge.

Our shooting was done at from 400 yards to 500 yards, with an occasional chance at under 400 yards. A sniper pal lay a few yards to our left, and our position was on the edge of the road, on the bank, where we were camouflaged by some fairly long grass. We each in turn had a cut at any Hun that showed, and the earth on the opposite side of the ridge being dry, we could see the whereabouts of our shot when we missed. Although we did miss some shots at the longer ranges, we 'winged' quite a few Huns, and a fair percentage of our bullets found spots where they did most good. At certain points the Boche had to leave their trenches and cross the open. Some did it in a hurry, whilst others were more blasé and took their time. The latter chiefly occupied our attention.

An absolute kill was good enough to tell. The human target lurched forward, appeared to hang an instant, and then crumpled up inert. A clean miss – yet possibly very close – generally seemed to put a kind of instantaneous jerk into the moving target, followed by a great increase in the latter's pace.

The first shot we got at the foot of one of the vertical trenches on the ridge was at a Boche who came down it – we could see his tin hat moving – who foolishly stopped instead of hurrying across a gap into a side trench. He caught it plumb centre, and went face downward, to move once or twice and then lie still. That trench opening proved quite a gold mine till the Hun 'got wise' and changed his tactics.

The gap party was subjected for a fair amount of rifle fire during the above happenings, but only one chap was put out for good. He, poor fellow, was not far off from the writer, and, like the Boche, fell, or rather dropped, on his face after incautiously showing himself. A hit, but not in a vital spot, apparently halted the human target, who immediately dropped whatever he was carrying and either recovered sufficiently from the temporary shock to run for cover, or got down in an awkward way behind whatever cover was available.

It was an afternoon to remember, for all the shooting was in the open, and there were plenty of individual targets to shoot at, and one could be pretty sure of the results of each shot.

Besides being able to shoot straight, a sniper must have the knack of proper observation, and be able to put down in the tersest shortest way what he has seen and its exact whereabouts. He is a killer first, but often he gets the chance to observe valuable information which may prove a chief factor in marring some scheme of the enemy's. Correct information gained by observation often saves the necessity of a raid by a fighting patrol, and nobody exactly loved such patrols if they could get out of them.

A sniper requires all the sleep he can get for he must keep a steady nerve. In summer his day is very long and trying unless the approach to his post can be negotiated in daylight. If not, he enters his post before dawn and is obliged to remain until after dusk. This means he cannot be relieved, so wherever possible, it pays to construct a post with a well camouflaged approach to it.

It is absolutely essential that the post itself be well camouflaged in the most expert manner. Once a post is spotted, the sooner you leave it the better for your health, as 'five nines' and other ironware are not conducive to happiness in life.

Never shoot from the post unless you are reasonably sure of a kill. Always remember to put the curtain down when you enter your post before opening the loop-hole, otherwise a bullet may come sizzling through the hole and get you.

A dead Boche is a good Boche, and tells no tales, but a wounded one who gets back to cover can give the show away and indicate your position, more or less, to his pals.

Space forbids a further description but, of all the jobs in the war, it was, to the writer, the most interesting and the most sporting. – R. CLAPHAM.

DEATH OF A MAN-EATER

HERE THE ELEPHANT paused and began to kick the earth and utter the low, tremulous sound by which some elephants denote the close presence of a tiger. We peered all about with nervous beatings of the heart; and at last the mahout, who was lower down on the elephant's neck, said he saw him lying beneath a thick jaman bush. We had some stones in the howdah, and I made the Lalla, who was behind me in the back seat pitch one into the bush. Instantly the tiger started up with a short roar and galloped off through the bushes. I gave him right and left at once, which told loudly; but he went till he saw the pad-elephant blocking the road he meant to escape by, and then he turned and charged back at me with horrible roars. It was very difficult to see him among the crashing bushes, and he was within 20 yards when I fired again. This dropped him into one of the channels; but he picked himself up, and came on again as savagely, though more slowly, than before. I was now in the act of covering him with the large shell rifle, when suddenly the elephant spun round, and I found myself looking the opposite way, while a worrying sound behind me, and the frantic movement of the elephant, told me I had a fellow passenger on board I might well have dispensed with. All I could do in the way of holding on barely sufficed to prevent myself and guns from being pitched out; and it was some time before Sarju (the elephant), finding he could not kick him off, paused to think what he would do next. I seized that placid interval to lean over behind and put the muzzle of the rifle to the tiger's head, blowing it into 50 pieces with the large shell. He dropped like a sack of potatoes; and then I saw the dastardly mahout urging the elephant to run out of the cover. An application of my gunstock to his head, however, reversed the engine; and Sarju, coming round with the utmost willingness, trumpeted a shrill note of defiance and rushing upon his prostrate foe, commenced a war-dance on his body that made it little less difficult to stick to him than when the tiger was being kicked off. – CAPT. J. FORSYTH.

A___ FACE

SIR, WHEN I first went to live in Co. Donegal, there was an enormous great fat lawyer, who used to go round all the Petty Sessions courts. He had a wonderful sharp tongue and plenty of bluff, and was in great demand among the country people, who were always having small law cases. Judge W. was sitting at one of the courts, and the great fat lawyer (he had an enormous great fat red clean-shaven face) was defending some case. An old country woman who was stone blind was called as a witness against his client. The big lawyer turned to Judge W. and said, 'My Lord, we are all sorry for the poor blind woman, but we can't take her evidence as she says herself she is quite blind.' The old woman turned to where she knew the judge was sitting and said, 'Sure, I am blind, but if I hear a man's voice and feel a man's face I can always tell who he is.' The lawyer said, 'My Lord, we really can't take her evidence.' The judge said, 'It's wonderful how blind people can tell by the voice and the feel of the face who it is.' The lawyer thought he would be very smart and put his great face close to the woman, and changing his voice, said, 'Now marm, who is talking to you?' The old woman said, 'I can't tell by your voice but put your face near me that I can put my hand on it.' He did so and the old woman put her hand on it and turned round to where the judge was sitting and said, 'Sure, Your Honour it's too bad making fun of a poor, blind decent woman. Still, it's not a face at all I'm feeling. It's a great, soft, fat A-se.' They say the whole Court went into roars of laughter, and for long afterwards the boys in the town where the big lawyer passed, used to call out, 'There goes old A-se face!'

Yrs., D.J.W. EDWARDES.

AMATEUR KEEPERS

SIR, IT WAS Boxing Day, and we wanted to shoot, but unfortunately the war and the absence of keepers had made game very scarce and vermin very general. Father J. and Brutus had, however, conceived a scheme overnight, and in the morning Uncle, the Major, Max, and Farmer R. were each presented with this card:

5s. SWEEPSTAKE

Jay +1	Woodcock +3
Pigeon +1	Stoat +3
Bat +2	Weasel +4
Magpie +2	Cock Pheasant −1
Dabchick +2	Moorhen −2
Little Owl +3	Owl (other) −3
Heron +3	Hen Pheasant −4

The Major wanted to know why a moorhen scored −2 and was told that Mrs J. liked to see them about. Uncle was made to understand that the satisfaction of shooting a cock pheasant was worth the loss of a point. The first drive produced three rabbits (Uncle 2, Farmer R. 1), a cock pheasant (Max), three jays (The Major 2, Max 1). The Major said he'd shot a stoat, but J., who was umpiring, and Uncle's dog could not find it and refused to accept his claim. The fun continued with various incidents. One jay must have been hit five times, but Max, being the fleetest of foot, secured the target. The Major got six jays and one sparrow-hawk (forgotten in the rules). At one stand Brutus spoiled his chances when in a narrow ride late in the day, for Uncle, the old dog, shouted 'cock over', and Brutus pulled down a hen pheasant. At one time Farmer R. was seen with his gun to his shoulder while busily studying the rules, held in his left hand. Max secured, we will not say shot, the woodcock. Father J. handed it to him, but you see, Father J. is Max's father.

The end of the day resulted in six pheasants (5 cocks, 1 hen), 18 rabbits, one partridge, one woodcock, 23 jays, one little owl, one dabchick, three pigeons, two magpies, and one sparrow-hawk. The Major gained the 25s. with 11 jays, one cock pheasant, one partridge and the owl, equals 13. A very enjoyable and amusing day's sport and a great benefit to the shoot.

Yrs., 'BRUTUS',
Great Missenden.

REMARKABLE GUN INCIDENT

THE FOLLOWING extraordinary incident appears in our American contemporary, *Field and Stream*. Two sportsmen were shooting ducks from a double battery on Great South Bay. In this form of shooting the gunners lie side by side in a coffin-like compartment of the battery which is anchored off shore. As the ducks come into the decoys which surround the battery, the gunners sit up and open fire. A flock of broad-bills arrived, and both gunners raised and fired one barrel. For the second shot Mr. Scofield was following a bird fairly well up in the air, while Capt. Ackerly had picked out a bird close to the water. Just as Mr. Scofield was about to pull the trigger, his bird crumpled and fell, and he felt a jar as though his gun had been discharged. However, he knew he had not shot and on opening his gun found the cartridge had not been fired. Mr. Scofield explains the incident in this way, and he has the gun to prove it. Just as he was about to fire, Capt. Ackerly, swinging ahead of his bird, pulled the trigger. The charge from the Captain's gun hit the barrels of Mr. Scofield's gun six inches from the muzzle, entered the left tube and followed on out of the barrel, killing the duck Mr. Scofield was aiming at.

THE DEATH OF A DOG

IT IS MOST wonderful how a dog can win one's affection and regard and, sad to say, the full extent to which it has accomplished this is seldom realised until it is gone for ever. Then the blank it has left is appreciated in all its intensity. Sportsmen long past middle age, as I am myself, indulge in much musing, in that way living over again the past; many reflections are most pleasant, but we all know sad moments as faithful four-footed friends which have passed away are brought to mind. The memory of two dear doggies are, and always will be, indelibly fixed in my mind, the one a black cocker spaniel, 'Panky' by name, and the other a black setter known to many besides myself as 'Rita'. One belonged to my youth, the other has just died, and both ought to have lived for years longer. In that fact rests much of the sadness, aye, and grief, felt at their decease. It is far easier to see a dog die which has lived out the fullness of its life, and especially if that life for some time has been marked by suffering, but it is grievous to lose one before its time. People who know dogs as mere appendages, mere chattels, kept for some ulterior reason, may wonder at, and be inclined to scoff at human affection extended to a dog, but I do not hesitate to say that in denying themselves a dog's love they lose more than can be ever understood by individuals possessing such a narrow outlook. The veriest cur appeals to me, and it is for the sake of dear doggies gone.

Both the dogs alluded to possessed intelligence almost human, and a wonderful capacity for interpreting one's exact meaning and desires, and this is developed only in dogs which have been with one since puppyhood. Many dogs, perhaps the majority, divide their affection, and if that affection is to be lavished on the owner alone, the latter must have the dog with him always from almost its babyhood. 'Rita', the black setter, was a wonderful example of devotion in a dog, for she was continually with me, and if by chance I had to leave her for a short period, her welcome on my return was pathetic to see. That is when I feel her loss most – when I go on a journey and return. Once, before I knew her character, I thrashed her, and never shall I forget her grief. She veritably sobbed for hours and behaved in such a way that I felt far the lower creature. A mere chiding would have been enough, had I known her disposition, and she scarcely ever deserved even that. And yet I feel assured the remembrance of that thrashing was with her to the last, for she shrank from a scowling look or word at all harsh. At midnight, although almost in extremis, she turned her brown eyes on me and my family, wagged her tail, and then I left her to die (for she was in no pain) feeling that indeed a friend was leaving me.

I wish I could confine the perusal of the foregoing paragraph to those readers who really love and appreciate dogs, and who, while valuing their helpful assistance, regard their dogs as real friends and companions. They will not feel inclined to ridicule or sneer at my expressed sadness, if only because they, too, have felt it at the death of doggie friends. Some may say that they would not have a dog if its loss affected them so keenly, but 'it is better to have loved and lost than never to have loved at all.' That remark was not intended to apply to love between human beings and animals, but it is the only reply I can give to those who make the query surmised. – 'HOVERER'.

MUSICAL SQUIRRELS

IT IS NOT generally known that squirrels seem to have an exact musical ear. It has been observed that they dance in allegro time of eight quavers to a bar; then they change to the time of six quavers divided into three quavers and a dotted crochet; then they return to common time, always resting between each change.

SMEUSE

SIR, IN YOUR issue of 21st August, page 16, column 2, the word printed 'Smense' should be 'smeuse', and of course 'smensed' should be 'smeused'.
Yrs., FRED.

1921

LARGE BAGS

AT BARON ROTHSCHILD'S shoot near Rambouillet, it is stated that over 4,000 pheasants were shot in one day and quite 15,000 pheasants were driven over the guns in the course of the day. Some shoot! And what about the cartridges? But they were not 25s. a hundred then. For England, we think the bag of 2,373 pheasants, shot by six guns, at Lord Sefton's place, Croxted Park, Lancashire on December 21st, 1883, holds the field, but the bag of 2,310, when King Edward was one of the party shooting at Elveden, Norfolk, in 1900, is a good runner up. In these days it fills us with amazement to reflect what these figures mean, because, as everyone knows, the bag only means a small proportion of the birds actually in the preserves, and then there is the staff of keepers, watchers, etc., etc.

A SIMILAR PSEUDONYM

SIR, I SEE that someone else in my *Shooting Times* of yesterday is using my *nom de plume* of 'Northerner'. I am surprised that you allow two people to use the same, and, although in my case it perhaps does not matter much, it is unsatisfactory. There would be a shindy if another 'Ptarmigan' arose. Many thanks for the answer in a recent issue to my query for a waterproof cloth. I have ordered and received a consignment of the genuine Harris tweed you recommend from Stornoway.

Yrs., A.W. THOMSON.

[We do not keep a register of our contributors' *noms de guerre*. We would suggest an alteration to 'Great Northerner'. – Ed.]

THE MOTORING POLICE PATROL

THE COMMISSIONER of the Metropolitan Police has decided to introduce motor police patrols, mounted on fast motor-cycles with side cars, to chase motorists guilty of exceeding the speed limit. Between the two, the public look like

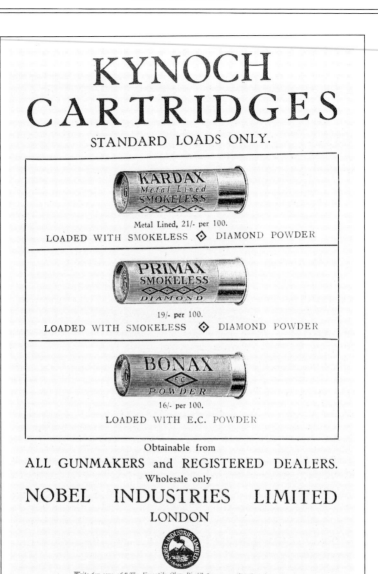
having a lively time, what with road hogs striving to escape arrest and patrols hot on their tracks. For one thing, it means giving an absolutely free hand to a body of men whose judgement and experience in driving can hardly be expected to compare with that of seasoned motorists. Methinks I can see great possibilities of long stern chases mile after mile along the great trunk roads leading out of London, leaving a track of corpses in their wake.

SHOOTING HUMMING BIRDS

IT IS, OF COURSE, for commercial purposes quite useless to shoot humming birds in the usual way. It is said the only successful method is to shoot them with a drop of water from a blow gun or a fine jet from a small syringe. Properly directed, the water stuns them and they fall into a silken net, and before reviving consciousness are suspended over a cyanide jar. This must be done quickly, for if the bird survives before the cyanide whiff puts an end to his life, he is sure to ruin his plumage in his frantic struggles to escape.

MYSTERIOUS ARROW

A VERY CURIOUS incident is reported from South Africa. A resident of Walkraal, Vaal River, noticing a large hawk hovering over his poultry yard, lay in wait, and was successful in shooting the bird as it was swooping on a chicken. The bird was somewhat larger than a red hawk, and through its body was an arrow about 2ft. 6in. in length, which had penetrated at a point between the breast and the bowels, and had remained firmly embedded. The arrow had evidently been there for a long period, probably for some years, so long in fact, that when it was withdrawn it was found that the centre portion had become partially rotted away by reason of the heat and the moisture of the bird's body. Thus, although not completely broken, the arrow had become bent at an angle, and those to whom it has been submitted for inspection are positive that the weapon was not made in the Transvaal, it being a completely different kind from what is used by natives in this part of the continent. The arrow was constructed from reed, and tipped with hard wood, the pointed part being carved into little barbs making it more difficult to extract. The butt was feather and the arrow junction was well bound with sinew. It is surmised that the hawk must have flown a long distance, perhaps from the interior of Africa, and it is certain that it carried the arrow, protruding about 12 in. on either side from its body, for a considerable period.

STAG IN MIST

A COUNTRY gentleman, well known in the South of Scotland, was spending some holidays in the historic region of Glencoe, and was much impressed by the abundance of wildlife and the grandeur of the scenery. One day, recently, he climbed to the top of

Buachaille Etive; and, the view of a wide extent of country, including Mull, Skye and other Western Isles was spread before him. Before he got half way back, however, a wisp of fog crept over the mountain side, and he soon realised that he was totally out of his bearings. With the aid of a pocket-compass he continued to grope his way along; and at length he came to the edge of a cliff which rendered impossible any further progress in that particular direction. He hastened back and was about to strike a different course, when he came face to face with a stag which was browsing the coarse herbage. The handsome creature raised its stately forehead, and regarded the intruder with a curious stare. In another moment he sprang backwards; but, discovering that all landmarks were obliterated by the fog, came to an instant standstill. The stranger approached him and found that he could handle the noble animal's horns and mane. By and by he became nobler, and opened the stag's mouth, speculating as to its age and antecedents. They were getting on very friendly and intimate terms when, a gentle breeze coming up the valley, the fog lifted, and each peak and corrie stood out clear and distinct, illuminated once again by the sun's golden beams. The bewildered stag cast one wondering glance around; and then, looking at its human companion, dashed off in mortal terror, and in a few seconds was lost from view beyond the nearest ridge. Is this a unique experience for a befogged hill climber?

BILL COX, 36, Manchester St., LIVERPOOL,
High-Class Taxidermist and Furrier.
Workmanship and Satisfaction Unconditionally Guaranteed.

GORILLAS

ONE LEARNS OF the shooting of 14 gorillas by Prince William of Sweden with mixed feelings. This bag of gorillas consisted of males, females and infants of all ages. These primitive folk are, we believe, somewhat rare and if shot wholesale will soon be exterminated.

MY FIRST SHOT

Long years ago, when I was ten,
I had a gun – a birthday gift –
And never boy more happy when
My first shot caused our cat to shift.
I missed my mark for many a day,
But joy! one morn I caught her pat,
And in the garden stowed away
The remnants of that pussy cat.

My father, digging up his plot,
Unearthed her – she was somewhat 'high',
Yet evidence that she was shot
Met father's cute, all-seeing eye.
He laid me firmly on his lap;
Said he: 'We'll have no more of that!'
And I did penance through a strap
For having shot that wretched cat.

Ah, Many a brace since then I've bagged
By well-stocked covert, moor, and fen,
And of my shooting prowess bragged,
To shine before my fellow men;
But give me back those days of ten,
The joys that came from shooting at
And potting in its native den
That prowling, poaching pussy cat.

HAL BERTIE

A FISH STORY

AN INTERESTING experiment was tried some little time ago with an ordinary salt water herring. The fish was put in a large bowl of salt water and every day a small quantity of the salt water was removed and an equal quantity of fresh water substituted, until eventually it lived and thrived in purely fresh water. The owner of the herring was so pleased with the success of this experiment that he then tried removing a very small quantity of water daily until the bowl was empty and entirely without water, and the herring was doing excellently without it, and as he was so lively in the empty bowl he had to put him in a cage. Here he lived happily, hopping from perch to perch just like a bird, until one day some sudden noise upset and startled him, and he fell into his water-trough and was drowned.

1922

PIGEON SHOOTING AT MONTE CARLO

AMONG THE attractions are tame pigeons, white, or shining with irridescent blues or greys, which strut among the flowers and take gifts out of the hands of visitors. These are now being caught, and, together with other victims bred for the purpose, have their tail feathers trimmed so that they fly in a baffling irregular fashion. They are then placed in little dark boxes set in a semi-circle on a central lawn between the terraces and the sea. Sportsmen take their turn on a stand facing the semi-circle; a trap is pulled, and a pigeon is suddenly released from one of the dark boxes. It may rise into the air at once, or only after it has been dislodged by a tennis ball. The alert marksman takes rapid aim; sometimes the bird plumps on the grass, a mass of lead and bloody feathers; sometimes it is only wounded, and flutters over to drown in the sea, or be retrieved by a clever dog or by one of the excited crowd of parasitic loafers; sometimes it escapes, and has the chance of being fed by ladies for a few days, until it has been caught again. The sportsman who brings down most birds with the fewest shots wins sweepstakes and various prizes up to a maximum of 10,000 francs, together with a silver-gilt medal.

OLD AGE

SIR, I CANNOT claim to have lived to an advanced age, but have been seriously troubled in my shooting by the slowing down in walking power which comes with middle age. I have worn Fox's spiral puttees for 20 years for slight varicose veins, and find that they give great support to the calf muscles, and at the same time keep the veins from getting distended. Puttees should be put on before getting out of bed in the morning, and must be worn next to the skin to be of any real value. They should be applied to the ankle where the leg is smallest, and, after fixing the first turn, every turn of the puttee should overlap about two thirds of the previous one.

Old age is thought to be the result of the gradual wearing out of the gastro-intestinal tract, and the poisons which get into the system through its excessive microbic infection. The Bulgarian peasants are a hardy, long-lived race, and it is thought that the sour milk which forms the principal part of their diet has a beneficial effect as regards longevity. Tablets having the power to turn milk sour can be obtained and the bacilli they contain will turn milk sour in from 24 to 48 hours. I know a man who has a small shoot here, and he is older than I am, but not so tired after a day on his heavy marshlands. He told me he has not eaten beef or mutton for years on the advice of his doctor, and is all the better for it. He also tells me he is never stiff after tennis or running after the beagles, while his daughters suffer stiffness after similar exercise. He certainly looks well.

Yrs., G.P. BARFF (Dr.),
Anglesey.

SPORT IN MALAYA

11 February

SIR, I HAVE a 12-bore hammerless non-ejector by a Birmingham maker, and also a Winchester self-loading .410 calibre rifle. On January 22nd, 1922, I shot 80 wood pigeons within four hours with only five misses. On 3rd inst., I shot a turkey at a distance of about 350 yards with my Winchester rifle, and its neck was smashed to atoms when I retrieved it. Early in the morning the next day I went hunting after big game, armed only with the Winchester and 100 soft point .250 grain bullet cartridges. When I returned home on the evening the following was my full bag: – a grizzly bear, a water-buck, four wild boars, a very young deer, two porcupines, eight napu, and three gila monsters. As to the cost of my hunting expedition, I hired five natives and paid them one dollar each for the day (five dollars the equivalent to about 11s. 6d.)

Yrs. 'ONG GIN PHOE', Kedah.

[We shall be pleased to hear further from our correspondent. – Ed.]

4 March

SIR, I HAVE just read a letter in your interesting paper, which, to put it mildly, has filled me with amazement, and not a little amusement. It is under the signature of 'Ong Gin Phoe'. During a residence of 14 years in British Malaya, I did a lot of shooting in that country, and so may lay claim to some knowledge of game, animal and bird, of that country. I find what your correspondent naively describes as 'his full bag' very interesting. In this 'full bag' he mentions a 'grizzly bear' and a 'waterbuck'. Neither of these animals has ever been seen in that country, for the simple reason that they do not exist there, neither has a turkey ever been seen in the country. The item 'eight napu' puzzles me. The 'Napoo', of course, flourished in France during the war! 'Three gila monsters' is also good, very good! 'Gila' is the Malay word for mad! Ho, ho, Mr. Editor. It won't do. Please tell your correspondent that he ought to take more soda with it, and wear a broader-brimmed hat when he goes out in the tropical sun. Should he tell his pathetic story in any of the clubs out there, some-one, it is to be hoped, will lead him gently and firmly to a doctor. There is an excellent asylum on a little island near Singapore, where patients can watch grizzly bears eating oysters and playing leap frog with the gentle 'Napoos'.

Yrs., B.H. HARRISON.

SALE – Handsome non-slip Golden Retriever bitch, two years, perfectly keeper trained, experienced, very steady, retrieves to hand, perfectly, alive or dead, land, water. £25.

PURDEY GUN FOR SALE 12-bore hammerless ejector, 30 inch Whitworth steel barrels, top lever; with lock up case. £78.

ANCHOVIES

A SPORTSMAN who thought of renting a shoot in Scotland was interrogating the resident keeper as to the position and prospects for game. 'How about the grouse?'

'In hundreds and thousands,' replied the keeper.

'And the black game?'

'More plentiful than ever,' was the cheerful reply.

'And the roe-deer?'

'Well, they're in large numbers.'

Indeed, according to Sandy's representa- tions the place swarmed with game, fea- thered, furred, and felled. The sportsman asked further questions, getting still roseate replies. At last, becoming suspicious and dubious at the stereotyped answers, the Saxon suddenly demanded, 'And how about the white-throated anchovies?'

For a moment the keeper looked per- plexed but, regaining his assurance, said, 'Oh, these are not so numerous this year as formerly, but they can be seen in the woods in twos and threes.'

GROUSE AT SAVOY

FOR THE FIRST time actually on the Twelfth itself, grouse, we are informed, was served at luncheon at the Savoy Hotel on Satur- day last. Some of the earliest birds shot on a well-known moor near Ripon were car- ried away by motor car and transferred to an aeroplane, and thus reached London in the forenoon.

MOREOVER THE DOG

A DORSET keeper who, when asked why he called one of his dogs 'Moreover', replied, 'Why sir, it's a real good Bible name for a dog. Aint we told that "Moreover the dog licked his sores"?'

OPPOSITE: Parrot shooting.

COST OF GAME BAG

SIR, I SAW a game bag in a shop window in Edinburgh the other day priced at 48s., but really worth no more than 30s. at the very most. Simply disgraceful! What have other readers to say on this subject? The price of cartridges too, is most unreasonable.

Yrs., 'SCOTTISH SPORTSMAN', Edinburgh.

NOVEL WAY OF CATCHING WILD DUCKS

THE CHINESE have a curious way of bagging wild ducks. Pumpkins are left floating on the surface of any pond frequented by the birds, in order that the latter may come to regard them as harmless objects. When a Chinaman wants a duck for his lunch he slips quietly into the pond and places over his head a pumpkin in which slits are cut for his eyes. He then moves gently through the water until he is near enough to catch a duck by the feet. With a sharp jerk, he pulls it under the water, wrings its neck and puts it into his belt. The other ducks are seldom disturbed, and he goes on until he has caught all he wants. – COUNTRY HOUSE NOTES.

POWER OF SNAILS

HOW MUCH weight can a snail draw? In order to put this problem to a test, two garden snails were fastened by narrow pieces of tape to a toy gun carriage made of lead. Not only did this novel steed pull along the burden with ease, but they also made steady progress when the gun carriage was filled with shot. To try their pulling powers further, a small brass cannon was then attached to the gun carriage, and although the combined weight amounted to 15oz., the snails continued on their course without difficulty. Two others were able to draw a wagon with a load of 2lb., and one undoubted champion was found who managed by himself to shift a weight of over 3lb. after only four days training. – COUNTRY HOUSE NOTES.

1923

LIGHTNING STRIKE ON GEESE

A NUMBER OF instances of gaggles of wild geese having been struck by lightning have been recorded, but we have never seen any explanation for the phenomenon. Here is an account of an incident of the kind which happened in Texas some time ago. A very large flock of wild geese, high up in the sky, were winging their flight to their far northern home. Their course was being watched by a few citizens, and the size of the flock commented upon, when suddenly a bar of lightning from a cloud seemed to strike the leader and then scintillate and play through the entire flock, causing terror and death, and immediately the air seemed to be filled with falling birds. They fell just across the slough, and Jack Hastings, a negro who was watching them from his door, waded over the slough, and after killing a few crippled ones, brought 52 into town, which he sold for 10 cents apiece. Some of them were badly bruised and torn, but it is not known whether this was caused by the lightning or the high fall. Some of the birds recovered and flew off after having fallen nearly to the ground. It is estimated that there were nearly 150 birds in the flock and of these at least 75 were killed.

GAME BIRDS IN CEYLON

SIR, I HAVE just been reading your issue of 6th January and a reference to winged gamebirds going to ground has brought to mind an experience I had on New Year's Day. My wife and her sister – both keen on sport and a day in the jungle on a brilliant Indian winter's day – accompanied me. I had arranged for 25 to 30 beaters to be waiting for us at a spot about four miles from the little construction bungalow I have built in the wilds 20 odd miles from Hazaribagh. We breakfasted at dawn, and left the bungalow at 7 a.m. in the ubiquitous Rolls-Ford, and arrived at the rendezvous at about 7.30. The rough road we had to travel over limited speed to 10 m.p.h. I found the beaters quite excited, and they all tried to enlighten me as to the reason at one and the same time. As they were chiefly Santals, who speak an extraordinary language of their own, I had to quell the clamour before I could make anything of their story, and eventually found that they had seen a decent nide (12 to 15) of peafowl go into a densely wooded ravine in the vicinity. One of the Santals, who knew the lie of the land, placed me (the single gun) in what he considered the best position to get a shot.

After about 15 minutes I heard the beat start, and as these jungles often have wild pig, barking deer and four-horned antelope, I was on the *qui vive* immediately. Ten minutes passed and a jungle cock came whirring over the tree tops in front of me, and as the clearing was only a trifle over 20 feet wide, it was a case of throw up and pull as quick as I could think. Fortunately I was well forward and he dropped with a much battered head. Two minutes later a hare gave me a good chance but clumsiness on my part allowed pussy to escape unhurt.

About five minutes later heavy rustlings in the jungle made me think a deer was coming along, so I hastily changed a No. 4 Manton's standard cartridge for a Lyon and Lyon lethal bore in the left barrel of my BSA gun. Silence for half a minute, and then up went a peahen about 60 yards away, and you can imagine the speed with which I extracted the bore cartridge and re-loaded with the No. 4. I had barely snapped the breech when a peacock rose within 25 yards and gave me a clean shot as he passed over the clearing. He had not covered more than 10 when he copped it and fell dead just inside the jungle on the far side. At the shot another cock rose and gave me a chance at about 40 yards. I saw him drop, but from the twist he gave I concluded he was a runner, so sent my cartridge carrier after him. The beaters came through very shortly after and flushed the remainder of the peafowl, but they all broke wide.

I then retrieved cock no. 1 and set off to where no. 2 had dropped in an isolated coppice, to find when I got to the spot that my cartridge carrier had called on his nearest confrères for assistance, as he was a very lively runner. The noise they made started him out of the scrub across a bit of open land, and we went after him, the beaters leading my by a long length, and the cock 25 yards ahead. When we got to the open not a sign of his cockship could we see. A bright youth of, perhaps, 14 who had outrun the rest of us, suddenly disappeared, and when we had got to the spot we found he had fallen into an erosion formed during the previous monsoons. He was quite uninjured, but very excited, and greeted me with the words, 'Sir, *morh hian hai*' – i.e., the peacock is here; and true enough when I looked into the hole I saw the end of his gorgeous tail sticking out of the underground tunnel the youth had broken into. We found the entrance to his hiding place quite 20 feet away, and but for the luck of the youth breaking through just at that point, we would have lost him for good.

Yrs., 'GYALA'.

GUN ACCIDENTS

SIR, IN MY opinion the majority of gun accidents can be divided into two classes – carelessness and ignorance. Although I myself have done it (albeit for the last time), it is morally criminal to put a gun into the hands of a man who has never used one, and expect him to handle that gun with safety to himself and others on a shoot. On one occasion we were walking a field when the gun next to me asked what the 'two' triggers were for, and the next moment had blown the hat clean off my head. Incredible as it may seem, this man had been in the army for two years. On another occasion, my next gun had a very nice 16-bore Browning automatic. He pulled at two successive birds without a click, and actually did not know how to get a cartridge into the breech from the magazine. Very conducive to good shooting on my part. Another time a man's gun went off three times in succession while crossing a hedge or ditch and then in the middle of an open field. If a man hasn't the love of a gun in him at a certain age then I don't think it is ever acquired, and the sooner some people realise they have a lethal weapon capable of disembowelling a man in their hands, and not a tennis racquet or a hockey stick, the better. How many readers have had their day spoiled by having to keep an eye on a neighbour's gun and not the birds? Then again, one of the most brilliant shots I knew, a man who loved a gun and knew through and through what he could do with it, would take the most hair-raising chances. He never hit anyone, but this, in my opinion, was sheer good luck. There is not a hare, a pheasant, or rabbit that ever breathed, worth a man's life, or eye, or even a dog's. Which reminds me of one occasion on a 'Go as you please' kind of rough shoot, seeing a lot of rabbits about the corner of a wood in the next field, I started crossing the fence for a shot, but was called back by the host, who said it was not his ground, and the owner of it had vowed he would shoot anyone he caught on it. I asked if they really thought this, and was informed by several who knew him well that he would, and had already been convicted for shooting at someone. I exclaimed, 'What! murder a man for a rabbit? Then by _ _ _ _ _ it's him or me.' Although a respecter of other people's preserves, I shot that wood through in the hope our bloodthirsty neighbour would turn up, but fortunately for both of us nothing happened.

Yrs., EDWARD MACEY,
Merton Park.

BULLET IN THE AIR

WOULD A BULLET fired vertically be likely to injure a marksman on its return to earth? is a question which Captain E.C. Crossman of the U.S.A. Army has endeavoured to resolve. As a result of tests, the Captain discovered that when a squad of riflemen had fired bullets which remained in the air more than a minute, the falling bullets had not sufficient penetration to bury themselves in sand more than two thirds of their length, and they would not injure a man's head if he had a fairly substantial cap. In these tests they used the standard infantry cartridge of the American service. But when they tried the new boat-tailed bullets – a remarkable new type with a tapering tail that doubles the range of the rifle – some of them nearly came to grief. After a

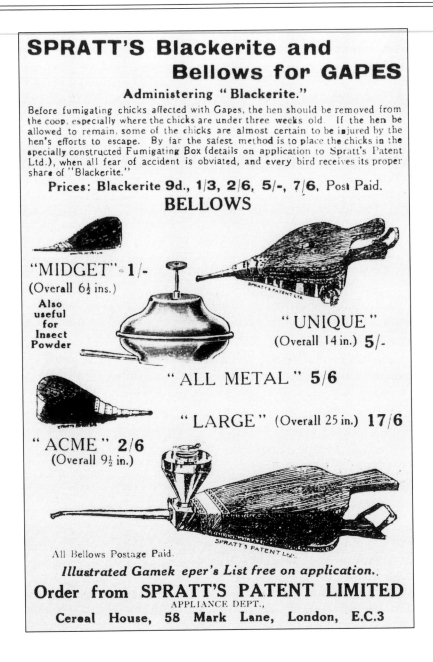
minute and seven seconds there came the bullet whirr, louder than those of the sevice rifle, and then the usual splashes on the surface of the lagoon. Then the splashes ceased, though not all the bullets had been accounted for. Some of the gunners had stepped out of their shelter, and the watches had been stopped – when

suddenly – certainly half a minute after the burst had landed, there came again the bullet whirr. Machine-gunners ducked for shelter, and down whirred eight or ten more shots. Whereupon they discovered an astonishing fact – that when fired from a machine gun, boat-tail bullets vary widely in their time of flight. In the next burst they found that the bullets returned in a cluster in about 67 seconds, while a second group returned fully 40 seconds later. The results show that almost any bullet fired into the air remained away 30 seconds or longer. The little .22 long rifle, with its 1,000 or 1,100 feet velocity, took 35 seconds. The large slow .45 automatic pistol bullet took 39 seconds. The Remington .35 auto-loader bullet, 200 grains at 2,000 feet per second, took 58 seconds. The quickest trip recorded was an inverted 175 grain boat-tail. It returned in 21 seconds, as compared with 67 to 107 seconds when fired normally.

UNSAVOURY TOAST RACK

A TEA PLANTER had neighbours drop in for tea, and ordered the meal to be prepared as soon as possible. It was a long time appearing, and he unwisely went to the kitchen to remonstrate with the cook. There he saw the gentleman toasting the last piece of toast, with four other pieces already toasted carefully held between the toes of the left foot, which rested on the fender and made a handy toast rack capable of keeping the toast warm.

THE LATE LORD RIPON

AS EARL DE GREY, this sportsman, who has recently died, was known as the best shot of his day, and probably of any other day; but there is no doubt he lived for it, denying himself many pleasures which he knew, or imagined, would interfere with his skill. So interested were other guns in his performance that they have, at a covert shoot, been noticed watching it, and allowing pheasants to pass overhead unshot at. A keeper who was employed by Earl de Grey when that nobleman was at his best, once told me that he had seen him bring down blackbird after blackbird with nothing more than a small-bore rifle loaded with bullets, although the birds were in full erratic flight. Lord de Grey, at that time, frequently indulged in such practice. He was a trying guest at times, for he lived for shooting, apparently, and would conform to nothing that might interfere. And I do not blame him! – 'HOVERER'.

MR. WINANS' DEER FORESTS

THERE IS NOTHING in all forest history to compare with the paying of £18,000 a year of rental for deer forests, a performance which the late Mr. Walter Winans kept up for many years, even after he stopped firing a shot or coming up North. He kept a big army of beaters and keepers, and we are probably not far from the mark in putting down his expenditure on the forests as exceeding quarter of a million pounds during the period when they were silent. We believe the cause of Mr. Winans' absence was brought about by a regrettable incident which happened near Tomish in Strath-glass; his carriage was passing along when a big stone was hurled through its top and narrowly missed him. Mr. Winans was not devoid of brains and he read in this cowardly attack more than he cared to confess. He was finished with the North, and he left it severely alone. Such is the true story of Mr. Winans' strange behaviour during the latter part of his tenancy of the forests of the North, where his area stretched from the North Sea to the Atlantic and embraced 12 separate lets. - SCOTTISH NOTES.

1925

PATSY HALLORAN

SIR, A SHORT time ago I had a letter from Patsy Halloran, of Kilkee, Co. Clare, the famous snipe shooting professional. He wrote to say that someone had sent him notes on snipe averages. I had mentioned in a note of mine he had killed over 30,000 snipe when I last shot with him, getting some seasons before that time 1,200 snipe for his season's shooting. I wrote to ask what his bag of snipe now was and, if he had one, to send me his photograph. You will see he mentions his bag is now over 40,000 snipe, and his best run of them was 23, getting five couple right and left. The following is an extract:- 'I have only missed two seasons' shooting (owing to the Troubles) since you were here, and I had very good shooting, as all this country is now open, and I practically had the whole place to myself. During the war snipe were a very good price, often getting over 4s. a brace. This was encouraging, and I stuck to it well, and shot better, in fact, than I ever did. Snipe were plentiful. Up to the middle of December 1924, I had shot 605 snipe. My best day was 38. One day last season I got nine snipe in six shots, getting two brace right and left; then three snipe rose and I killed them with one shot. This is my fiftieth season after snipe. I am now 69 years old and shot very well this season but do not take the long walks I used to.' His bag for this season was 762 snipe.

Yrs., D.J.W. EDWARDES.

Patsy Halloran.

THE PARTING OF THE WAYS

I HAVE JUST been meditating on a remark a sportsman made to me a couple of hours ago. 'I wonder,' said he, 'how you and I will feel when our shooting days are over. How will we feel on our last day with a gun?'

So far as shooting is concerned, I do not suppose that many men know that a certain day is their last day with a gun. As the years advance, they drop out imperceptibly. Each season sees them shooting a little less, perhaps just a stroll around for an hour or two on a fine day. But I do not suppose that any man ever has to say to himself, as he goes out in the morning, 'This is my last day's shooting.' No, we taper off instead. And it is good that this should be so. Some, indeed, of my acquaintance, have been compelled to do so through physical infirmity, and for them one feels the deepest sympathy.

It is good to realise that, almost as long as life remains, most men can participate in field sport with credit to themselves. For the love of rod and gun, of horse and hound, is deeply rooted in the sportsman. He can never bear to think of the day when he shall meet the parting of the ways. And so it comes about that he reaches that parting of the ways without ever knowing it.

But even when we have reached a stage at which we can only just potter about with a gun for an hour or two on a fine day, with, possibly, a sturdy grandson or two in attendance to see that the old man does not do anything foolish, I am quite sure that the glamour of sport will remain for us, we shall still 'follow the gleam'. I have just spent a week in the company of a sportsman whose memories of shooting go back to the 'sixties: he is as keen as ever he was; we spent solid hours in talking of sport and exchanged reminiscences. He is not able to do much shooting now, but he enjoys an occasional day. Twenty years ago he could walk and shoot from early morning till late at night, but now 'Anno Domini!' He manages two or three hours in a day, where the going is not too heavy; and, best of all, he is quite contented and happy about it. He is gradually tapering off, though I know that for him the tapering process will continue as long as he lives. It will be a little less of his beloved gun every successive year, but never will he lay it aside for good and all. May it be so for all of us. The time slips by us imperceptibly, almost without our noticing it, year is added onto year of our lives. A few grey hairs appear, we are a bit more tired at the end of a day than we used to be. The young folk are growing up around us, we talk to our friends of 20, 30, 40 years ago, but we still shoulder our guns and go off as eagerly as ever. The keenness always remains and it helps to keep us young. Does one ever think of the parting of the ways? No. And even when old age has really overtaken us, when we realise how little remains in our power, and how much has slipped from our power, we are still following the gleam of sport. The aged sportsman in his armchair by the fireside still murmurs to himself:-

For me the sunlight spaces call, to me the breakers cry,
And I must hit the trail again, once more before I die.
Home-coming's sweet for weary feet when evening dusks are falling,
But sweet and near and loud and clear, I hear the lone trail calling.

F.W.E. WAGNER, M.A., Sc.D.

LORD WALSINGHAM'S BAG OF GROUSE

MANY OF OUR readers have manifested some curiosity to know the guns and charges used by Lord Walsingham on August 30th, 1888, when, as subsequently recorded in our columns, he killed 1,070 to his own gun in one day. His Lordship, in reply to our inquiry, supplied the information:

'I shot with four breech-loaders: No. 1, a gun made by Purdey, subsequently converted from pin-fire to central principle, to which new barrels were made last year; Nos. 2 and 3, a pair of central-fire breech-loaders, made also by Purdey about 1870, for which I have likewise had new barrels; No. 4, a new gun made by Purdey this year, to match the two mentioned above, but with Whitworth steel instead of Damascus barrels. The guns are all 12-bore with cylinder 30 inch barrels, not choked. My cartridges were loaded by Johnson, of Swaffham; those used in the down-wind drives containing 3½ drs. Hall's Field B Powder to 1⅛oz. No. 5 Derby shot; those used in the up-wind drives (where birds of course came slower) had 3 drs. only of the same powder with the same shot; not hardened shot in any case. I find I never go out shooting without learning something. If I had the day again I should cut off the extra ⅛oz. of shot, not on account of recoil and discomfort of any kind, from which I never suffer, although always using black powder, but because I failed to get as much penetration at long distances as I do with one ounce only. I distinctly remember firing three barrels at one bird, striking well in the body every time, but killing dead only with the last shot; the powder seemed to burn too slow. Another thing I learnt was that Whitworth steel barrels are not desirable for a heavy day's shooting; the explosion makes quite a different sound from

Remember always — restraint in dress, speech + movement

that given off by Damascus barrels, there is more of a ring about it, and I can imagine that this might prove a serious annoyance to anyone who minds the noise of shooting. I have no recollection myself of ever having a headache from gun-firing. Moreover, the Whitworth barrels become hot much more rapidly than the Damascus, and this is a serious drawback, especially to the man who shoots with one gun. I can imagine that they last much longer and are in many ways suited for ordinary light work; but I am now replacing them with Damascus as in all my other guns.

Yrs., WALSINGHAM.

A FAMOUS INDIAN DUCK SHOOT

IN NEARLY all parts of India it is possible to get quite good wild duck shooting, but there are certain well-known places which are famous for this form of sport. Bharatpur, the capital of the native state ruled by His Highness Maharajah Kishen Singh, is one of them. Here in the swamp known as the Ghanna, from the impenetrable jungle which surrounds it – Ghanna being an Indian word for thick – the wild duck come in their thousands every cold weather, and due toll is taken of the flocks by the many guests which His Highness invites to the shoots. Among the guests there are, as a rule, several distinguished persons, many of them crack shots, for the Ghanna's fame is widespread. The late Lord Curzon, during his Viceroyalty, was a frequent visitor, and was perhaps the best shot of all India's Viceroys. Lord Hardinge, who left Bharatpur for Delhi only the night before the eventful day on which an attempt was made on his life, and later both Lord Chelmsford and Lord Reading stayed there. His Royal Highness the Prince of Wales, Prince Arthur of Connaught, and the ex-Crown Princes of Germany and Rumania have been among the Royal personages to take part in the shoots in recent years; while among India's own princes are numbered some of the finest shots in all India. Their Highnesses of Bikanir and Dholpur are perhaps the most renowned, while the present Maharajah of Kashmir, Sir Hari Singh, and the Heir Apparent of Bikanir are no mean performers.

To describe the actual shooting ground, one should try to visualise a large swampy area with patches of tall grass, reed beds and stretches of open water – the whole covering about 20 square miles, with a wide, tree-bordered road raised above flood level, running through the centre of the swamp. From this raised 'bunds', or in ordinary language, raised footpaths, lead out into the swamp at frequent intervals. Around the main swamp area are also a number of lesser 'jheels', and on days when a big shoot is to take place these are lined with men to keep the duck from settling. Through the main swamp a whole army of beaters and a dozen or so elephants are continually keeping the birds on the move.

There are, of course, certain favourite stands, which get the cream of the shooting, and those which are not set apart for some famous personage are eagerly sought after. At the 'bund' known as the 'Viceroy's Bund', His Excellency, if present, is always posted. Here, although there are always a tremendous number of duck coming over, the shooting is none too easy as they fly very high. Most of the other stands are merely distinguished by numbers – the one exception being 'Rao-ji's Bund', where the uncle of His Highness invariably shoots and at times makes the biggest bag. This, however, falls more often, or did in days gone by to the Princes of Bikanir and Dholpur, whom it was a pleasure to watch. True, they both paid no heed to the expenditure of ammunition, but the number of duck that were pulled down out of the sky from extraordinary heights testified to their skill. Another great shot of his time was a Mr. Cruickshank, the Engineer of the state, who frequently got over 200 birds to his own gun, and on more than one occasion topped the list. Fifty guns is the average number at a shoot, and a good bag totals, as a rule, over 3,000, although the record in a certain very good year reached just over 5,000.

With the exception of mallard of which only a few are shot, nearly every other kind of wild duck figure extensively in the bag; gadwall, pintail, spot bills, pochard of all kinds, and teal being the most common, not counting the ubiquitous shoveler, a bird not much sought after owing to its slow flight and poorness for the table. The large red-headed pochards are in some years very numerous, while the number of wigeon too vary from year to year. Occasionally one or two rare visitors, such as marble teal, are accounted for. A few geese of both greylag and bar-headed varieties meet their fate in the first 10 minutes, before they have had time to rise to those heights from which no man can bring them down.

Shooting starts usually about 9.30 a.m.

and a bugle blows the 'Commence fire' as a signal, while the 'Cease fire' at one o'clock gives a respite of about an hour for lunch. After that firing continues until it is too dark to see, many a keen sportsman adding greatly to his bag in the last half hour, when the teal commence flighting just before dusk. The 'butts' are screens of coarse grass, each containing a stool, two bottles of soda water, some cigarettes, and a wood receptacle for cartridges.

Seated in one of these, with the three attendant coolies, the latter well oiled against their immersion in the chill water, you await for the sound of the bugle. When it comes, and with the sound of the first shot the noise of beating wings is terrific, and after the first few minutes the tyro is apt to get confused by the large numbers of duck flying in all directions. If your butt happens to be near a tree-bordered road, or near a clump of trees, you will find some real high birds as they soar to clear the foliage. One of the prettiest sights is perhaps a flock of pintail whizzing by high in the heavens, the gleaming black and white of the male birds showing up clear in the bright sunny skies. They call for good straight shooting, do these pintail, while the small pochards coming downwind present perhaps an equally difficult task, as do the circling, twisting teal, searching for some quiet backwater away from the constant banging of the guns, which so often bring them hurtling earthwards, lifeless and crumpled.

Towards evening, as the setting sun starts to transform the already picturesque scene into a maze of ever-changing and glorious colouring, the Ghanna presents a truly beautiful picture. But to view it in its proper setting one must visit it on an evening when no shooting is taking place to desecrate its glories. Seated in some quiet corner you may watch in peace the wonders of the fading light until with the short Indian twilight at an end, darkness comes on apace and the Ghanna settles down for the night. - 'TRAVELLER'.

WITHIN TEN MILES OF VICTORIA

MANY OF US have heard of pheasants being shot in London on ground which is now covered by fields and streets, but in the Year of Grace 1925 it is difficult to believe that three guns in three and a half hours could bag 12½ brace of partridges and one leveret within 10 miles of Victoria Station. Yet it is true; so true that if the shooting had been good, the bag ought to have totalled at least 16 or 17 brace. Further, if a whole day had been devoted to the sport five guns could have bagged 30 brace.

Let me tell you all about it. On Friday, September 24th, I left Victoria Station, feeling that I was embarking on a wasted day; so much so that I almost begrudged the railway ticket for the dog. As it was, I only put about a score of cartridges in the gun case, but for my little faith I had the mortification of having to borrow half-a-dozen from my host. True, I had the lion's share of the shooting, but, even so, the fact that I had failed to bring sufficient cart-ridges was not a compliment to my host.

I should explain that the shoot covered about 120 acres of market garden land and is all in one piece, with not a fence on the place. The area is all worked in plots of rhubarb, potatoes, beans, cabbages, kale and vegetable marrows. The land is sur-rounded by factories, besides being bord-ered by a new arterial road, over which thousands of cars pass daily. I knew the land well, as I had passed it on trams scores of times! So, perhaps it was not to be wondered that I should think there was little sport to be obtained.

Three of us, W.W.P., J.M. and myself set off at mid-day. The day was stifling hot, so hot that I discarded my waistcoat and hat. We had to dodge across the road to escape cars travelling at 45 m.p.h. We then passed a group of bricklayers erecting a row of houses. Within 30 yards of this group, we came to a patch of rhubarb about an acre in extent. To my surprise, our host suggested lining up and walking it down. On one side was a mortar mixing machine clinking away, on the other was a man horse-hoeing, whilst at the bottom was a close-boarded fence surrounding a pumping station. I obediently got into line, and, when we had got to within 25 yards of the fence, a covey of five got up practically out of range. The situation was so novel and appeared so ludicrous, that I roared with laughter. All this time my spaniel had been hunting about, and, to my astonishment, put up a single bird which, no doubt, had failed to rise with the others. This time I made no mistake. All this within 50 yards of a high road and workmen erecting houses!

J.M. said that the birds had settled in a piece of lucerne; some made for this on a piece of land sown to spring cabbage. Here a 'Frenchman' rose and paid the penalty. As he was a young bird, I knew there must be a covey somewhere, but, although we finished the cabbages, we failed to find them. Adjoining the cabbages was a piece of recently ploughed potato ground. Here we saw a covey of 12 get up just out of shot and settle 200 yards away. They were then close to the boundary, so J.M. suggested that we should creep round the fencing, onto which back private dwellings, and try to get the covey into a piece of kale. Round we crept and had the satisfaction of seeing the covey run into the centre of the plot, away from the boundary fence. We got behind them and set them off into the kale, but one bird broke to the right and settled in the cabbage we had just left. As I had the dog, I volunteered to go and try to drive it into the kale also, but, instead of going round the boundary fence, I made straight across the potato ground. I had almost got to the cabbages, when a 'Frenchman' got up wide and was flying back. To turn him, I fired two shots well in front, but he still sailed on and disappeared into a private garden.

The sound of my shots had caused the inhabitants of the houses to forsake their labours in the garden to look over the fence. One of these told me that the bird had settled half-way up the cabbages. I warned the other two to come back, and together we walked up the cabbages. Running through the cabbages was a footpath which had recently been closed to the public, but we saw a policeman walking along this towards us. I suddenly remembered that I had not got my game licence in my pocket, and knew that it was a certainty I would be asked for it. The P.C. was almost upon us when the loose bird rose, which J.M. knocked down almost at the feet of the arm of the law. He picked up the bird and seemed very interested in it. He was quite a baby, and I should say quite

new to the force. 'That's a partridge,' J.M. remarked. 'I know that,' the P.C. replied, but I feel certain that if he had been told it was a woodcock, he would have said, 'I know that.' Even the law never gives itself away.

We next tried the kale, and as this bordered the road, we took that side first. Cars had stopped to watch us and we had quite a 'gallery'. Up and down the kale we went, but failed to find the covey until the last few yards. We took heavy toll out of it, but one bird went away with both legs down. We carefully noted the spot and went back for it. We here put up two single birds we had obviously walked over. The dog could make nothing of the bird, so I took him to a neighbouring house for a drink. Back he came, but with no result. We then tried a piece of marrows in which men and women were working. We had not gone many yards before the dog put up a leveret. This accounted for the set-off. Within 20 yards of some men working, we put up a covey of six. I was lucky in getting a right and left. J.M. pulled down one whilst W.W.P. had two towered birds. One fell by a steam engine and the other in a private garden, the owner of which would not let us pick up the bird as he said it was his property. A piece of beet was next tried and, even though there were some women on it, we found birds. J.M. got one down which proved a runner, and I picked another which fell on the plough. We tried the dog on the runner, but he was panting with heat. The marrow plot had been hard work for him. As we were close to the road, I took him to a factory where men were putting down concrete floors, where I knew water would be. In crossing the road, an obvious American, who had been watching us, spoke to me.

'What are you shooting – larks?' he asked.

'No,' I replied, laughingly, 'partridges.'

'Go on, you're jossing me,' he replied.

'Very well,' I said, pulling a partridge out of my pocket, 'just look at this lark, then; even you've got no larks this size on the other side of the herring pond.'

'Hell, that's prime; sure I believe you now.'

With this I threw the bird to him. 'Better taste it and you will be sure then.'

'Thanks, I will; you're sure spunk.'

I found a large tank, so dipped the spaniel in it and being much refreshed, he went back to make a good find in a strong runner.

It was getting close on three o'clock and we wanted to catch the 4.18 train, but we tried a rough piece of grass on the other side of the road, and in not more than four acres shot 2½ brace. As this was close to the road, on account of the 'spectators', we had to take it down-wind, but even then the birds lay well.

To me it had been a wonderful day. Twelve and a half brace gathered, 1½ not gathered in 3½ hours, on land surrounded by houses, and spotted with workmen and tractors, and aeroplanes buzzing overhead. The shooting had not been of the best, but as W.W.P. remarked, going home, 'How the devil could you shoot when every time you lifted your gun, you saw either a workman or a spectator.' - 'SALTINGS'.

THE NEW SPRING FERRET MUZZLE.
Registered, No. 24326.
Post paid, 13 stamps.

MACNAUGHTON, GUNMAKER, EDINBURGH.

1927

IRISH AGENT

IN THE OLD Land League days in Ireland a certain agent wrote to a landlord living in London. He stated that the tenants on the estate threatened to shoot him unless the landlord reduced the rents. To which the landlord replied: 'Will you please inform the tenants that if they think they can intimidate me by shooting you they are making a great mistake.'

TRAGIC LOSS

WE FEEL SURE that we shall be echoing the wishes of a large number of our readers by conveying to our old contributor, Mr. Nicholas Everitt, of Oulton Broad, their, as well as our own, deepest sympathies to him in the great loss he has recently sustained through the death of his favourite Labrador bitch, Pedham-Peggy.

STRANGE FRIENDSHIP

A FARM LABOURER living in the neighbourhood of Preston once found a nest of young wild rabbits, and threw them to a couple of ferrets, one of which was expecting a family. Three of the little creatures were immediately dispatched, but the fourth was discovered a few days later nestling up to the ferret, which had clearly adopted it. The ferret was employed at its usual work but the attachment thus strangely begun continued till one day the lid of the box was left open and the rabbit, now full grown, escaped to its native burrows. Two days later it was found to be struggling to enter the hutch and rejoin its foster-parent. The door was opened, and to the labourer's astonishment, the ferret welcomed her lost companion with the liveliest tokens of delight and satisfaction.

1928

MUGGER LAND

ONLY THOSE OF us who have been on a mugger shoot can realise its fascination. By muggers, of course, I mean all types of crocodiles, from the man-eating kinds down to the veriest baby measuring, perhaps, a little more than a foot (the latter are mostly netted by fishermen and sold alive as curiosities).

For many years I lived on the banks of the Ganges, one of India's most sacred rivers, which abounds in muggers. Often, as a child, I have gone without breakfast because I had seen a dead body in the river; and for years I never ate fish for this same reason, though I knew definitely that only 'certain' fish touched dead bodies or even ate other fish.

But to come to the actual shoot. We hired boats, and after laying in stores, usually were rowed back on our return journey if it was not too far; otherwise we came back in tikka gharies (a two-horsed carriage). Perhaps for the first two hours we met nothing worth having a shot at; then suddenly someone in the party would discover what was just a huge log of wood basking in the sun (because that is exactly what a mugger looks like). After looking through the glasses and getting the boat within decent range, someone fired and missed, and then tried again, yet nothing moved. So that this time, apparently, it was real wood and not a mugger. But such little troubles are all part of the game, so we had lunch to recuperate after such

wasted energy, and then to work again.

Meanwhile, all of a sudden, there would be a frightful row and on looking we should find we were passing quite near a burning ghat, where five or six pariah dogs were fighting for their share of a body. It is horrible at the time, but after a while one gets used to looking the other way. On one occasion I remember my mother being frightfully upset on getting out of a boat at night, because her foot was fixed firmly in a woman's skull (we knew it was a woman because their bodies are wrapped in red cloth and a man's in white). Another time we were all terrified at discovering one of my brothers in sinking sands, and waited breathlessly while my father went to his assistance and got him out.

Towards nightfall we put up at a Dak bungalow and had our dinner under the shade of a dirty paraffin lamp. I don't know why, but on these occasions we usually had Palethorpe's sausages and tea sweetened with condensed milk. It was good, anyway. And to this day if I wish to indulge in memories, I have only to shut my eyes to see that horrible lamp and the sausages rubbing shoulders on the bare table. After dinner it was early to bed and early to rise to be ready for the next day's shoot.

After an early breakfast we start back, this time being towed by boatmen clad in the scantiest garments. Very soon there is a halt because one of them has discovered a mugger with two or three little ones, some distance away. This time we shot it successfully, and when the boat reached the spot where it lay, then began the work of skinning it, as it is usually too heavy to take home as it is. This time we retrieved from its stomach a pair of silver bracelets and two pairs of small anklets. It made us think of the poor young mother who probably brought her first-born to bathe in the sacred river and offer the usual marigolds to the gods. A cruel river, a hungry mugger, and a people steeped in religion. Not much romance in it, surely!

I remember once, having little time to waste, we placed a dead mugger on the boat without skinning it. It was securely fastened with ropes, except for its mouth. I was sitting right next to it when, judge my astonishment and terror, it suddenly opened its huge mouth and bellowed. I screamed and shifted my quarters at once even though everyone tried to convince me of its incapability to hurt me at all.

After one of our shoots, which lasted two days, we bagged nine muggers. My father met my mother with the words 'no mugger'; at which she was frightfully disappointed, till she realised he meant nine ('no' being the Hindustani word for that number).

On the way home we passed the usual crowd of gaily-attired holiday makers (old men, young women, and babies in arms), come to bathe in the sacred waters. Sometimes an old man would fill a bottle with the water, apparently to take home, believing it would ease his final moments. At last we would come to the end of our journey, tired out but happy. And now all we have left to remind us of those thrilling days are some mugger attaché-cases and handbags, not forgetting the silver jewellery, blackened with age; but as I touch them what memories they revive! – ELSIE STRINGER.

VEGETARIAN WEAKNESS

THIS IS A sentimental age, but sentiment when carried beyond a certain point becomes irrational weakness; for it shows that people have lost their balance in logical reasoning power. From the fundamental standpoint, man is a carnivorous creature and to sustain and retain his physical and mental qualities he is all the better for a moderate flesh diet, at least in temperate and northern climates. When he becomes a vegetarian in such climes he will undoubtedly become weaker in stamina and other ways. Our grand Empire was not made by molly-coddles and sentimentalists and it will certainly be never retained by such; so let our people practise manly sports and deal with them by word and deed in the spirit of truth, for nothing else has any lasting value. – 'CHIMKANGO'.

BABOON

A BECHUANALAND trader, spending the Sunday afternoon reading the three day-old newspaper which had just reached his remote store, looked up in annoyance as the deep grunting bark of a baboon reached his ears. For days past a troop of baboons had been harrying his ripening mealie crops, and now apparently here they were again. He rose from the long chair in the shade of his verandah and called to his house-boy to bring him his rifle. Whilst awaiting for the arrival of the boy with the rifle he looked eagerly round for his enemies, but none were for the moment to be seen, but stay! What is that? From the midst of the high maize he fancied that a slinking figure emerged – yes, it had perched itself on the target rock. The trader smiled grimly, for his enemy had played into his hands. What he called his target rock was a small outstanding stone about five feet high, distant from the verandah exactly 800 yards, as he well-knew, having got the exact range through frequently shooting at it. The animal was clearly outlined against the sky, the rock being at the top of a rise in the ground – the trader distinctly saw it move a little.

The houseboy arrived bringing the rifle. He fixed his sights for the well-known range, took steady aim and fired. The baboon fell in a crumpled heap at the base of the rock. Very pleased with himself he resumed his chair with the newspaper while the houseboy went to fetch the ape. After a while, the houseboy returned empty-handed.

'Baas! baas!,' he said, in a terrified voice, 'that's not a baboon, that's a boy you shot!'

The horrified trader hurried to the spot. Alas! his aim had been all too true. There dead before him lay a small native boy, apparently about eight or nine years old. He wore no single stitch of clothing – not even the cheap brass bangle which most of his kind affect. The unhappy trader prepared himself mentally to face a bereaved mother and family of this poor little victim (and incidentally to be blackmailed indefinitely by every native near at hand who could claim relationship with the dead child) and reported the matter to the police. Strange to say, the child's identity was never established – no one knew him, and no report was made of a missing boy from any neighbouring district. It was generally surmised that the boy must have been a member of a party of travelling natives, who had either deliberately abandoned him, or had lost him on the veldt and gone on their way without troubling to make a sufficient search for him.

– E. MARKHAM HEALE.

NAPOLEON'S SHOOTING

THE EMPEROR Napoleon was somewhat of a sportsman, and was as terrible to his friends by the covert-side as he was to his enemies in the field. Once, shooting with Berthier and Masséna, he raked the line and shot Masséna in the eye. He was as fond of stag hunting as he was of shooting. As well as being a bad shot, he was a dangerous one. He used light guns with short barrels, which belonged to Louis XVI, and had them so heavily charged that his hands and shoulders suffered severely.

PEPPERED

ONCE A LINE of guns were walking through thick cover when a woodcock rose and a gun fired and dropped it and peppered a man painfully. When they got out into the open he shouted: 'The chap who got that 'cock put his hand up,' and the reckless sportsman did, and the next moment he found his arm and hand full of No. 6, for the infuriated sufferer (an Anglo-Indian colonel with a liver) retaliated in this drastic way.

HELPING A NEIGHBOUR

IT IS MARVELLOUS how a man who understands the game may make shooting for his neighbours in a drive. For instance, once at a partridge drive, I was next to a sportsman who provided me with many an unexpected chance. We were standing some 30 yards behind a tall fence, and directly a covey topped the fence this gun took them in hand most successfully. His quick shooting caused each covey to split up, and the gun on either side stood in, sometimes getting a brace. The gun on my left was more slow, killed the majority of his birds behind, and never dispersed a covey. Partridges are always more easily broken up than grouse.

ROYAL SHOTS

IT IS STRANGE to learn that the King is not grouse shooting in Yorkshire, for the opening of the grouse shooting generally sees His Majesty at Bolton Abbey. The scarcity of birds and the consequent doubtful prospects are the explanation. The King has gone to Balmoral and will spend the next few weeks shooting over the moors there. Several years ago, if we remember correctly, there was taken a census as to opinions as to the best game shot in Great Britain. On that list we think the King was

OVER THE LUNCHEON TABLE

Young Sportsman : "That was a very high bird you had in the drive just before lunch, sir."

Old Hand : "Yes, I'm glad you spotted it. Sometimes partridges get right up at that particular drive."

Young Sportsman : "You killed him stone dead, sir—wonderful fine shot, wasn't it? What sort of lead did you give him?"

Old Hand : "Oh, the usual, couldn't tell you exactly—you see I always shoot partridges with the same load, the same powder and the same cases. I don't believe in experimenting. Find a powder and a load that suits you, and then stick to it. You then shoot instinctively. You know just what your cartridges will do, so long as they are scientifically loaded, with a powder of uniform excellence and regularity, such as 'SMOKELESS DIAMOND' or 'E.C.'"

Young Sportsman : "I must have a talk with my Gunmaker."

Insist on either

ELEY *or* KYNOCH

The following cartridges, loaded by the makers, are obtainable from all Gunmakers and Ammunition Dealers.

ELEY "GRAND PRIX"	ELEY GASTIGHT	KYNOCH "PRIMAX"
Loaded with Smokeless Diamond	*Water resisting, loaded with Smokeless Diamond, E.C., Schultze or Empire.*	*Loaded with Smokeless Diamond*

BRITISH THROUGHOUT AND BEST

IMPERIAL CHEMICAL INDUSTRIES LIMITED, NOBEL HOUSE, LONDON, S.W.1.

placed third, but were such a census taken today there can be little doubt that he would head the list. His Majesty uses a gun with 30 inch barrels and handles it with the left arm fully extended. His guns are really hammerless, but they are fitted with 'dummy' hammers. It is said that he has one old gun to which he is most attached. It is not, perhaps, generally known that both the Prince of Wales and the Duke of York are excellent shots, though it is not likely that either of them will rival their illustrious father.

WOODCOCK IN IPSWICH

SIR, I LIVE quite in the town of Ipswich, and have a good garden. I have a brace of good gundogs, and in walking round the garden on Sunday morning my dog made a point in a bunch of nettles and flushed a woodcock which, as it took some time to rise, the dog jumped up and got. He retrieved the bird to me alive, and all my neighbours wondered what it was. I have shot all my life and in all parts of Suffolk, but do not recollect getting a woodcock so early as October 14th. I thought this was very early indeed. I may say my dog is a splendid dog, between pointer and labrador, and very quick.

Yrs., H.W.T. CROSS, Ipswich.

1929

ROYAL FISHERMAN

THE 'XI HUSSARS JOURNAL' gives an extract from a French paper which describes King George salmon fishing. The extract runs: 'He is an angler of the first force this King of Britain, behold him there, as he sits motionless under his umbrella patiently regarding his many-coloured float. How obstinately he contends with the elements. It is a summer day in Britain. That is to say, a day of sleet, fog and tempest. Presently the King's float begins to descend. My God, but how he strikes; the hook is implanted in the very bowels of the salmon. The King rises. He spurns aside his footstool. He strides strongly and swiftly towards the rear. In due course the salmon comes to approach himself to the bank. Aha! The King has cast aside his rod, he hurls himself flat on the ground on his victim. They splash and struggle in the icy water. The ghillie, a kind of outdoor domestic, administers the *coup de grâce* with his pistol. The King cries with a shrill voice, "Hip, Hip, Hurrah!" On these red-letter days His Majesty King George dines on a haggis and whisky grog. Like a true Scotsman he wears only a kilt.'

TRESPASSERS W

'NOTIS - Any persins found trespasing on this hear propperty will be persecuted to the extent of two mungrel dorgs what ain't never been over parshal to straingers and one dubble barrel gun what ain't loaded with no sofer cushions dam if I ain't tired of all this hear hell raising on mi propperty.'

CHARITY

SOME TIME ago I watched a number of people passing into a large hall where an anti-sport meeting was to be held. It was on a winter evening and the weather was bitterly cold. Standing there, also watching, were two little boys in ragged clothes, blue with cold, looking pinched and hungry. All those people passed them by. Then I saw one man speak to the children for a moment or two, and he went off towards a coffee stall, each child clutching one of his hands. That man is a famous sportsman; he is known to every reader of this paper, but it would be as much as my life is worth were I to give a hint of his identity. I only mention this incident now to point a moral. – 'DIANA'.

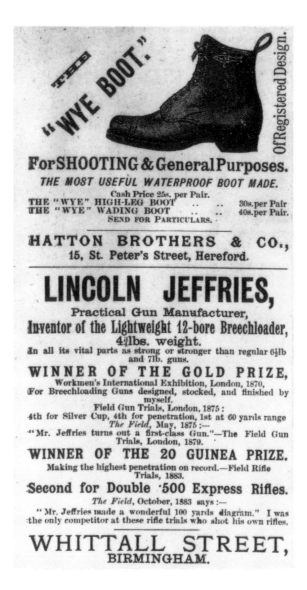

1930

FLOATING PIGEON

Sir, Whilst fishing a dry fly on a smooth, deep stretch of the Usk last year in very hot weather, I was astonished to see a wood pigeon alight slap in the middle of the river and, holding its wings half-open and well above its head, float downstream for a distance of 35 or 40 yards. After this cooler it flew off the water with little effort and disappeared.

Yrs., 'MEDICO', Newport.

'WARE STRONG TOBACCO

Sir, At the foot of Mr. C. W. Buckwell's letter in a recent issue, you said you are spending the close time smoking strong tobacco. I would not be surprised if your shooting does not fall off at least 40 per cent when next season commences. Chuck smoking altogether and you will not know yourself. I chucked it suddenly six years ago and never regretted it. I am 69 next August, yet I feel tireless, have a capital appetite and am full of vim. I was a very heavy smoker for years. What makes ladies of all classes take it up I fail to see, only I have a great regard for the man at the helm of the *Shooting Times*, or I would not pen the above. I bet you the Scottish team in the International smoke less than the English, Irish, or Welsh. Rain still continues. I have seen in the paper that an iceberg several hundred feet high was in Dog's Bay, Roundstone, Galway. They are breaking it up for summer fish. Where did that 'berg come from? All the way from the Arctic, I suppose, no wonder the cold is still severe here.

Yrs., 'PTARMIGAN'.

[We might mention that the famous 'All Blacks' Rugby team that toured Great Britain and Ireland in 1904–5 – probably the greatest team in the annals of the game – were practically all smokers. They were frequently seen contentedly puffing their pipes in the dressing room just before going out to play a match. Yet they put up a marvellous record of scores and seemed tireless athletes. All good wishes to you, old friend. - Ed.]

HATS AND SUITS AND BOOTS

A GADGET WAS brought to my notice by Mr. John Ritchie. It is what I call the Ritchie hat and I will say that it is far and away the most comfortable headgear for shooting in that I have ever come across. Here is the recipe, as given to me by the inventor. Take an old, soft felt hat, one for which you think you will have no further use, the sort of hat which, if you lived in a city, would induce the charitably disposed to press sixpence into your hand murmuring, 'My poor fellow,' etc. Sneak your wife's sharp scissors and remove the band of the hat, then remove also the band and the binding from inside the hat. Then put on the hat, and you will be surprised to find how comfortable it is. I here and now give due warning to all concerned, that in such a hat I propose to do all my shooting in future.

I must say that I like to shoot in comfort, and comfort in this respect means for me an old and utterly disreputable suit of clothes. In fact, my shooting suit is so patched and mended that it would not be easy to sort out the original material from the rest. It has, to my sorrow, long passed the stage in which I could, so to speak, shoot in public with it, and its usefulness is now confined to those occasions on which I make solitary expeditions. Mud and blood, salt water and rain, barbed wire and thorns – all have left on it indelible traces of their oft-repeated contact.

Boots? I will have the oldest and most battered, with holes to let the water out as well as to let in. Such are almost the official badge of the inveterate snipe shooter. I do not believe in trying to keep your feet dry when you are walking up snipe. The best thing to do is to get wet right away, and then you do not care what

happens. I generally walk into the first water I come across and get thoroughly and comfortably wet up to the knees. If you are constantly worrying about getting wet you cannot enjoy your shooting, but once you are wet, you are wet, and it does not matter what happens after that. You will get wet sooner or later, and you might as well get wet sooner! – F.W.E. WAGNER, M.A., ScD.

MODEL SHOT

WHEN A mannequin working in a Paris dressmaking house recently shot a magpie she had no thought of the French game laws or fame. Now she has heard much of both. The magpie stole the mannequin's ring and swallowed it, whereupon the girl drew a revolver from her purse and shot the bird dead. Police officers arrested her for an infraction of the game laws, and when her case came before the court she was sentenced in her absence. She has now achieved a measure of fame by appealing to the higher courts and the newspapers.

A MIXED BAG

SIR, ON ONE occasion last season the conversation turned to an argument on how many varieties of game one gun, unaided but for a dog, could shoot in one day on one estate, and having a day to spare, I decided to try my luck. It was a morning in early October, one of those grand mornings with bright sun and a slight touch of frost. I had no dog with me; it was only 7.30 a.m., and later she would have an energetic day before her. I had decided to try for the easy ones first, the homely rabbit and perhaps a hare and a pheasant from a nearby turnip field, but things were to turn out differently. I soon had the rabbit, one of 50 or so feeding within shot of a convenient rhododendron bush. How rudely the sound of my shot echoed round the woods. It was as though by pressure on the trigger I had declared war on the wild life. Rabbits raced for cover, and the woods gave back an answering challenge with the clatter of pigeons' wings. But this was no time for silly reflections; I still had 15 or more possible varieties to bring home, so I set off for the roots. An inquisitive pigeon flying out of the wood gave me a lucky chance, and I was very glad to get him. Many times have I walked and walked and never seen one in shot, and I had been afraid a pigeon might still be missing from the bag with the light fast failing. Perhaps I might have a look at the flooded quarry hole in the hope of seeing a mallard. Last year I shot a pintail there. An easy pond to stalk, too, provided one of those silly moorhens did not give me away. A noisy old cock pheasant got up, but no sign of a duck as yet. Five yards further on and up got two pheasants (no idea there were so many up here). Another yard and there were a pair of mallard. Yet another yard or two, and up they got six of them. To my great surprise I got a right and a left, a great feat for me. How I wished I had my dog, for both fell into the water and I was soaked to the waist before I reached one. The other mysteriously revived and flew strongly away. To make matters still more dampening, it had now begun to pour with rain. A walk round a flood pond, sadly dried up, where a spring of 30 teal had risen yesterday, showed nothing but a distant snipe, so picking up the bedraggled bag I started home for breakfast, soaked to the skin, but otherwise in pretty good form.

Fortified with eggs and bacon, I set out in the car with my dog. First, I had decided to visit a secluded point in a wood, always a sure find for teal and mallard. Having stalked the pond with infinite care, I found to my disgust a man cutting reeds at the water's edge. My dog, however, put out a mallard from the far shore, which I shot. A moment later she flushed a shoveller, which are not infrequent here, but I missed it, and shortly afterwards shot a coot. My next draw was a field of 'neeps' where I had an easy shot at an old cock pheasant. My grouse and blackgame were going to be a problem, unaided as I was. I decided a stubble, close to a flow, would be a likely venue for the former. Two hundred yards away I thought I could see a small covey, close to a good wall. An easy stalk and a sudden pounce over the wall showed a covey of seven, and an easy shot added one more variety to the bag. Shortly afterwards I got a hare – seven varieties and it was still only 11.30 a.m. The rain had stopped too; in fact things were going surprisingly well and I was feeling in good form.

Half an hour later and I felt better still. I had been walking a young spruce plantation in the hope of seeing a roe and a woodcock, when I surprised a wily blackcock, which was a tremendous stroke of luck. And I had been reckoning him among the most improbables too. Immediately afterwards I had a shot at a deer at 10 yards range, but lost sight of him and missed. Followed then a long walk over a flow for snipe, but although I had a shot at a teal and a woodcock, all the snipe had gone. So we got to work on biscuits and apples. A period of stagnation seemed to have set in. From noon to 3.30 p.m., I never fired a shot. At last I did get a snipe, however, and very glad I was. I had begun to get very anxious about him, and I can never be quite certain of hitting even the easiest of snipe. And it was then, while I was whistling frantically at some golden plover, that I saw them – gaggle after gaggle of pinkfoot geese leaving a large flow and settling on a big stubble field. I did not think there was the remotest chance of getting within shot of them, but after leaving the dog I set out to see what could be done.

To describe the excitement of that stalk would fill a book. Lying like a turnip when they flew over, and rushing on when the air was clear, I got near enough to hear them eating, a sound just like a lot of tiny waterfalls interspersed with a good deal of goose language. Still they came, easily within shot overhead, but I simply had to wait and have just one look into the field, only 15 yards on now. For the moment the air was clear, and I lifted my head cautiously and peered through a thin bit of hedge. Never have I seen such a sight. The whole field was just geese – and more geese, just stuffing on the stubbles. However, now for it; and clutching my gun (hope to goodness it's loaded) I pounced up over the hedge. How I missed I do not know, but both my shots legged a goose, I am sorry to say. And then I discovered I had left all my other cartridges behind, not that they would have been very much use. A friend watching a quarter of a mile away said it was an astonishing sight; the whole field rose in one grey screaming sheet. The last I saw of my wounded goose, it was one of a thousand (or was it two thousand?) odd geese settling on to the flow across the marsh half a mile away. After such birds as geese, the plover I got seemed tame, still more so the partridge. There only remained a last look for the teal on the flood I had visited in the morning. But the only sign of life in the gathering darkness was one lonely heron, which flapped slowly off as my dog and I splashed over the mud. The total bag was 11 varieties, and I had hoped for 13. But (and this is just as important) I had been within range of, and fired at, 16; had I been a better shot I would have undoubtedly killed the 16. I was also within shot of green plover, curlew and jack snipe, but we never shoot them here. I never saw a quail, though the keeper said he saw a single bird the week before. And so home to dinner for us both, after what was certainly one of the most interesting and hardest day's shooting I have ever had.

Yrs., B. J.–F.

A loaded panier pony taking home the bag.

1931

DISAPPEARING SIGHTS AND SOUNDS

IN MY YOUNGER days the sound of cow-bells was a very familiar one, as was also that of sheep bells. I can remember so well the leathern collars with a bell attached to each, which used to be placed round the neck of the cows, and what a pleasant tinkling sound they made as the animals fed hither and thither in the fields. It is a long time since I heard cow-bells, but more recently I have heard the sheep-bells on the Sussex Downs. Probably they have also survived in other parts, and that can be understood, since, so utilitarian have we grown in our outlook, they serve a useful purpose. But I am afraid the cow-bells have disappeared.

When I was a child I often heard my grandfather talk about the early days of muzzle-loaders, and the old man would tell us, with half-wistful regret, about the pleasant thud of the ramrod on the wads as it drove home the charge; and he would speak about the tang of the black powder that he loved, even though the smoke was a nuisance on a damp morning. Well, that pleasant thud is no longer heard in the shooting field, and you can no longer locate the guns by the smoke that used to hang around their position. All that belongs to the past.

Among the birds of the countryside the quail, which has well been described as a miniature partridge, has practically disappeared. It is nearly 20 years since I flushed a bevy of quail in the British Isles. At one time they were very common. Again, and this has lately been noticed by some writers in the *Shooting Times*, it looks as if we should soon have to add the corncrake to our list of extinct birds. There was a time, and not so long ago, when this bird was almost a plague; but now we miss its hoarse calls from the sounds of the countryside. I was amused to read of 'Hoverer's' expedient of turning an energetic tom-cat loose at night to drive the corncrakes away from the house. They often kept me awake at night, but I never thought of that! It is three years now since I heard a corncrake. Here is another problem for the naturalists.
– E.M.C.

WILDFOWLER'S ASSOCIATION

THE ASSOCIATION was founded near the mouth of the Humber, west of Spurn Point. Mr. Proctor, one bitter winter's night in the month of February 1907, walked six miles in a driving snowstorm to be present at the lonely gathering appointed to consider the business of forming a wildfowlers' association. He arrived at 1 a.m. and was greeted with a warm welcome, a hot glass of 'toddy' and a glowing fire. It was as great a reception as could be shown since the shelter was but a rude wooden hut, made as comfortable, however, as circumstances would allow. Not until the affairs of the Wildfowlers' Association had been moulded to a shape of satisfaction did the party retire. This was 4 a.m.

1932

NARROW ESCAPE

I WAS OUT IN Corrievalagan, in the forest of Dibiedale, when there was a deer drive, and I was sent to flank, and if the occasion arose, keep the stags from breaking out to the west. The shooting tenant was none too careful and had two rifles and fired nearly 20 shots. Unfortunately the deer were coming out east of me, and the shooting proceeded. I had no cover whatever but short heather, and at last a bullet cut the turf about two yards from me and splashed moss and turf all over me. I got a great fright, and I am not ashamed to say that I lay flat, and used the deerhound, Oscar, that I had with me as a sandbag, behind which I crouched, although he did not lie very quiet. No more bullets came, however, and poor Oscar and myself were saved for the time being. When later on we met, I told what had happened, and the shooting tenant merely laughed, and said: 'Your own and Oscar's time to go to another sphere hasn't arrived yet evidently. We have secured two Royals and such a feat was worth a certain amount of risk.' That was how the shooting tenant of over 40 years ago looked at matters. Possibly they are more careful and polite today.
– A. ROSS.

TRAGEDY OF A TURKEY'S EGG

A STRANGE STORY comes from the village of Esebey, near Brusa. When the storks returned this year, the same, or apparently the same, pair came to their old nest on the house of one Mehmet Effendi, and until a few days ago all went well with them. Then came tragedy. The pair were seen to return together to the nest from a foraging expedition, whereupon a fierce altercation took place. The male was apparently remonstrating with his spouse, and she stoutly defending herself. After some minutes the male flew away, and having collected all the other storks from the village, returned with them to the nest, which they all examined. Then, leaving the female behind, they flew into the air and circled overhead, engaged in a lively discussion. At the end of half an hour the male and two other storks, detaching themselves from the rest, returned to the nest and solemnly killed the female. This sad task performed, the male was seen to carry one of the young from the nest and deposit it gently on the ground. Imagine the astonishment of the onlookers when they saw that the young bird left on the ground was not a stork but a turkey. The dead female had been convicted of infidelity and paid the penalty. The whole village was in a state of excitement, and it was some hours before an explanation for the tragedy that they had all witnessed was forthcoming. It was this. A small boy had climbed up to the nest just after the stork had laid her eggs, and substituted a turkey's egg for one of them. In due course the eggs were hatched, but at first Father Stork detected nothing wrong. Then, returning one day to the nest, he suddenly realised that one of the young was no offspring of his, with the result here related.

TERMS USED IN SPORT

TWO GAME BIRDS of any species are called a *brace*. Note that it is not correct to speak of a brace of snipe or a brace of woodcock; the proper term being a *couple* of snipe and a *couple* of woodcock. A *covey* of grouse or partridge. Of grouse and blackgame, a *pack* (i.e. a collection of coveys). A *bevy* of quail. A *nide* or *brood* of pheasants. A *flight* of woodcock. A *wisp* of snipe. To *raise* grouse or blackgame. To *push* or *spring* a pheasant or partridge. To *flush* a woodcock. To *spring* a snipe. To *raise* a quail.

A *paddling* or *team* of wild duck. A *company* of wigeons. A *sege* of herons or bitterns. A *herd* of swans. A *spring* of teal. A *covert* of coots. A *gaggle* of geese. A *skein* of geese (in flight). A *sord* of mallard. A *dopping* or *dropping* of shell-drakes. A *congregation* of plover. A *wing* of plover (in flight). A *trip* of dotterel. A *cast* of hawks. A *building* of rooks. A *murmuration* of starlings. A *muster* of peacocks. A *flight* of swallows. A *host* of sparrows. A *watch* of nightingales. A *charm* of goldfinches. An *exultation* of larks. A *desert* of lapwings. A *fling* of oxbirds. A *hill* of ruffs.

The term *trip* is often applied to any small number of wildfowl, about 30 or 40 such as ducks and geese. A *bunch* is a similar number of wigeon, pochard or teal, and a *knob* is a still smaller number of these birds.

The following terms are used in angling: A *cloud* of fry. A *shoal* of perch. We talk about the *lair* of the pike, but the *lie* of a salmon or trout. A trout *hovers* in the stream. A *rise* of trout, when numbers of them are rising freely over a considerable area. A *hatch* of flies. A fisherman is said to have *had* so many salmon, but to have *got* so many trout. A salmon *takes hold* of a fly or bait; a trout *takes*, and a pike *seizes*.

HINTS AND TIPS

SIR, 'SHENZI' of Tanganyka wants to know how an amateur can tighten the action of a gun. Well, he can do it by simply putting a piece of thin brass between the catch of the barrels and the breech pin. It will tighten up all right and last a long time. The brass is easily obtained. He has only to cut a piece that will fit from the brass end of a cartridge case. I am afraid a hole, no matter how small, in a barrel is unsafe for nitro powder. The weather has been most unpleasant here since the Twelfth, except for a day or two. Guns complained of shooting badly, yet there were plenty of birds. I am not surprised at bad shooting; I could not hit a dreadnought in such muggy weather. I do not care how hot or bright a day may be, provided there is a bit of a breeze. I rarely shoot all day in such weather. I prefer going to the bog or moor at daybreak, and after getting what birds I want, return before the heat of the day. Both dogs and I are fresh and eager for the next morning. It is impossible to keep birds in the larder for any length of time in the muggy, hot weather.

When one robin has haunted a house and then dies, its place is immediately taken by another. My poor old robin, unknown to me, took up its quarters in the kitchen. One night, to my horror, I found it dead in a mouse-trap. The new bird comes in and out as if he had been used to the place all its life. He is a young bird of this year's brood.

The second rise of mayfly and dapping with daddy-longlegs, I hear, did not go well.

'The Leprechaun' writes that grouse are of different colours in parts of Ireland. I have found this also. Those of the Bog of Allen are fine big brown birds, some almost black; but they are very old and worthless for eating. Those on small bogs are small and light-coloured. I have seen the same sort in a bag of a dozen from the Sligo moors. I am told the southern birds are the biggest of all.

If 'Footsore' gets a small bottle of Rexall corn solvent, there is a sponge attached to the cork. Wet the corn with it, when dry apply again, three or four times on the first day. Do that daily, then after four days leave it for a week. Soak the feet then in hot water, and the callosities will be easily removed. If only a portion of them comes off apply the solvent again till the foot is free of them, otherwise they reappear quickly.

I wonder if we will see a good old-fashioned winter, like the good old times years ago when hunting was stopped by snow and frost for weeks. What times for wildfowling and snipe shooting! I remember one night, when six huntsmen were snow-bound by a sudden storm, and they had to stay overnight in our big house which had plenty of stables in the yard. In the middle of the night one of them, a great practical joker, got up and set all the row of bells in the hall ringing by getting on top of the table and dancing on it, his head setting the bells ringing furiously. That made all the others tumble out of bed. They seized the joker, brought him out, rolled him in the snow, then all began to pelt each other in their nightshirts with snowballs. Those were gay times!

Yrs., 'PTARMIGAN'.

STATUESQUE MOUNT

A MAN I know tried hard a season or two ago to purchase a pony trained for shooting off its back, but continued advertising revealed not one. He could not walk owing to an accident, and had to fall back on an old cavalry trooper, which proved as steady as a rock as far as shooting was concerned. Unfortunately, the horse was near 17 hands, and when the sportsman appeared in the field, it all resembled the Duke of Wellington's statue on the loose. Partridges could see him a mile away and rose right out of shot, much to his disgust. So the poor old troop horse proved of no use and was turned over to the home farm, where he ended his days. – 'HOVERER'.

The late Sir R. Payne-Gallwey in the Gun Room, Thirkleby Park.

1933

PIG POINTER

Sir, Most shooting men have had a variety of experiences in the training of dogs for the gun, but few would ever dream of attempting to train a pig as a pointer. 'Slut' was a unique example of porcine intelligence, for she loved to accompany the guns and could more than hold her own with the best of trained pointers working alongside her in the field. This wonderful animal started life like many other animals of its kind, living half-wild in the New Forest. Her owner and his brother, called Toomer, were keepers in the Forest and trained dogs for the shooting field. Slut was about 18 months old before any notice was taken of her, and then she accidentally walked past the brothers one day when they were bemoaning the indifferent behaviour of several dogs then under training. Being attracted by the confident way the pig approached them for some food that they threw here, the brothers suddenly conceived the idea of training her for the gun. She fully repaid their experiment, answering to her name on the first day. At the end of a fortnight, Slut would point both partridges and rabbits, and soon after would retrieve runners as well as the best sporting dog. She would point all kinds of game, excepting hares for which she had an unaccountable objection. She showed a most amiable temperament when working with dogs, backing readily when they pointed, but dogs did not like working with such a plebeian companion. However, Slut usually circumvented any attempt to exclude her from a shooting day, for she unfailingly turned up later in the day to take her due share in the sport. Slut's speed was a steady, piggy, jog-trot which was accelerated into a headlong gallop on hearing the whistle, which meant a walk with the gun – any appearance of shooting equipment causing her much excitement as a keen gundog. Her owner was amazed at Slut's wonderful scenting powers. She would stand a single partridge at 40 yards, as steady as a rock, and then drop like a setter, drawing slowly up if the bird moved. Poor Slut, who kept up her love of shooting for many years, unhappily shared the fate of many fat pigs, and this rarely intelligent animal met its death at the hands of the local butcher, which seems an ignominious end for such a faithful companion.

Yrs., SARAH J. SHARP.

SWAN SHOOTING

Sir, In your last issue I notice remarks on prejudice against the shooting of wild swans in the Highlands. Perhaps he has overlooked the fact that all this nonsense – which I hoped was as extinct as the prehistoric monsters unearthed by scientists from time to time – had its origins in the superstitions of our imaginative race. Superstition was one of the weak points of the Highlander in the past. There is the well-known example of the wild swans which cast the evil eye upon a certain minister's cows on the west coast. The cows were supposed to give no milk for this cause. Swans were popularly supposed to be akin to angels, and to shoot one was to bring disaster on the shooter. This nonsense is responsible for any past feeling on the subject, and in the interests of sport it is best to dispel it once and for all. One word of advice to the swan shooter may not come amiss. You want a big game bag.

Yrs. H.E.B. MACPHERSON, Kingussie.

NEW RICH

Mr X. had made a huge fortune out of war provisions of some description between the fateful years of 1914 to 1918. He purchased an estate which had been allowed to run down owing to the sacrifices caused by the very conflict that enriched the new purchaser.

As the purchase was completed too late for rearing pheasants, the head keeper, only too pleased to have any sport to show at all, sensibly advised the purchase of a couple of thousand well-grown poults from a game farm, that hastened, naturally, to supply the welcome order. The feeds were put in order, the necessary foods supplied, and all looked as merry as a wedding bell.

Shortly after the first eventful day of October the new boss decided to open out in more ways than one, and to have a shoot. He sent down peremptory orders in very different terms from those which the head-keeper had been used to receive from his well-beloved former master. But the leaves were still thick on the trees, the foliage dense everywhere, and it would be a well-nigh hopeless proposition to show good sport so early in the season.

The keeper wrote a civil and apologetic letter to the new master, stating that owing to the leaves in the woods he could not possibly show the guests the good sport he might do if only a much later date could be fixed. In a still more peremptory epistle, the employer said, 'leaves be d_ _ _ _ _, put plenty of men on and have them all swept up. The days were fixed, and no alteration would be made!' Collapse of head-keeper in consequence.

1934

WOODCOCK IN THE METROPOLIS

As I passed through London, the woodcock I was carrying met with many envious glances. Altogether four persons spoke to me, referring to the birds as snipe! I said to one man, as I leaned against the refreshment counter at Paddington, devouring a sandwich, 'You are wrong; those birds are not snipe.' 'Then what might they be?' he asked. 'I will tell you if you buy me a bottle of Bass,' I replied. So he bought me the Bass and I told him 'woodcock'. 'Woodcock be d_ _ _ _ _,' said he, and, turning on his heel, left the place, evidently under the impression he had been swindled! I wonder what his definition of a woodcock is! – 'TOWER BIRD'.

INDIAN BEATERS

On occasions Indian beaters are the source of much amusement, but more often than not are unutterably exasperating. Woe betide the unfortunate *shikari* who is careless enough to pepper an advancing line of beaters. Although this seldom happens, when it does the injured can be relied on to make the most of the occasion. It can become very expensive for the unfortunate offender who, rather than listen to the moans and outpourings of malingerers, will meet any demands to bring them back to some sort of sanity again. Beaters have an uncanny understanding of the laws of extortion, and will inveigle anything up to a rupee a pellet wound from the distressed sportsman; they will even add to the number of these wounds with the point of a knife, making themselves into an unearthly mess of gore.

When tigers are unexpectedly found on a drive, beaters in the neighbourhood will

The 'Paradox' gun for big and winged game shooting.

go at once to a tree, allowing the tiger to break back. Thus he will be lost to the infuriated guns, who on occasions will have to go to the rescue of some half-demented idiot who refuses to come to earth again.

On many occasions they are badly mauled by tiger or leopard, and sometimes bones are broken by charging stag or boar, but it is all part of the day's work with them. – 'TURSA'.

BEAR SHOOTING

IN THE Ak Sai region in the Tien Shan, and also in the Pamirs, where there are numerous caverns in the limestones, the Kirghiz will not hesitate to go right into the deep caverns and shoot bears in their dens. These bears attain an immense size, but are not famed for their fierceness or courage. Still, it requires nerve on the part of the sportsman who, armed with a candle and his *multuk* or muzzle-loader, walks boldly in. On entering, he advances carefully, peering into all the nooks and dark corners. When he catches sight of the animal's eyes, glistening in the candlelight, he walks right up to the astonished creature, which, as a rule, remains motionless and stares at the phenomenon of a light in his gloomy lair. The man then puts the candle on the ground, sits down beside it, rests the heavy barrel of the rifle upon its prop, quietly and unhurriedly takes aim at the bear between the eyes, and fires. The Kirghiz do not often miss, but even if they do the result is not necessarily fatal to them, as these bears are very timid and extraordinarily quiet. Still, the patience of even so phlegmatic a creature has some limit.

THE MARSH TIDE

FOR SOME YEARS I have been after a really hard-hitting gun for the roughest of rough work by the sea – the sort of gun that would knock a goose cold at extreme range, but also show a decent pattern at ordinary distances. After a lot of poignant thought I became the possessor of a double hammer 8-bore. A hefty tool with 36-inch barrels and an under-lever like a 4-bore. I chose an under-lever hammer gun because I wanted a gun that would not jam when shooting in a gale amongst sandhills.

There is a delectable spot on the east coast that I visit on certain winter tides. A glorious place of winding, odorous creeks and grey saltings; of shingle ridges and gleaming low tide sloblands and zostera beds; of distant sandhills shimmering in the winter sunshine like giant wave crests, and great billows of slowly moving clouds.

It was to this place, far from mankind's petty squabbles, but full of gull voices and sounds of the sea, that I went one day last February to test the 8-bore. There was a marsh tide at five o'clock, but I wanted wind as well, a gale in fact. There was not enough wind to sway the dead stems of the sea lavender and the sun shone coldly from a hard, cloudless sky.

We had our lunch, the Labrador and I, in a hole scooped out of the shingle behind some little bushes, just above where the drift from the last tide lay. The 8-bore lay on the cartridge bag. She was loaded with ancient green shells with waxed turnover and black powder.

The tide had turned but it was a long way off. Every now and then came the distance voice of curlew. Westwards, flocks of knots wheeled and twisted. A grey crow left the shore and came inland over the shingle ridge. I cocked and raised the gun and took him well forward at about 60 yards. There came a hollow boom and a dense cloud of smoke; a slight push was the only recoil. The dog dashed through the smoke screen and returned with the crow, which might have been dead for hours. At the report a mob of gulls rose in a clamouring cloud. All along the tide line the

[209]

curlews called. Redshanks flew like twisting arrows over the pools and gullies, piping sadly as they flew. Now and again the lonely voice of a grey plover came hauntingly from afar.

As the tide grew and little sleepy waves, scarcely turning in their langour, lifted the zostera on the flats and floated the pod weed on the shingle, a flight of sheld duck came in from the open sea and settled to feed. Clouds of stints scudded over the water in an ecstasy of motion, and a cluster of golden plover rose high in the air and flew inland. Curlew moved all along the tide line. I got two and missed a third. There was no wounding with the 8-bore. Everything hit was killed dead in the air.

The sheld duck departed for the shore by the sandhills, but another lot came circling in to settle and feed, to be joined by six brent geese. Then small flights of duck showed on the skyline and several more brent came in to settle with the others.

A woodpigeon came wearily from over the sea. When about 200 yards from the shore, a peregrine swooped from out of the sky like a falling stone. The pigeon turned and flopped into the water. The falcon rose on sizzling wings, just avoiding hitting the sea, the rush and tear of his mighty pinions fanning the water. A score of scolding godwits mobbed him, following him up until circling high, he vanished like a black star in the purpling east. The pigeon floated in with the tide and then heaved itself out of the water and flew slowly inland over my hide. I watched him go.

Good luck to him. The sun sank, flushing the sandhills far away. The tide reached its full and the long dreamy waves rolled in like a poem over the open sea. A seal swam lazily in the languid, lifting swell and the plaintive, melancholy call of the green plover came from the inland marshes.

The ducks were strung out along the tide line. Wigeon voices came with the gathering dusk. A small lot came over and left two to the single shot. Then in from the sea came a wild swan, a young bird not in his full plumage. He passed behind me but fell stone dead at the shot. In pacing it out, it was 91 yards; the only swan I have ever shot. I am sure a magnum 12-bore would not have done that. They are fine guns for all inland wildfowling and inland duck flighting; but I have fallen in love with the 8-bore and I think it cannot be equalled for a real tough gun for heavy winter seacoast wildfowl. My 8-bore was too long in the barrels for easy swinging, and this year I have had it fitted with 32 inch barrels chambered for 3¾ inch paper cases and proved for 2½oz. of big shot. The gun now handles like a dream and I long for a really rough day with a north-easter thundering in the sandhills and the brent coming in long black lines, rising and dipping over the surf. The sort of day when one leans against the wind and the spume, and the spindrift plasters a crust of salt over one's face. Then perhaps I will learn a little more about what I consider an absolutely ideal winter wildfowl gun. – ALAN F. SAVORY.

RATTING ETC.

SIR, LAST SUNDAY week, after reading the *Shooting Times* from cover to cover, I went to the shed for a few sods, and saw a freshly-eaten potato there. Thereupon I called in 'Sot', the clever half-bred terrier and cocker. He came, smelt, cast a professional eye, then went outside. Here he searched the hedge, dislodged a large rat, and chased it on and off for the length of more than 400 yards of hedge. Finally, he scratched it out with four more which he killed. I set some traps but got no rats till yesterday morning, when I had a very large one. I flung it across the road from the yard as a motor car was passing, and the 'flying deceased' went right into it, through the open window. I looked after the car, expecting to see the rat thrown out. But no! The driver probably took it home as a curiosity! We are having terrible summer-like weather. I wrote to a friend and asked him where one could get a few snipe. The reply was he wished to know the same, as he was out for hours daily and only met one. I have heard of only one woodcock being shot. Wild fowl are utterly unapproachable, though numerous.

Yrs., 'PTARMIGAN',
Westmeath.

1935

OLD CARTRIDGES

SIR, WITH REFERENCE to the above, may I tell you a terrible story, containing a horrible warning? Let me say at once I have been shooting geese for 40 years and over, and am old-fashioned and prejudiced. One pitch-dark Sunday night in January, about 20 years ago, we had a violent thunderstorm with a lot of lightning. A north-west gale came in with one terrific squall about eight o'clock. All the pink-foot geese resting on the sand were terrified, and came south-east over my house, straight in front of the storm, making a great noise. I expected them to come back in the morning, so, before I turned in, I got all my gear ready. I usually use a 10-bore, but on this occasion some evil spirit prompted me to get out an 8-bore of my brother, and some mixed cartridges he had left with me. Next morning, about six o'clock, I went out to find it blowing north-west heaven's hard. For a moment my guardian angel urged me to get out the 10-bore instead, but the devil of laziness won, and I walked off about a mile with the 8-bore, which was all ready. I can weep now at what happened. Before dawn, in fact while still pretty dark, the geese started to come back in small bunches of six to 10. They were so low that they had to rise over the field fence as they came in to them. I was under a little cliff with a fence on the top, the whole about 20 feet high. They poured over me bunch after bunch. The 8-bore went off like a damp squib; at 15 to 20 yards I could hear the shot literally dribble against the goose I had shot at, and he went on without any damage with the others. I fired off all the 8-bore cartridges and ran home cursing and weeping for the 10-bore, grabbed it up with a pocketful of cartridges, and killed two right-and-lefts with the last four shots I got that day. I picked up three of the geese and the other towered and fell in the sea. The flight was over. I honestly believe that with a 12- or 16-bore gun, I could that morning have killed 30 or 40 geese by deliberately shooting them in the head or neck at 10 to 15 yards rise. It came out afterwards that those 8-bore cartridges were seven years old, and had been on a couple of trips to West Africa and back. 'Never no more.' I now cremate all 'left overs', but, alas! it is too late, and I can never expect to see such a chance again.

Yrs., PHILIP HAMOND,
Norfolk.

WOLVES' MUZZLES

'YES,' SAID THE man who had just returned from a hunting trip, 'I thought it was all up with me. I was running for all I was worth, but the wolves were drawing nearer and nearer at every moment until I could feel their muzzles touching me.' 'You must have been glad,' put in one fair young thing at this point. 'Glad?' said the hunter in astonishment. 'Why?' 'Because they had their muzzles on,' said the sympathetic girl.

POACHER'S ODE

A HIGHLAND POACHER, whom I had detected from a distance, affected not to see me coming. He was seated at a rock, two lurchers lying at his feet, and he was writing. 'Good morning, Mac,' I said. 'You have a fine view up here. Are you poaching?' 'Not me!' he said. 'Am jist up here consultin' the Muse, as I may say, for that's the best view in Scotland.' I asked him to let me see his 'poem' and after some demur he handed it over. As far as I remember it went:-

'Oh! the Loch, the beautiful Loch, the Loch!

I wish I was in you up to my hoch,

THE LOCH, THE LOCH, THE BEAUTIFUL LOCH, THE LOCH.'

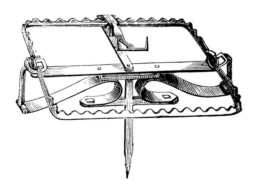

Heron trap.

1936

SAFE BET

I WAS ONCE listening to a rather heated argument regarding the value of October pheasants, one party contending that they could be equal to those of November and the other maintaining the reverse. I was called in as arbitrator, but refused to express an opinion. The end of it all was, for the time being, a rather heavy bet that one of the parties would show the other as fine an October shoot as he had ever enjoyed in November or even later on in the season. The result was that he did, the first week in that month as arranged, the pheasants being plentiful and all flew high and strong. The secret of the success was that those pheasants had been reared the previous season and not shot, but fed and kept over to win the bet. The secret was well kept, did not leak out, and the man who lost failed to learn how he had been tricked.

DEFENCE AGAINST BULLS

SIR, WHEN attacked by a bull, stand your ground. You are perfectly safe, provided, of course, you do not lose your head. Now it is not generally known that when a bull makes a charge it always shuts its eyes. All one has to do is to step to one side and let the beast pass. As soon as it has missed, you turn round sharply, catch hold of its tail, and give it a tremendous twist. The bull will be at once brought down to the ground. Now make a bee-line for the nearest fence. If you are overtaken by the bull before you reach the fence, repeat the performance.

Yrs., 'JUDGED', Yorkshire.
[Hm! - Ed.]

1937

THE MASTER

IT WAS IN either Austria or Hungary that a bit of marksmanship by the late Marquis of Ripon was witnessed which definitely disproved the suggestion that he was not such a fine performer in an emergency as he was under the ordered conditions of driven sport. He was one of a party engaged in carrying out a huge encircling movement by which an area of ground is walked inwards towards a central point. His gun was lying on the stubble and he was busy doing up his bootlace when a shout from a beater warned him that game was on the move. Lord Ripon picked up his gun and saw a covey of six partridges heading straight at him. He promptly killed a brace in front, changed guns with his attendant, and killed a second brace overhead, and finally bagged the third and surviving brace in the rear with his reloaded first gun. All birds were stone dead. – 'SCOLOPAX'.

1938

BRIGHT DOG

WE EXTRACT THE following from a letter received from a correspondent whose veracity is without question:- 'You are always speaking about the intelligence of dogs, but how about this for common sense? We were out partridge shooting, and an old colonel had a partridge down which he thought was a dead bird. I sent Brutus out for it, remarking to the colonel, 'That bird is a runner, sir.' 'It most certainly is not,' replied the Colonel; 'it is a dead bird.' The dog was away an unusually long time, nearly 10 minutes, to be exact, but eventually showed up with an old tin kettle in her mouth, held, of course, by the handle. Everyone was highly amused to see old Brutus returning with the kettle and a lot of uncomplimentary things were said. However, when the kettle had been delivered to hand, lo and behold, there was the partridge inside, full of life, for it had only been tipped in the wing.'

DOUBLE TAKE

SIR, RECENTLY MY friend, Mr. Brown, was fishing Loch Awe on an exceptionally stormy day, when it was difficult to keep a fly in the water. Eventually a small bay was found where there was a temporary shelter. In a few minutes he rose and hooked a good trout. It bored deep and fought for five minutes. Slowly raising it towards the surface, the top of the cast emerged, then the dropper fly. At that instant a house martin skimming over the water seized the fly and hooked itself. Its struggles alarmed the trout, which again went deep, dragging the bird down with him. The lifting process was repeated and then the martin appeared, still alive and struggling. The commotion caused another descent, and this time the trout broke away, leaving Mr. Brown to play the bird in the air. He succeeded in retrieving it. The hook was in the gullet and took some time to extract. On being released, the martin flew away, apparently none the worse for the experience.

Yrs., G.M. FORMAN,
Blairgowrie.

ACCOUNTS OF A ROUGH SHOOT

Sir, I wonder if you would care to print a copy of the following account of my shoot for last season. The shoot is in Hertfordshire.

SHOOT, 1937–8

	£	s.	d.
Rent of land, about 1,000 acres	107	0	0
Cartridges and vermin money	14	12	2
Keepers' (2) wages	180	17	6
Coal	3	14	0
Clothes	8	15	6
Rent of cottages	18	0	8
Health insurance	6	18	4
Licence and keepers' dog food	5	0	6
Wire netting	10	5	4
Pheasant eggs (1,000)	40	5	0
Sitting hens and eggs for chicks	13	12	6
Rent of rearing field and cartage	16	7	0
Lime	1	6	0
Corn and food for birds	72	16	7
Extra payment for watching birds	4	15	0
Beaters' wages	30	11	6
Lunches	8	5	2
Sundries and beaters' insurance	8	1	9
Traps, tools, etc.	6	0	8
Cutting drives in woods	3	10	5
Compensation for damage	7	0	0
Christmas boxes to keepers	15	10	0
	583	12	7
Less sale of game	89	1	9
Cost of shoot	£494	10	10

Approximate bag, 1937–8:- Partridges, 156; pheasants, 410; hares, 16; woodcock, 3; rabbits, 200; pigeon, 20; total, 805

Yrs., O.L.S.

Additional List of Used Guns

(Rebuilt or reconditioned, and fully guaranteed by Churchill)

PURDEY.
Pair 12-bore 30 in. Finest Quality Sidelocks chambered for 2½ in. cases. Weight 7¼ lbs. Left barrels choked. Excellent condition **£110**

EVANS.
Pair 12-bore 28 in. Sidelock Ejectors weighing 6 lbs. 7 ozs. and fitted with straight hand stocks. Length 13½ in. An excellent pair of game guns. Complete in case .. **£85**

CHURCHILL.
Pair 12-bore "Premiere" Model Finest Quality Sidelock Ejectors fitted with 25 in. barrels. All barrels bored ¼ chokes. Half Pistol Grips. Long stocks. Condition as new **£160**

COGSWELL & HARRISON.
Pair 12 30 in. Ejectors with right barrels Cylinder and left barrels Half Choke. Fitted with finely figured walnut stocks and cast-off for shooting from right shoulder with left eye master. Weight 6 lbs. 9 ozs. 15 in. stocks. In case. **£60**

LANG.
Pair 12-bore 28 in. sidelocks weighing 6 lbs. 11 ozs. Half Pistol Grips. Length of stocks 14¼ in. All barrels ¼ chokes. Long forends. **£75**

CHURCHILL.
Pair 12-bore "XXV" UTILITY Model Guns with Easy-opening mechanism. Weight 6 lbs. Bored Right ¼ chokes and Left ¾ chokes. In new condition and complete in double leather case **£80**

CHURCHILL.
Pair 12-bore "XXV" "UTILITY" Model guns standard opening mechanism, with cast-off stocks. Weight 6 lbs. 2 ozs. An ideal pair of game guns in lightweight case. **£70**

PURDEY.
Pair 12-bore 29 in. Finest Quality Sidelocks right barrels ¼ chokes and left barrels Half-chokes. Weight 6 lbs. 10 ozs. 14¾ in. stocks. Condition as new and complete in box leather case **£150**

CHURCHILL.
12-bore "UTILITY" "XXV" Model gun with cross-stock for shooting from right shoulder with left eye master. Weight 6 lbs. 6 ozs. 15¼ in stock with recoil pad. Condition as new **£40**

CHURCHILL.
12-bore "UTILITY" "XXV" Model gun weighing 6 lbs. 3 ozs. with recoil pad and 15¼ in. stock. Very little used and guaranteed perfect in every respect **£35**

JEWSON.
12-bore 28 in. A. and D.. engraved ejector weighing 6½ lbs. Right barrel cylinder and left barrel Full Choke . In new condition **£20**

WILD.
12-bore 29 in. Fully Engraved A. and D. action. Selective Single Trigger gun, both barrels Full Choke and chambered for 2½ in. cases. Weight 7 lbs. Half Pistol Grip. Condition as new **£35**

JEFFERY.
12-bore Engraved A. and D. action fitted with 3-in. chambered 30 in. barrels. Both barrels Full Choke. Weight 8 lbs. 4 ozs. 15⅛ in. stock. Recently thoroughly overhauled and re-conditioned **£25**

CHURCHILL.
12-bore 28 in. A. and D. action Ejector with cross-stock. Weight 6 lbs. 12 ozs. Bored right barrel ⅛ choke and left barrel Half Choke. 15 in. stock with recoil pad. Good condition **£25**

CHURCHILL.
12-bore "UTILITY" "XXV" Model easy-opening ejector weighing 6 lbs. 1 oz. Bored both barrels Half-choke. 14¼ in. straight hand stock. As new **£40**

LANG.
12-bore 28 in. Sidelock with 14½ in. stock and straight hand grip. Weight 6 lbs. 11 ozs. Ideal for driven game. **£25**

ADKIN.
12-bore 28 in. Engraved A. and D. action. Weight 6¼ lbs. Bored right barrel Cylinder and left barrel Full Choke. Straight Hand stock 13⅞ in. with recoil pad .. **£22 10s**

COGSWELL & HARRISON.
12-bore 30 in. engraved Ejector weighing 6 lbs. 10 ozs. with straight hand stock and a length of 16 in. Right barrel ¼ choke and left barrel Full Choke **£17 10s**

COGSWELL & HARRISON.
12-bore 26 in. ejector weighing 6 lbs. 1 oz. 14 in. stock. Cylinder barrels. Good order **£10**

SMYTHE.
12-bore 30 in. engraved ejector. Weight 6¼ lbs. Straight hand grip with recoil pad. Length 14⅜ in. Right barrel Cylinder and Left ¼ choke. Good order .. **£17 10s**

CHURCHILL.
12-bore "CROWN" "XXV" Model as new. Right barrel ¼ choke and left barrel ½ choke. Weight 6 lbs. 3 ozs. 14 in. stock **£30**

CHURCHILL.
12-bore 30 in. Finest Quality A. and D. action with both barrels ¼ chokes. Weight 6 lbs. 12 ozs. Straight Hand stock with recoil pad and cast-off. Good condition .. **£30**

PURDEY.
Pair 20-bore Finest Quality Sidelocks fitted with 28 in. barrels and extra choke barrels 25 in. by Westley Richards. Chambered for 2½ in. shells. In perfect condition. The complete outfit **£125**

CHURCHILL.
16-bore "Crown" Ejector with 25 in. barrels. 14¼ in. stock. Weight 5¼ lbs. Right barrel ¼ choke and left barrel Full Choke. As new **£22 10s**

LANG.
20-bore A. and D. ejector with 28 in. barrels. Weight 5 lbs. 11 ozs. Right cylinder and Left Half Choke. Length of stock 14⅜ in. **£20**

SMITH.
16-bore A. and D. Engraved Ejector with 29 in. barrels. Right cylinder and left Half Choke. Weight 5 lbs. 15 ozs. Length of stock 14¼ in. In excellent condition .. **£15**

TURNER.
16-bore Engraved A. and D. ejector with 28 in. barrels. Right cylinder and left Full Choke. Absolutely as new. Weight 5 lbs. 15 ozs. **£25**

CHURCHILL.
20-bore "CROWN" "XXV" Model gun with 25 in. barrels. Weight 5 lbs. 3 ozs. 13¾ in. stock with recoil pad. Recently renovated as new. Right cylinder and left Half Choke .. .. **£22 10s.**

LEESON.
28-bore Sidelock Ejector with 26 in. barrels. Weight 5¼ lbs. Length of stock 14⅛ in. New barrels bored right cylinder and left full choke. Good condition **£18**

Send details of your requirements and full particulars of most suitable weapons will be forwarded by return together with latest XXV Booklet.

E. J. CHURCHILL (Gun Makers) LTD.

ORANGE STREET GUNWORKS, LEICESTER SQUARE, LONDON, W.C.2

Printed and Published by the Burlington Publishing Company, Limited, 74 to 76, Temple Chambers, E.C.4, in the City of London.

WELL-READ POACHERS

TEN CARDIFF MEN were summoned at Weston-super-mare for poaching on Steepholm, a small island in the Bristol Channel. It was stated that they journeyed to the island in two small boats with a dog and guns, but on seeing the approach of a motor-boat containing police constables and other members of a pursuit party, they took to their boats, hoisting sails as well as oars. In the chase they threw overboard a volume of *Encyclopaedia Britannica*.

KEEP SHOOTING

SIR, AFTER OVER 30 years experience, I am confident there is nothing like shooting for keeping you strong and fit. No doctor's medicine will ever keep a man in such robust health. Should any sportsman in middle life or older contemplate giving up shooting, my advice is the same as *Punch's* – DON'T! – or probably your days will be numbered. An uncle of mine was the finest game shot I ever saw. For 35 years, his gun was his constant companion, but he gave up shooting when about 50 and at 53 years of age passed away. Sir Harry Lauder says, 'Keep right on to the end of the road', and I agree with him.

Yrs., 'RUSTIC', Devon.

INDEX